Chilterns an[d West Anglia]
Bus H[andbook]

British Bus Publishing

Body codes used in the Bus Handbook series:

Type:

A	Articulated vehicle
B	Single-deck bus
C	Coach - High-back seating
D	Low floor double-deck bus (4-metre)
DP	Express - high-back seating in a bus body
H	Full-height double-deck
L	Low-height double-deck
M	Minibus
N	Low-floor single-deck bus
O	Open-top bus (CO = convertible, PO = partial open-top))

Seating capacity is then shown. For double-decks the upper deck first,

Door position:-

C	Centre entrance/exit
D	Dual doorway
F	Front entrance/exit
R	Rear entrance/exit
T	Three or more access points

Equipment:-

L	Lift for wheelchair
T	Toilet

e.g. - H32/28F is a high-bridge bus with thirty-two seats upstairs, twenty-eight down and a front entrance/exit.
     B43D is a bus with two doorways.

Re-registrations:-

Where a vehicle has gained new index marks the details are listed at the end of each fleet showing the current mark, followed in sequence by those previously carried starting with the original mark.

Other books in the series:

The 1998 Stagecoach Bus Handbook
The 1998 FirstBus Bus Handbook
The 1999 Arriva Bus Handbook (New in Autumn 1998)
The Scottish Bus Handbook
The Ireland & Islands Bus Handbook
The North East Bus Handbook
The Yorkshire Bus Handbook
The Lancashire, Cumbria and Manchester Bus Handbook
The Merseyside and Cheshire Bus Handbook
The North and West Midlands Bus Handbook
The East Midlands Bus Handbook
The South Midlands Bus Handbook
The North and West Wales Bus Handbook
The South Wales Bus Handbook
The East Anglia Bus Handbook
The South West Bus Handbook
The South Central Bus Handbook
The South East Bus Handbook (New in Autumn 1998)

Associated series:

The Hong Kong Bus Handbook
The Leyland Lynx Handbook
The Model Bus Handbook
The Police Range Rover Handbook
The Toy & Model Bus Handbook - Volume 1 - Early Diecasts
The Fire Brigade Handbook (fleet list of each local authority fire brigade)
The Fire Brigade Handbook - Special Appliances Volume 1
The Fire Brigade Handbook - Special Appliances Volume 2

Contents

The Chilterns and West Anglia Bus Handbook

The Chilterns and West Anglia Bus Handbook is part of the Bus Handbook series that details the fleets of stage carriage and express coach operators. Where space allows other significant operators in the areas covered are also included. These handbooks are published by British Bus Publishing and cover Ireland, Scotland, Wales and England outside central London. The current list is shown on page 2 of this book. These provide comprehensive coverage of all the principal operators' fleets in the British Isles.

Considerable time has been expended to ensure the accuracy of the fleet detail. However, the publisher would be keen to learn of anything which is incorrect, or any later information about the fleets so we can ensure that the future books reflect that information.

British Bus Publishing,
The Vyne,
16 St Margaret's Drive
Wellington
Telford,
Shropshire TF1 3PH

Series Editor: Bill Potter

Principal Editors for The Chiltern and West Anglia Bus Handbook: Keith Grimes and Colin Lloyd

Acknowledgements:
We are grateful to David Donati, Mark Jameson, Jef Johnson, Bill Potter, Steve Sanderson, Tony Wilson, the PSV Circle, LOTS and the majority of the operating companies for their assistance in the compilation of this book. To keep the fleets up to date we recommend Buses, published monthly by Ian Allan while the news-sheets of the PSV Circle provide more in-depth information.

The front cover photograph is by Tony Wilson.

Contents correct to August 1998
ISBN 1 897990 43 X
Published by British Bus Publishing
The Vyne, 16 St Margaret's Drive, Wellington,
Telford, Shropshire, TF1 3PH

Fax & Evening orderline - 01952 255669 - 🔳 VISA

A TO B TEAM BUS & COACH
SMART COACH

B R Le Blond, 9 Vicarage Road, Marsworth, Buckinghamshire, HP23 4LR

HIL2833	Volvo C10M-70	Ramseier & Jenser	C49FT	1986	Watson Enterprise, Corringham, 1995
D849CRY	Volkswagen LT55	Optare City Pacer	DP25F	1987	R & I, Park Royal, 1994
F791TBC	TAZ Dubrava	TAZ D3200	C49FT	1989	Dalybus, Eccles, 1996
H741LHN	CVE Omni	CVE	B23F	1990	JC, Widnes, 1997

Previous Registrations:-

HIL2833   C346GSD

Livery:- Grey, two-tone blue and pink.

Depots:- Airfield Industrial Estate, Cheddington and High Street, Dunstable.

Pictured in Victoria Street, London, is a rare example of a TAZ Dubrava. Operated by AtoB Team Bus & Coach, F791TBC was built by the Yugoslavian company, Tvornica Autobusa, which is associated with FAP-Famos. Many of the products of both manufacturers are integral vehicles assembled from locally manufactured Mercedes-Benz running units, a company with which links had been established. *Colin Lloyd*

ABC TRAVEL

J M Lunt, The Chequers, 46 Elmlea Drive, Olney, Buckinghamshire, MK46 5HX

XRN716R	Bedford YMT	Plaxton Supreme III	C53F	1977	Hyde, Tilsworth, 1998
TDL419S	Bedford YMT	Duple Dominant II	C51F	1977	Wightline, Newport, 1998
WDA968T	Leyland Fleetline FE30AGR	MCW	H43/33F	1979	Travel West Midlands, 1997
WDA689T	Leyland Fleetline FE30AGR	Park Royal	H43/33F	1979	Travel West Midlands, 1997
JNK238V	Bedford YMT	Plaxton Supreme IV	C53F	1979	First Choice, Slough, 1994
TJH882Y	Bedford YNT	Plaxton Paramount 3200	C53F	1983	Prosser, Bratton Fleming, 1991
D149HML	Bedford YNT	Plaxton Paramount 3200 II	C53F	1987	Smith, Liss, 1993
E677GRF	Mercedes-Benz 609D	Reeve Burgess	C19F	1987	R & I, Park Royal, 1993
E940RWR	Freight-Rover Sherpa	Carlyle	B18F	1987	East Midland, 1996
E235ADO	Mercedes-Benz 609D	Advanced	C21F	1988	
G968WNR	Mercedes-Benz 609D	Yeates	C19F	1990	Shire Coaches, Garston, 1993
G37HDW	Freight-Rover Sherpa	Carlyle Citybus 2	B20F	1990	Bakewell, Longnor, 1998
G500MFV	Ford Transit VE6	Jubilee	M7	1990	Jubilee, West Bromwich, 1993
H27LHP	Leyland-DAF 400	Jubilee	M16	1990	private owner, 1993
J828JFG	Volkswagen Transporter	Devon Conversions	M7	1992	private owner, 1994

Named Vehicle:- TJH882Y *Silver Rocket*

Livery:- Blue, silver and red.

Depot:- Newport Road, Moulsoe

When pictured TJH882Y of ABC Travel carried the name Silver Rocket. Many of the vehicles in the fleet are used on school contracts, a duty many coach operators have chosen for their Plaxton Paramount 3200s. However here it is seen on its way to Wembley Stadium. *Keith Grimes*

The Chilterns and West Anglia Bus Handbook

ABBEY COACHES

J L Robinson, 134 Desborough Road, High Wycombe, Buckinghamshire, HP11 2PU

GBF79N	Bristol VRT/SL2/6G	Eastern Coach Works	H43/31F	1974	Stephenson, Rochford, 1996
RKY878R	Leyland Leopard PSU3E/4R	Plaxton Supreme III	C53F	1977	Hudson, Downley, 1995
LBL990W	Ford R1114	Plaxton Supreme IV	C49FT	1981	Douglas, Slough, 1992
A33PFE	Mercedes-Benz L307D	Whittaker	M12	1983	Ruffle, Castle Hedingham, 1989
A481WCA	DAF MB200DKFL600	LAG Galaxy	C49FT	1984	Shevill, Wishaw, 1993
F797MGB	Volvo B10M-61	Plaxton Paramount 3200 III	C49F	1988	Silver Choice, East Kilbride, 1998
G726CEM	Mercedes-Benz 814D	North West Buffalo	C30F	1989	Roberts, Bootle, 1991
H319OEV	Ford Transit VE6	Ford	M8	1991	private owner, 1994

Previous Registrations:-

LBL990W	OPR508W, 681KAU	RKY878R	SDD148R, NIB8927

Livery:- White, lilac and pink.

Depot:- Westbourne Street, High Wycombe

Abbey Coaches operate a single DAF coach and this carries a LAG Galaxy body. A481WCA is seen in Parliament Square before returning to High Wycombe with a private school party. *Colin Lloyd*

ACCLAIM TRAVEL/ HOWLETTS

GA & RS Durham, 2 Station Road Industrial Estate, Winslow,
Buckinghamshire, MK18 3DZ

YOD567L	Ford R192	Plaxton Panorama Elite	C45F	1972	Howlett & Durham, Winslow, 1980
GDN704N	Ford R1114	Duple Dominant	C53F	1974	Bennett, Gloucester, 1983
CFX305T	Ford R1114	Plaxton Supreme III	C53F	1979	AC, Bournemouth, 1981
KBM647Y	DAF MB200DKFL600	Plaxton Paramount 3500	C44F	1983	
A691ERB	Bedford YNT	Plaxton Paramount 3200	C53F	1984	Felix, Stanley, 1991
C875JCP	DAF MB200DKFL600	Plaxton Paramount 3500 II	C53F	1985	
D516WNV	DAF SB2300DHS585	Caetano Algarve	C53F	1987	Dunn-Line, Nottingham, 1996
F628OHD	DAF MB230LB615	Plaxton Paramount 3500 III	C55F	1988	

Livery:- Black, white, gold and beige.

ALEC HEAD / RELIANCE

J & A M Head & S J Johns, Reliance Garage, Lutton, Northamptonshire, PE8 5NE

KJD268P	Scania BR111DH	MCW Metropolitan	H43/33F	1976	Whippet, Fenstanton, 1994
RCH511R	Bedford YMT	Plaxton Supreme III Express	C53F	1976	Whyatt, Woodston, 1997
YTA612S	Volvo B58-61	Duple Dominant II	C57F	1977	Holloway & McGrey, Partington, 1997
7195BY	Volvo B10M-60	Jonckheere Jubilee P50	C51FT	1983	West Kingsdown, 1987
TXI2427	DAF SB2300DHS585	Jonckheere Jubilee	C57F	1983	Morris Travel, Pencoed, 1996
WSV509	Van Hool TD824	Van Hool Astromega	CH55/21FT	1983	AML, Hounslow, 1995
NIL1787	Scania K112CRS	Jonckheere Jubilee P50	C57F	1983	LB Travel, Pytchley, 1996
6447PO	Volvo B10M-61	Jonckheere Jubilee P50	C49F	1983	Hallmark, Luton, 1987
A111OAV	Volvo B10M-61	Plaxton Paramount 3200	C57F	1983	
4388WX	Volvo B10M-61	Jonckheere Jubilee	C55F	1984	
RBD215	DAF SBR2300DHS570	Jonckheere Jubilee P99	CH57/14CT	1984	Rapson, Alness, 1993
3085KX	Scania K112CRS	Jonckheere Jubilee P599	C57FT	1984	Derek Randall, Harlesden, 1986
LIL7234	DAF SB2300DHS585	Jonckheere Jubilee	C51F	1984	
MIL8741	Scania K112TRS	Plaxton Paramount 4000 II	CH54/21CT	1985	Limebourne, Battersea, 1997
TIB8567	Scania K112CRS	Jonckheere Jubilee P599	C57F	1985	Scancoaches, North Acton, 1996
MJI6251	Scania K112TRS	Plaxton Paramount 4000 II	CH55/20CT	1986	Martindale, Ferryhill, 1997
RJI1649	Scania K112TRS	Plaxton Paramount 4000 II	CH55/20CT	1986	Taylor, Widnes, 1998
E777MCE	Volvo B10M-61	Caetano Algarve	C49FT	1988	
F222BFL	DAF SB2305DHTD585	Plaxton Paramount 3200 III	C49DL	1989	
A8EAD	DAF SB2305DHS585	Jonckheere Deauville P599	C43FT	1990	
8098NK	MAN 16-290	Jonckheere Deauville P599	C51FT	1990	Eardley, Leek, 1991
A11EAD	Scania K113TRB	Van Hool Alizée SH	C44FT	1990	Wilfreda-Beehive, Adwick-le-Street, 1995
G702LKW	Scania K93CRB	Plaxton Paramount 3200 III	C49DL	1990	C & G, Chatteris, 1992
H809RWJ	Scania K93CRB	Plaxton Paramount 3200 III	C57F	1990	McLeans, Witney, 1995
K230WNH	MAN 16-290	Jonckheere Deauville P599	C51FT	1992	Budden's, Romsey, 1996
K231WNH	MAN 16-290	Jonckheere Deauville P599	C51FT	1992	Budden's, Romsey, 1996
M111EAD	Scania K113TRB	Irizar Century 12.37	C51F	1995	Silver Choice, East Kilbride, 1998

Previous Registrations:-

3085KX	A62JLW	MIL8741	C400JOO, 9242FH, C678NHJ
4388WX	A777RAV	MJI6251	C351DWR
6447PO	ONV636Y	NIL1787	DLX33Y, AEF368A, RBD536Y
7195BY	JNV531Y	RBD215	A131MFL, 318DHR, A675VSK
8098NK	G373RNH, A8EAD	TIB8567	C409LRP
A8EAD	G184UAV	TXI2427	EEW123Y
A11EAD	G700LKW, WLF5, A8EAD	WSV509	NDS842Y
LIL7234	B555XEG	YTA612S	CCW936S, 8933CD
M111EAD	M25XSC	RJI1649	C350DWR

Named Vehicles:- 6447PO *Volvo Executive*; 7195BY *Volvo Executive*; 8098NK *MAN Executive*; A8EAD *DAF Executive*; A11EAD *Scania Executive*; G702LKW *Scania Executive*; M111EAD *Scania Executive*

Livery:-Two tone blue and white.

As the supply of Ford and Bedford coaches has reduced, Acclaim Travel have chosen DAF products for their later models. All bar one carry Plaxton Paramount 3500 bodywork represented here by KBM647Y. The livery styling used here was common on contemporary vehicles supplied by Plaxton in the mid 1980's. *Colin Lloyd*

Three MAN-chassied coaches are employed by Alex Head, and all carry Jonckheere Deauville bodywork, a style that provided the bodybuilder with many orders from British operators. There are variations of the Deauville, this example with split windscreen being the P599. *Colin Lloyd*

ANGLIA

Hilo Transport Ltd, 36 High Street, Offley, Hitchin, Hertfordshire, SG5 3AH

D654BPL	LAG G355Z	LAG Panoramic	C49FT	1987	Berryhurst, Lambeth, 1995
H448VNH	EOS E180Z	EOS 100	C53FT	1990	Boorman, Henlow, 1996
LAZ5827	Bova FHD12.290	Bova Futura	C51FT	1991	Clarkson, South Elmsall, 1997

Previous Registrations:-
LAZ5827   H624FUT

Livery:- White and orange

Depot:-Stopsley Holes Farm, Ley Green, Offley

ANITA'S

Anita's Coach & Minibus Hire Ltd, 1 Yewlands, Sawbridgeworth, Hertfordshire, CM21 9NP

E413YLG	Mercedes-Benz 609D	PMT	C26F	1988	
E658UNE	Volvo B10M-61	Plaxton Paramount 3500 III	C53F	1988	Turners, Bristol, 1997
F996SVX	Mercedes-Benz 814L	North West Buffalo	C29F	1989	
H832JNK	Mercedes-Benz 811D	Reeve Burgess Beaver	C33F	1991	
K3ERN	Dennis Javelin 12SDA1929	Caetano Algarve II	C49FT	1992	
M6ERN	Dennis Javelin 12SDA2136	Caetano Algarve II	C55F	1994	
P3ERN	Volvo B10M-62	Caetano Algarve II	C51FT	1996	

Previous Registrations:-
E658UNE   E658UNE, YBP692

Livery:- White, red and maroon.

Depot:- Star Garage, London Road, Sawbridgeworth

AR TRAVEL

AR Travel Ltd, 40 Perry Green, Hemel Hempstead, Hertfordshire, HP2 7ND

E681MWP	DAF SB2305DHS585	Van Hool Alizée DH	C51FT	1988	Rutter, Hertford, 1997
M581BVL	Mercedes-Benz 410D	Autobus Classique	M16	1994	Rutter, Hertford, 1997
M582BVL	Mercedes-Benz 814D	Autobus Classique Nouvelle	C29F	1994	Rutter, Hertford, 1997

Previous Registrations:-
E681MWP   E441LNP, DSK593

Livery:- Silver, grey blue and red.

Depot:-Unit 1, Warrenwood Industrial Estate, Stapleford, Hertford

Shown here are two Mercedes-Benz minibuses from Hertfordshire operators. Above is Anita's F996SVX with Buffalo bodywork by North West Coach Sales, while the lower picture shows AR Travel's M582BVL which carries the Nouvelle style built by Autobus Classique. *Colin Lloyd*

ARRIVA serving The Shires

Arriva The Shires Ltd, Castle Street, Luton, Bedfordshire, LU1 3AJ
Arriva Watford Ltd, Castle Street, Luton, Bedfordshire, LU1 3AJ
Lutonian Buses Ltd, Castle Street, Luton, Bedfordshire, LU1 3AJ

Minibuses

2020w	E990DNK	MCW MetroRider MF150/83	MCW	B23F	1988	London Country NW, 1990
2033w	E486CNM	MCW MetroRider MF150/74	MCW	B23F	1987	Sovereign, 1990
2037	F122TRU	Mercedes-Benz 709D	Reeve Burgess Beaver	B25F	1988	Kentish Bus, 1991
2038	F123TRU	Mercedes-Benz 709D	Reeve Burgess Beaver	B25F	1988	Metrobus, Orpington, 1991
2039	F124TRU	Mercedes-Benz 709D	Reeve Burgess Beaver	B25F	1988	Kentish Bus, 1991
2040	F125TRU	Mercedes-Benz 709D	Reeve Burgess Beaver	B25F	1988	Metrobus, Orpington, 1991
2041w	E341DRO	Iveco Daily 49.10	Dormobile	B25F	1988	
2043	F128TRU	Mercedes-Benz 709D	Reeve Burgess Beaver	B25F	1988	Metrobus, Orpington, 1991
2045w	E335DRO	Iveco Daily 49.10	Dormobile	B25F	1988	
2048	F598CET	Mercedes-Benz 709D	Reeve Burgess Beaver	B25F	1988	Argyll Bus & Coach, 1992
2050	G58BEL	Mercedes-Benz 811D	Wadham Stringer Wessex	DP31F	1989	Buffalo, Flitwick, 1995
2051w	F985GKJ	Iveco Daily 49.10	Robin Hood City Nippy	B21F	1990	Buffalo, Flitwick, 1995
2052w	MBZ6455	Iveco Daily 49.10	Carlyle Dailybus	B25F	1988	Buffalo, Flitwick, 1995
2053w	F969GKJ	Iveco Daily 49.10	Robin Hood City Nippy	B21F	1989	Buffalo, Flitwick, 1994
2054	G360FOP	Mercedes-Benz 709D	Carlyle	B25F	1989	Yellow Bus, Stoke Mandeville, 1995
2055	G896TGG	Mercedes-Benz 811D	Reeve Burgess Beaver	B33F	1990	Stevensons, 1995
2056	H523SWE	Mercedes-Benz 709D	Whittaker Europa	B29F	1990	Rhondda, 1995
2057	H407FGS	Mercedes-Benz 811D	Reeve Burgess Beaver	B31F	1991	Sovereign, 1996
2058	H408FGS	Mercedes-Benz 811D	Reeve Burgess Beaver	B31F	1991	Sovereign, 1996
2059	H406FGS	Mercedes-Benz 811D	Reeve Burgess Beaver	B31F	1990	Sovereign, 1996
2060	H848AUS	Mercedes-Benz 709D	Reeve Burgess Beaver	B25F	1990	Argyll Bus & Coach, 1992

Arriva colours are now displacing The Shires former livery, though the former colours still remain in large numbers. Newly delivered is 2185, R185DNM, pictured here in Hemel Hempstead.
Keith Grimes

Shown with Watford lettering and route-branding for service 8 is Mercedes-Benz 2128, N908ETM, one of the 1995 intake that featured Plaxton Beaver bodywork. *Tony Wilson*

2061	H641UWE	Mercedes-Benz 814D	Europa Enterprise	B31F	1991	Buffalo, Flitwick, 1995
2062	H642UWE	Mercedes-Benz 814D	Europa Enterprise	B31F	1991	Buffalo, Flitwick, 1995
2063	H35DGD	Mercedes-Benz 811D	Dormobile Routemaker	B33F	1991	Pathfinder, Newark, 1995
2064	H614CGG	Mercedes-Benz 709D	Dormobile Routemaker	B33F	1991	Pathfinder, Newark, 1995
2065	F121TRU	Mercedes-Benz 709D	Reeve Burgess Beaver	B25F	1988	Kentish Bus, 1991
2066	J917HGD	Mercedes-Benz 709D	Reeve Burgess Beaver	B25F	1991	Argyll Bus & Coach, 1992
2067	H231KBH	Mercedes-Benz 709D	Carlyle	B27F	1992	Buffalo, Flitwick, 1995
2068	H408BVR	Mercedes-Benz 709D	Reeve Burgess Beaver	B25F	1990	Star Line, Knutsford, 1995
2069	H409BVR	Mercedes-Benz 709D	Reeve Burgess Beaver	B25F	1990	Star Line, Knutsford, 1995
2070	J65UNA	Mercedes-Benz 709D	Plaxton Beaver	B23F	1992	South Lancashire, St Helens, 1996
2071	K8BUS	Mercedes-Benz 811D	Wright NimBus	B33F	1993	Patterson, Birmingham, 1995
2072	K578YOJ	Mercedes-Benz 709D	Dormobile Routemaker	B29F	1993	Patterson, Birmingham, 1995
2073	K543OGA	Mercedes-Benz 811D	Dormobile Routemaker	B29F	1992	Pathfinder, Newark, 1995
2074	K579YOJ	Mercedes-Benz 709D	Dormobile Routemaker	B29F	1993	Patterson, Birmingham, 1995

2075-2079

		Mercedes-Benz 709D	Made-to-Measure	B24F	1992	Birmingham Omnibus, Tividale, 1995

2075	K25WND	2076	K26WND	2077	K27WND	2078	K28WND	2079	K29WND

2080	K580YOJ	Mercedes-Benz 811D	Wright NimBus	B33F	1993	Patterson, Birmingham, 1995
2081	K31WND	Mercedes-Benz 709D	Made-to-Measure	B24F	1992	Birmingham Omnibus, Tividale, 1995
2082	K32WND	Mercedes-Benz 709D	Made-to-Measure	B24F	1992	Birmingham Omnibus, Tividale, 1995
2083	K203FEH	Mercedes-Benz 709D	Dormobile Routemaker	B27F	1993	Stevensons, 1995
2084	L864BEA	Iveco Daily 49.10	Marshall C29	B23F	1993	Buffalo, Flitwick, 1994
2085	L863BEA	Iveco Daily 49.10	Marshall C29	B23F	1993	Buffalo, Flitwick, 1994
2086	L326AUT	Mercedes-Benz 709D	Leicester Carriage Builders	B25F	1994	Midland Fox, 1994
2087	L327AUT	Mercedes-Benz 709D	Leicester Carriage Builders	B25F	1994	Midland Fox, 1994
2088	L328AUT	Mercedes-Benz 709D	Leicester Carriage Builders	B25F	1994	Midland Fox, 1994
2089	K202FEH	Mercedes-Benz 709D	Dormobile Routemaker	B27F	1993	Stevensons, 1995

2090-2094 — Iveco TurboDaily 59-12 — Marshall C31 — B27F — 1994

2090 M150RBH	**2091** M151RBH	**2092** M152RBH	**2093** M153RBH	**2094** M154RBH

2095 K184GDU	Mercedes-Benz 811D	Wright NimBus	B31F	1993	Yellow Bus, Stoke Mandeville, 1995

2096-2100 — Iveco TurboDaily 59-12 — Marshall C31 — B27F — 1994

2096 M156RBH	**2097** M157RBH	**2098** M158RBH	**2099** M159RBH	**2100** M160RBH

2101	J171GGG	Mercedes-Benz 709D	Dormobile Routemaker	B29F	1991	Yellow Bus, Stoke Mandeville, 1995
2102	L600BUS	Optare MetroRider MR11	Optare	B31F	1995	Lucky Bus, Watford, 1997
2103	L700BUS	Optare MetroRider MR11	Optare	B32F	1996	Lucky Bus, Watford, 1997
2104	L800BUS	Optare MetroRider MR11	Optare	B31F	1996	Lucky Bus, Watford, 1997
2105	M45WUR	Mercedes-Benz 709D	Plaxton Beaver	B25F	1995	
2106	M46WUR	Mercedes-Benz 709D	Plaxton Beaver	B25F	1995	
2107	M47WUR	Mercedes-Benz 709D	Plaxton Beaver	B25F	1995	
2108	M38WUR	Mercedes-Benz 811D	Plaxton Beaver	B25F	1995	
2109	M39WUR	Mercedes-Benz 811D	Plaxton Beaver	B25F	1995	
2110	N906ETM	Mercedes-Benz 709D	Plaxton Beaver	B27F	1995	
2111	M41WUR	Mercedes-Benz 811D	Plaxton Beaver	DP31F	1995	
2112	M42WUR	Mercedes-Benz 811D	Plaxton Beaver	DP31F	1995	
2113	M43WUR	Mercedes-Benz 709D	Plaxton Beaver	B25F	1995	
2114	N918ETM	Mercedes-Benz 709D	Plaxton Beaver	B27F	1995	
2115	N919ETM	Mercedes-Benz 709D	Plaxton Beaver	DP27F	1995	

2116-2137 — Mercedes-Benz 709D — Plaxton Beaver — B27F — 1995

2116 N186EMJ	**2121** N191EMJ	**2126** N196EMJ	**2130** N910ETM	**2134** N914ETM
2117 N187EMJ	**2122** N192EMJ	**2127** N907ETM	**2131** N911ETM	**2135** N915ETM
2118 N188EMJ	**2123** N193EMJ	**2128** N908ETM	**2132** N912ETM	**2136** N916ETM
2119 N189EMJ	**2124** N194EMJ	**2129** N909ETM	**2133** N913ETM	**2137** N917ETM
2120 N190EMJ	**2125** N195EMJ			

2138-2162 — Mercedes-Benz 709D — Plaxton Beaver — B25F — 1996

2138 N368JGS	**2143** N373JGS	**2148** N378JGS	**2153** N383JGS	**2158** N366JGS
2139 N369JGS	**2144** N374JGS	**2149** N379JGS	**2154** N384JGS	**2159** N367JGS
2140 N370JGS	**2145** N375JGS	**2150** N380JGS	**2155** N385JGS	**2160** P670PNM
2141 N371JGS	**2146** N376JGS	**2151** N381JGS	**2156** N386JGS	**2161** P671PNM
2142 N372JGS	**2147** N377JGS	**2152** N382JGS	**2157** N387JGS	**2162** P669PNM

2165	WIB1114	Mercedes-Benz 609D	PMT	C26F	1987	Checker, Garston, 1997
2166	J465UFS	Mercedes-Benz 609D	Crystals	C24F	1992	Checker, Garston, 1997
2167	SLU261	Ford Transit VE6	Deansgate	M12	1987	Checker, Garston, 1997
2168	G40OHS	Ford Transit VE6	Dormobile	B16F	1989	Checker, Garston, 1997
2169	G715PGA	Ford Transit VE6	Deansgate	M14	1989	Checker, Garston, 1997
2170	J964NLL	Ford Transit VE6	Crystals	M13	1992	Checker, Garston, 1997

2171-2184 — Mercedes-Benz Vario O810 — Plaxton Beaver 2 — B27F — 1997

2171 R171VBM	**2174** R174VBM	**2177** R177VBM	**2180** R180VBM	**2183** R183VBM
2172 R172VBM	**2175** R175VBM	**2178** R178VBM	**2181** R181VBM	**2184** R184VBM
2173 R173VBM	**2176** R176VBM	**2179** R179VBM	**2182** R182VBM	

2185-2198 — Mercedes-Benz Vario O810 — Plaxton Beaver 2 — B27F* — 1998 — *2196-8 are B31F

2185 R185DNM	**2188** R188DNM	**2191** R191DNM	**2194** R194DNM	**2197** R197DNM
2186 R186DNM	**2189** R189DNM	**2192** R192DNM	**2195** R195DNM	**2198** R198DNM
2187 R187DNM	**2190** R190DNM	**2193** R193DNM	**2196** R196DNM	

2199	L429CPC	Mercedes-Benz 709D	Danescroft	B27F	1994	Arriva Guildford & W Surrey, 1998
2200	L426CPB	Mercedes-Benz 709D	Danescroft	B27F	1994	Arriva Guildford & W Surrey, 1998

Opposite:- **Arriva The Shires has Dennis Darts with bodywork from several manufacturers. The upper picture shows 3173, P673OPP, one of four low-floor examples built in 1996 that carry East Lancashire bodywork (then an associated company) while the lower picture shows a Plaxton Pointer 2-bodied example. This vehicle, 3187, P187SRO, formed the main delivery of midi buses in 1997, many of which are based at Watford.**

2204w	G276HDW	Freight Rover Sherpa	Carlyle Citybus 2	B20F	1990	Lutonian, Luton, 1998
2205	G277HDW	Freight Rover Sherpa	Carlyle Citybus 2	B20F	1990	Lutonian, Luton, 1998
2206	G145GOL	Iveco Daily 49.10	Carlyle Dailybus 2	B23F	1990	Lutonian, Luton, 1998
2207	G146GOL	Iveco Daily 49.10	Carlyle Dailybus 2	B25F	1990	Lutonian, Luton, 1998
2208	G148GOL	Iveco Daily 49.10	Carlyle Dailybus 2	B25F	1990	Lutonian, Luton, 1998
2209w	G225GSG	Iveco Daily 49.10	Carlyle Dailybus 2	B25F	1990	Lutonian, Luton, 1998
2210	H475KSG	Iveco Daily 49.10	Carlyle Dailybus 2	B25F	1990	Lutonian, Luton, 1998
2212	J32UTG	Leyland-DAF 400	Carlyle Citybus 2	B20F	1992	Lutonian, Luton, 1998
2213	J37VDW	Iveco Daily 49.10	Carlyle Dailybus 2	B25F	1992	Lutonian, Luton, 1998
2214	N124GNM	Iveco TurboDaily 59.12	Marshall C31	DP29F	1996	Lutonian, Luton, 1998
2215	P860PBH	Iveco TurboDaily 59.12	Marshall C31	B27F	1996	Lutonian, Luton, 1998
2216	P861PBH	Iveco TurboDaily 59.12	Marshall C31	B27F	1996	Lutonian, Luton, 1998
2217	P570TBH	Iveco TurboDaily 59.12	Marshall C31	B27F	1997	Lutonian, Luton, 1998
2218	P571TBH	Iveco TurboDaily 59.12	Marshall C31	B27F	1997	Lutonian, Luton, 1998
2219	P26KOP	Iveco TurboDaily 59.12	Marshall C31	B27F	1997	Lutonian, Luton, 1998
2220	P981PKX	Iveco TurboDaily 59.12	Marshall C31	B27F	1997	Lutonian, Luton, 1998
2221	M239XLV	Iveco TurboDaily 59.12	Marshall C31	B27F	1995	Arriva North West, 1998
2222	M240XLV	Iveco TurboDaily 59.12	Marshall C31	B27F	1995	Arriva North West, 1998
3014	SBD524R	Leyland National 11351A/1R		B49F	1977	United Counties, 1986
3015w	BVV545T	Leyland National 11351A/1R		B49F	1978	United Counties, 1986
3027w	MNH577V	Leyland National 11351A/1R		B49F	1979	United Counties, 1986
3031	NRP581V	Leyland National 2 NL116L11/1R		B49F	1980	United Counties, 1986
3033	SVV588W	Leyland National 2 NL116L11/1R		B49F	1980	United Counties, 1986

3035-3043

		Leyland National 2 NL106AL11/2R		B44F	1981	Parfitt's, Rhymney Bridge, 1995

3035	GUW465W	3037	GUW457W	3039w	GUW447W	3041	GUW461W	3043	GUW475W
3036	GUW456W	3038	GUW441W	3040	GUW494W	3042	GUW462W		

3044	IIL4821	Leyland 10351/1R/SC(6HLX)	East Lancs Greenway (1993)	B41F	1974	Crosville Cymru, 1995
3045	IIL4822	Leyland 10351/1R/SC(6HLX)	East Lancs Greenway (1993)	B41F	1976	Crosville Cymru, 1995
3046	TIB4873	Leyland 10351B/1R(6HLX)	East Lancs Greenway (1993)	B41F	1979	Crosville Cymru, 1995
3047	IIL4824	Leyland 10351/1R(6HLX)	East Lancs Greenway (1994)	B41F	1975	Crosville Cymru, 1995
3048	BAZ6869	Leyland 10351B/1R(6HLX)	East Lancs Greenway (1994)	B41F	1979	Crosville Cymru, 1995
3049	RJI6861	Leyland 10351B/1R(6HLX)	East Lancs Greenway (1994)	B41F	1979	Crosville Cymru, 1995
3050	BTX152T	Leyland 10351A/2R(6HLX)	East Lancs Greenway (1994)	B44F	1979	Parfitts, Rhymney Bridge, 1995
3052	IAZ4037	Leyland National 11351A/1R(Volvo)		B49F	1977	United Counties, 1986
3053	CAZ6852	Leyland 10351B/1R(6HLX)	East Lancs Greenway (1994)	B41F	1978	Crosville Cymru, 1995
3054	TIB7835	Leyland 10351B/1R(6HLX)	East Lancs Greenway (1994)	B41F	1979	Crosville Cymru, 1995
3055	RJI6862	Leyland 10351B/1R(6HLX)	East Lancs Greenway (1994)	B41F	1979	Crosville Cymru, 1995
3056	IIL4823	Leyland 10351B/1R(6HLX)	East Lancs Greenway (1993)	B41F	1978	Crosville Cymru, 1995
3057	TIB4886	Leyland 10351B/1R(6HLX)	East Lancs Greenway (1993)	B41F	1975	Crosville Cymru, 1995
3058	GHB574V	Volvo B58-61	East Lancs EL2000(1994)	B53F	1980	Parfitt's, Rhymney Bridge, 1995
3061	D603ACW	Leyland Lynx LX112L10ZR1R	Leyland Lynx	B51F	1987	Sovereign, 1990
3062	E970NMK	Leyland Lynx LX112TL11ZR1S	Leyland Lynx	B49F	1987	Sovereign, 1990
3063	E420EBH	Leyland Lynx LX112TL11ZR1R	Leyland Lynx	B51F	1988	Sovereign, 1996
3064	E969PME	Leyland Lynx LX112L10ZR1R	Leyland Lynx	B49F	1988	Atlas Bus, Harlesden, 1994
3065	E965PME	Leyland Lynx LX112TL11ZR1R	Leyland Lynx	B49F	1988	Yellow Bus, Stoke Mandeville, 1995
3066	E966PME	Leyland Lynx LX112TL11ZR1R	Leyland Lynx	B49F	1988	Yellow Bus, Stoke Mandeville, 1995
3067	H407ERO	Leyland Lynx LX2R11C15Z4S	Leyland Lynx	DP45F	1990	
3068	H408ERO	Leyland Lynx LX2R11C15Z4S	Leyland Lynx	DP45F	1990	
3069	H409ERO	Leyland Lynx LX2R11C15Z4S	Leyland Lynx	DP45F	1990	
3070	H410ERO	Leyland Lynx LX2R11C15Z4S	Leyland Lynx	DP45F	1990	

3071-3075

		Leyland Lynx LX112L10ZR1R	Leyland Lynx	B51F	1989	

3071	F401PUR	3072	F402PUR	3073	F403PUR	3074	F404PUR	3075	F400PUR

3076	E970PME	Leyland Lynx LX112L10ZR1R	Leyland Lynx	B49F	1988	Atlas Bus, Harlesden, 1994
3077	NIB8459	Volvo B10M-61	East Lancs EL2000(1991)	B55F	1988	Buffalo, Flitwick, 1995
3078	F314RMH	Volvo B10M-56	Plaxton Derwent II	B54F	1988	Buffalo, Flitwick, 1995
3079	F151KGS	Volvo B10M-56	Plaxton Derwent II	B54F	1988	Buffalo, Flitwick, 1995
3080	F152KGS	Volvo B10M-56	Plaxton Derwent II	B54F	1988	Buffalo, Flitwick, 1995
3081	F153KGS	Volvo B10M-56	Plaxton Derwent II	B54F	1988	Buffalo, Flitwick, 1995
3089	L133HVS	Volvo B10B-58	Alexander Strider	B51F	1993	Buffalo, Flitwick, 1995

Arriva The Shires was recently known as Luton & District and it was for that operation's airport services that a batch of Leyland Lynx were delivered in 1995. When new the seating was reduced to just 25 to accommodate extra luggage space. One of these vehicles, 3068, H408ERO, is seen with a full set of high-back seating and in the new colours. *Colin Lloyd*

3091-3098

Dennis Dart 9.8SDL3004   Carlyle Dartline   B40F   1991   London Country NW, 1991

3091	H922LOX	3093	H925LOX	3094	H926LOX	3096	H243MUK	3098	H245MUK
3092	H923LOX								

3099	K447XPA	Dennis Dart 9.8SDL3017	Plaxton Pointer	B40F	1992	Buffalo, Flitwick, 1995
3100	K448XPA	Dennis Dart 9.8SDL3017	Plaxton Pointer	B40F	1992	Buffalo, Flitwick, 1995
3101	L100BUS	Dennis Dart 9.8SDL3035	Plaxton Pointer	B39F	1994	Lucky Bus, Watford, 1997
3102	L200BUS	Dennis Dart 9.8SDL3035	Plaxton Pointer	B39F	1994	Lucky Bus, Watford, 1997
3103	L300BUS	Dennis Dart 9SDL3031	Marshall C36	B34F	1994	Lucky Bus, Watford, 1997
3104	L400BUS	Dennis Dart 9SDL3031	Marshall C36	B34F	1994	Lucky Bus, Watford, 1997

3105-3136

Volvo B6-9.9M   Northern Counties Paladin   B40F   1994

3105	L305HPP	3112	L312HPP	3119	M719OMJ	3125	M725OMJ	3131	M711OMJ
3106	L306HPP	3113	L313HPP	3120	M720OMJ	3126	M726OMJ	3132	M712OMJ
3107	L307HPP	3114	L314HPP	3121	M721OMJ	3127	M727OMJ	3133	M713OMJ
3108	L308HPP	3115	L315HPP	3122	M722OMJ	3128	M728OMJ	3134	M714OMJ
3109	L309HPP	3116	L316HPP	3123	M723OMJ	3129	M729OMJ	3135	M715OMJ
3110	L310HPP	3117	M717OMJ	3124	M724OMJ	3130	M710OMJ	3136	M716OMJ
3111	L311HPP	3118	M718OMJ						

3137	L43MEH	Volvo B6-9.9M	Plaxton Pointer	B40F	1994	Stevensons, 1994
3138	L922LJO	Volvo B6-9.9M	Northern Counties Paladin	B40F	1994	Yellow Bus, Stoke Mandeville, 1995
3139	L923LJO	Volvo B6-9.9M	Northern Counties Paladin	B40F	1994	Yellow Bus, Stoke Mandeville, 1995

3143-3149

Scania L113CRL   East Lancashire European   N51F   1995

3143	N693EUR	3145	N695EUR	3147	N697EUR	3148	N698EUR	3149	N699EUR
3144	N694EUR	3146	N696EUR						

3151-3166 — Scania L113CRL — East Lancashire European — NDP49F — 1995

3151	N701EUR	3155	N705EUR	3158	N708EUR	3161	N711EUR	3164	N714EUR
3152	N702EUR	3156	N706EUR	3159	N709EUR	3162	N712EUR	3165	N715EUR
3153	N703EUR	3157	N707EUR	3160	N710EUR	3163	N713EUR	3166	N716EUR
3154	N704EUR								

3167	N28KGS	Scania L113CRL	East Lancashire European	N51F	1996
3168	N29KGS	Scania L113CRL	East Lancashire European	N51F	1996
3169	N31KGS	Scania L113CRL	East Lancashire European	N51F	1996
3170	N32KGS	Scania L113CRL	East Lancashire European	N51F	1996
3171	P671OPP	Dennis Dart SLF	East Lancashire Flyte	N41F	1996
3172	P672OPP	Dennis Dart SLF	East Lancashire Flyte	N41F	1996
3173	P673OPP	Dennis Dart SLF	East Lancashire Flyte	N41F	1996
3174	P674OPP	Dennis Dart SLF	East Lancashire Flyte	N41F	1996

3175-3190 — Dennis Dart SLF — Plaxton Pointer 2 — N39F* — 1997 — *3175-8 are B41F

3175	P175SRO	3179	P179SRO	3182	P182SRO	3185	P185SRO	3188	P188SRO
3176	P176SRO	3180	P180SRO	3183	P183SRO	3186	P186SRO	3189	P189SRO
3177	P177SRO	3181	P181SRO	3184	P184SRO	3187	P187SRO	3190	P190SRO
3178	P178SRO								

3191-3205 — Scania L113CRL — Northern Counties Paladin — N49F — 1997

3191	R191RBM	3194	R194RBM	3197	R197RBM	3201	R201RBM	3204	R204RBM
3192	R192RBM	3195	R195RBM	3198	R198RBM	3202	R202RBM	3205	R205RBM
3193	R193RBM	3196	R196RBM	3199	R199RBM	3203	R203RBM		

3206-3215 — Dennis Dart SLF — Plaxton Pointer 2 — N31F — 1997-98

3206	R206GMJ	3208	R208GMJ	3210	R210GMJ	3212	R212GMJ	3214	R214GMJ
3207	R207GMJ	3209	R209GMJ	3211	R211GMJ	3213	R213GMJ	3215	R215GMJ

3241-3247 — Volvo B6-9.9 — Alexander Dash — B40F — 1993 — Arriva Scotland West, 1998

3241	M841DDS	3243	M843DDS	3245	M845DDS	3246	M846DDS	3247	M847DDS
3242	M842DDS	3244	M844DDS						

3899	GFR799W	Leyland National 116690/1R		B52F	1979	Surrey & West Sussex, 1998

Originally purchased by National Bus for Green Line services, A157EPA is now fleet number 4007 in the Arriva The Shires fleet. Five of these early Leyland Tigers, all of which carry the express version of Plaxton Paramount bodywork, remain in service. Shown here, 4007 is one of the recent repaints into the new colours.
Colin Lloyd

For the main single-deck bus requirement Scania L113s were added to the fleet from 1995. The initial deliveries carry East Lancashire European bodywork represented here by 3158, N708EUR which carries previously used *Gadevalley* lettering which will disappear from vehicles after their next repaint.

4002	A152EPA	Leyland Tiger TRCTL11/3R	Plaxton Paramount 3200 E	C57F	1984	London Country NW, 1990
4003	A153EPA	Leyland Tiger TRCTL11/3R	Plaxton Paramount 3200 E	C57F	1984	London Country NW, 1990
4006	A113EPA	Leyland Tiger TRCTL11/2R	Plaxton Paramount 3200 E	C53F	1983	London Country NW, 1990
4007	A157EPA	Leyland Tiger TRCTL11/3R	Plaxton Paramount 3200 E	C57F	1984	London Country NW, 1990
4008	A143EPA	Leyland Tiger TRCTL11/2RH	Plaxton Paramount 3200 E	C51F	1984	London Country NW, 1990
4009	FIL4919	Volvo B10M-61	Duple 320	C49FT	1987	Lucky Bus, Watford, 1997
4015	HIL7595	Volvo B10M-61	Plaxton Paramount 3500 III	C53F	1988	Moor-Dale, 1994
4016	SIB4846	Leyland Tiger TRCTL11/3ARZA	Plaxton Paramount 3200 III	C53F	1988	London Country NW, 1990
4017	C147SPB	Leyland Tiger TRCTL11/3RH	Berkhof Everest 370	C53F	1986	London Country NW, 1990
4019w	C149SPB	Leyland Tiger TRCTL11/3RH	Berkhof Everest 370	C53F	1986	London Country NW, 1990
4020	SIB7480	Leyland Tiger TRCTL11/3ARZA	Plaxton Paramount 3200 III	C51F	1988	London Country NW, 1990
4021	E881YKY	Leyland Tiger TRCTL11/3ARZ	Plaxton Paramount 3200 III	C53F	1988	
4022	E882YKY	Leyland Tiger TRCTL11/3ARZ	Plaxton Paramount 3200 III	C53F	1988	
4023	E323OMG	Leyland Tiger TRCTL11/3ARZA	Plaxton Paramount 3200 III	C53F	1988	London Country NW, 1990
4025	SIB8529	Leyland Tiger TRCTL11/3ARZA	Plaxton Paramount 3500 III	C51FT	1988	London Country NW, 1990
4026	SIB7481	Leyland Tiger TRCTL11/3ARZA	Plaxton Paramount 3500 III	C51FT	1988	London Country NW, 1990
4027	HIL7597	Volvo B10M-61	Plaxton Paramount 3500 III	C53F	1988	Moor-Dale, 1994
4028	MIL2350	Dennis Javelin 12SDA1919	Duple 320	C57F	1990	Lucky Bus, Watford, 1997
4034	H198AOD	Volvo B10M-60	Plaxton Expressliner	C50FT	1996	Trathens, Plymouth, 1996
4035	H199AOD	Volvo B10M-60	Plaxton Expressliner	C50FT	1996	Trathens, Plymouth, 1996
4036	L500BUS	Iveco Country Rider 48-10-21	WS Coachbuilders Vanguard	B47F	1995	Lucky Bus, Watford, 1997
4037	P100LOW	Dennis Javelin	UVG Unistar	C55FTL	1996	Lucky Bus, Watford, 1997
4039	WIB1113	Volvo B10M-61	Plaxton Paramount 3200 II	C53F	1985	Checker, Garston, 1997
4040	YIB2396	Volvo B10M-61	Plaxton Paramount 3200 II	C53F	1986	Checker, Garston, 1997
4043	YIB2397	Leyland Tiger TRCTL11/3RZ	Duple 320	C57F	1987	Checker, Garston, 1997
4046	TIB5906	Leyland Tiger TRCTL11/3RH	Duple 320	C51F	1986	Kentish Bus, 1997

4047-4056		DAF DE33WSSB3000	Plaxton Prima	C53F	1997

4047	R447SKX	**4049**	R449SKX	**4051**	R451SKX	**4053**	R453SKX	**4055**	R455SKX
4048	R448SKX	**4050**	R450SKX	**4052**	R452SKX	**4054**	R454SKX	**4056**	R456SKX

4057	M947LYR	DAF SB3000WS601	Van Hool Alizée	C493FT	1994	Arriva London North East, 1998
4058	M946LYR	DAF SB3000WS601	Van Hool Alizée	C493FT	1994	Arriva London North East, 1998

The Lucky Bus operation, Lucketts, was absorbed into Arriva The Shires during 1998. One of the vehicles to transfer is Dennis Javelin P100LOW, which now carries fleet number 4037. The vehicle is seen in its old silver, red and blue livery in Millbank. This vehicle features a UVG Unistar body, the additional centre door being where the lift access is based. *Colin Lloyd*

5000	BKE847T	Bristol VRT/SL3/6LXB	Eastern Coach Works	H43/31F	1979	Maidstone & District, 1997	
5011w	PRP802M	Bristol VRT/SL2/6LX	Eastern Coach Works	H43/31F	1974	United Counties, 1986	
5013	LBD837P	Bristol VRT/SL3/6LX	Eastern Coach Works	H43/31F	1975	United Counties, 1986	
5014w	OVV851R	Bristol VRT/SL3/501(6LXB)	Eastern Coach Works	H43/31F	1976	United Counties, 1986	
5016	OCY916R	Bristol VRT/SL3/501	Eastern Coach Works	H43/31F	1977	South Wales, 1987	
5017w	IAZ3977	Bristol VRT/SL3/501	Eastern Coach Works	H43/31F	1977	South Wales, 1987	
5018	OVV852R	Bristol VRT/SL3/501(6LXB)	Eastern Coach Works	H43/31F	1976	United Counties, 1986	
5019w	OVV853R	Bristol VRT/SL3/501(6LXB)	Eastern Coach Works	H43/31F	1976	United Counties, 1986	
5022	YVV893S	Bristol VRT/SL3/6LXB	Eastern Coach Works	H43/31F	1978	United Counties, 1986	
5023	YVV894S	Bristol VRT/SL3/6LXB	Eastern Coach Works	H43/31F	1978	United Counties, 1986	
5024	YVV895S	Bristol VRT/SL3/6LXB	Eastern Coach Works	H43/31F	1978	United Counties, 1986	

5025-5030		Bristol VRT/SL3/6LXB	Eastern Coach Works	H43/31F	1978-80	United Counties, 1986	
5025	CBD897T	**5027**w CBD900T	**5028** ONH928V	**5029** ONH929V		**5030** CBD904T	
5026	CBD899T						

5032	SNV932W	Bristol VRT/SL3/6LXB	Eastern Coach Works	H43/31F	1980	United Counties, 1986	
5033	SNV933W	Bristol VRT/SL3/6LXB	Eastern Coach Works	H43/31F	1980	United Counties, 1986	
5034	SNV934W	Bristol VRT/SL3/6LXB	Eastern Coach Works	H43/31F	1980	United Counties, 1986	
5035	ONH925V	Bristol VRT/SL3/6LXB	Eastern Coach Works	H43/31F	1980	United Counties, 1986	
5036	UDM448V	Bristol VRT/SL3/6LXB	Eastern Coach Works	H43/31F	1980	Crosville Cymru, 1995	
5037w	JPE237V	Leyland Atlantean AN68B/1R	Roe	H43/30F	1980	London Country NW, 1990	
5038	SNV938W	Bristol VRT/SL3/6LXB	Eastern Coach Works	H43/31F	1980	United Counties, 1986	

5039-5043		Leyland Atlantean AN68B/1R	Roe	H43/30F	1980	London Country NW, 1990	
5039	JPE233V	**5040** JPE236V	**5041**w KPJ241W	**5042** KPJ242W		**5043**w KPJ243W	

5046-5052

Bristol VRT/SL3/6LXB   Eastern Coach Works   H43/31F   1981   United Counties, 1986

5046	URP946W	5049	VVV956W	5050	VVV960W	5051w	VVV951W	5052	VVV957W
5047	URP947W								

5053-5060

Leyland Olympian ONLXB/1R   Eastern Coach Works   H45/32F   1981-82   United Counties, 1986

5053	ARP613X	5055	ARP615X	5057	ARP617X	5059	ARP619X	5060	ARP620X
5054	ARP614X	5056	ARP616X	5058	ARP618X				

5061	MUH287X	Leyland Olympian ONLXB/1R	Eastern Coach Works	H45/32F	1982	Rhondda, 1994
5062	ARP612X	Leyland Olympian ONLXB/1R	Eastern Coach Works	H45/32F	1981	United Counties, 1986
5063	MUH290X	Leyland Olympian ONLXB/1R	Eastern Coach Works	H45/32F	1982	Rhondda, 1995
5064	MUH284X	Leyland Olympian ONLXB/1R	Eastern Coach Works	H45/32F	1982	Rhondda, 1994
5065	BPF135Y	Leyland Olympian ONTL11/1R	Roe	H43/29F	1983	Sovereign, 1990
5066	BPF136Y	Leyland Olympian ONTL11/1R	Roe	H43/29F	1983	Sovereign, 1990
5067	IAZ2314	Leyland Olympian ONLXB/1R	Eastern Coach Works	H45/32F	1982	Rhondda, 1995
5068	A141DPE	Leyland Olympian ONTL11/1R	Roe	H43/29F	1983	Sovereign, 1990
5069	A149FPG	Leyland Olympian ONTL11/1R	Roe	H43/29F	1984	London Country NW, 1990
5070	A143DPE	Leyland Olympian ONTL11/1R	Roe	H43/29F	1983	Sovereign, 1990

5071-5075

Leyland Olympian ONTL11/1R   Roe   H43/29F   1984   London Country NW, 1990

5071	A151FPG	5072	A152FPG	5073	A153FPG	5074	A154FPG	5075	A155FPG

5076	B262LPH	Leyland Olympian ONTL11/1R	Eastern Coach Works	H43/29F	1985	Sovereign, 1990
5077	B273LPH	Leyland Olympian ONTL11/1R	Eastern Coach Works	H43/29F	1985	London Country NW, 1990
5078	A698EAU	Leyland Olympian ONTL11/1R	Northern Counties	H47/33D	1984	Buffalo, Flitwick, 1995
5079	A699EAU	Leyland Olympian ONTL11/1R	Northern Counties	H47/33D	1984	Buffalo, Flitwick, 1995
5080	B270LPH	Leyland Olympian ONTL11/1R	Eastern Coach Works	H43/29F	1985	London Country NW, 1990
5081	B271LPH	Leyland Olympian ONTL11/1R	Eastern Coach Works	H43/29F	1985	London Country NW, 1990
5082	B272LPH	Leyland Olympian ONTL11/1R	Eastern Coach Works	H43/29F	1985	London Country NW, 1990

5083-5094

Leyland Olympian ONCL10/1RZ   Alexander RL   H47/32F*   1988   *5086/91 are DPH47/29F

5083	F633LMJ	5086	F636LMJ	5089	F639LMJ	5091	F641LMJ	5093	F643LMJ
5084	F634LMJ	5087	F637LMJ	5090	F640LMJ	5092	F642LMJ	5094	F644LMJ
5085	F635LMJ	5088	F638LMJ						

5095-5107

Leyland Olympian ON2R50C13Z4   Alexander RL   H47/32F*   1989-90   *5104 is DPH47/29F

5099-5103 are H47/34F

5095	G645UPP	5098	G648UPP	5101	G651UPP	5104	G654UPP	5106	G656UPP
5096	G646UPP	5099	G649UPP	5102	G652UPP	5105	G655UPP	5107	G657UPP
5097	G647UPP	5100	G650UPP	5103	G653UPP				

5108	F506OYW	Leyland Olympian ONTL11/1RH	Northern Counties	H47/30F	1988	Yellow Bus, Stoke Mandeville, 1995
5109	G129YEV	Leyland Olympian ONCL10/2RZ	Northern Counties	H49/34F	1989	London Country NW, 1990
5110	G130YEV	Leyland Olympian ONCL10/2RZ	Northern Counties	H49/34F	1989	London Country NW, 1990

5111-5125

Leyland Olympian ONCL10/1RZ   Leyland   H47/31F   1989-90   London Country NW, 1990

5111	G281UMJ	5114	G284UMJ	5117	G287UMJ	5120	G290UMJ	5123	G293UMJ
5112	G282UMJ	5115	G285UMJ	5118	G288UMJ	5121	G291UMJ	5124	G294UMJ
5113	G283UMJ	5116	G286UMJ	5119	G289UMJ	5122	G292UMJ	5125	G295UMJ

5126	H196GRO	Leyland Olympian ON2R50C13Z4	Leyland	H47/29F	1991	
5127	H197GRO	Leyland Olympian ON2R50C13Z4	Leyland	H47/29F	1991	
5128	H198GRO	Leyland Olympian ON2R50C13Z4	Leyland	H47/29F	1991	
5129	H199GRO	Leyland Olympian ON2R50C13Z4	Leyland	H47/29F	1991	
5130	F747XCS	Leyland Olympian ONCL10/1RZ	Alexander RL	H47/32F	1989	A1 Service (McMenemy), 1995
5132	H202GRO	Leyland Olympian ON2R50C13Z4	Leyland	H47/29F	1991	
5133	H203GRO	Leyland Olympian ON2R50C13Z4	Leyland	H47/29F	1991	
5134	G131YWC	Leyland Olympian ONCL10/2RZ	Northern Counties	H49/33F	1989	Ensign, Purfleet, 1991
5135	G132YWC	Leyland Olympian ONCL10/2RZ	Northern Counties	H49/33F	1989	London Country NW, 1990

5136-5145

Volvo Olympian YN2RV18Z4   Northern Counties Palatine II   H47/30F   1996

5136	N36JPP	5138	N38JPP	5140	N46JPP	5142	N42JPP	5144	N35JPP
5137	N37JPP	5139	N39JPP	5141	N41JPP	5143	N43JPP	5145	N45JPP

Representing Arriva The Shires' double-deck fleet is 5076, B262LPH, an Eastern Coach Works-bodied Leyland Olympian previously with Sovereign. The latest delivery of Volvo Olympians has further reduced the numbers of remaining Bristol VRs. Beside these two models, the only other double-deck vehicles are seven Leyland Atlanteans.

5146-5161

| | | | | | | | | | | Volvo Olympian | Northern Counties Palatine II | DPH39/29F | 1998 |

5146	S146KNK	5149	S149KNK	5152	S152KNK	5156	S156KNK	5159	S159KNK
5147	S147KNK	5150	S150KNK	5153	S153KNK	5157	S157KNK	5160	S160KNK
5148	S148KNK	5151	S151KNK	5154	S154KNK	5158	S158KNK	5161	S161KNK

5852	VPA152S	Leyland Atlantean AN68A/1R	Park Royal	H43/30F	1978	London & Country, 1998
5866	FKM866V	Bristol VRT/SL3/6LXB	Eastern Coach Works	H43/31F	1979	Maidstone & District, 1997
5874	FKM874V	Bristol VRT/SL3/6LXB	Eastern Coach Works	H43/31F	1979	Maidstone & District, 1997

Heritage fleet:-

| 1178 | FEV178 | Leyland Titan TD5 | Eastern Coach Works (1949) | L28/27R | 1937 | preservation, 1987 |

Ancilliary fleet:

1005	F273CEY	Iveco Daily 49.10	Robin Hood City Nippy	B21F	1988	Crosville Cymru, 1994
1007	F266CEY	Iveco Daily 49.10	Robin Hood City Nippy	B21F	1988	Crosville Cymru, 1994
1008w	F696GMA	Iveco Daily 49.10	Robin Hood City Nippy	B21F	1988	Crosville Cymru, 1994
1201t	YMB938T	Bedford YLQ	Plaxton Supreme IV	C49F	1979	ADS, Wem, 1993
1203t	RDS83W	Volvo B58-56	Duple Dominant	B53F	1980	Buffalo, Flitwick, 1990
1204t	RDS84W	Volvo B58-56	Duple Dominant	B53F	1980	Buffalo, Flitwick, 1990
1205t	NJF204W	Bedford YMQ	Plaxton Supreme IV	C45F	1980	Lee & District, 1990
1206t	FJR776L	Bedford YRT	Plaxton Parnorama Elite III	C53F	1972	Rodham, Washington, 1994
1207w	K657KNL	Iveco Daily 49.10	Carlyle Dailybus 2	B23F	1989	OK, Bishop Auckland, 1996
2163t	D208SKD	Mercedes-Benz L608D	Reeve Burgess	B20F	1986	London & Country (GWS), 1997
2164t	D210SKD	Mercedes-Benz L608D	Reeve Burgess	B20F	1986	London & Country (GWS), 1997
3087t	G97VMM	Leyland Swift LBM6T/2RS	Wadham Stringer Vanguard II	B39F	1989	London Country NW, 1990
4038	ADZ4731	Volvo B10M-56	Plaxton Viewmaster IV Express	C51F	1982	Checker, Garston, 1997

Previous Registrations:

ADZ4731	KNP3X	MBZ6455	E295VOM, 7178KP
BAZ6869	JTU577T	MIL2350	G171BLH
BTX152T	AYR329T, NIW4810	NIB8459	E637NEL
CAZ6852	HMA561T	RJI6861	HMA569T
FEV178	From new	RJI6862	MCA677T
FIL4919	D614FSL, D448FSP	SIB4846	E321OMG
GHB574V	EYH802V, NIW2309	SIB7480	E325OMG
H231KBH	CMN414C	SIB7481	E326OMG
HIL7595	E663UNE	SIB8529	E324OMG
HIL7597	E660UNE	SLU261	WET880, D969MDB
AZ2314	MUH288X	TIB4873	MCA671T
IAZ3977	RTH917S	TIB4886	HPF322N
IAZ4037	VRP532S	TIB5906	C264SPC
IIL4821	XPD299N	TIB7835	JTU594T
IIL4822	LPB180P	WIB1113	B504CGP
IIL4823	GMB659T	WIB1114	E428YDM
IIL4824	HNB20N	YIB2396	C510LGH
J65UNA	J59MHF, J6SLT	YIB2397	D296RKW
J964NLL	J413UUK		
L500BUS	M289CUR		

Allocations & Liveries:-

Livery: Arriva turquoises and stone; yellow; green and white (Green Line ♣ and Jetlink) grey, red and blue♥ (Lucketts).

Aylesbury (Smeaton Close, Brunel Park) - Aylesbury & The Vale

Outstation - Leighton Buzzard

Mercedes-Benz	2054	2068	2069	2073	2083	2089	2095	2101
	2105	2106	2107	2113	2116	2117	2118	2119
	2145							
Greenway	3044	3045	3047	3048	3049	3054		
Lynx	3067							
Scania	3163	3164	3165	3166	3203	3204	3205	
Bristol VR	5874							
Olympian	5053	5054	5055	5056	5057	5058	5059	5060
	5061	5062	5063	5064	5067	5068	5070	5078
	5079	5083	5085	5088	5097	5099	5100	5101
	5102	5103	5104	5156	5157	5158	5159	5160
	5161							

Dunstable (Tavistock Street) - Luton & Dunstable

Mercedes-Benz	2037	2038	2039	2040	2043	2048	2061	2062
	2064	2065	2067	2121	2122	2124	2126	
Dart	3091	3092	3096					
National	3035	3036	3040					
Volvo B6	3123	3130	3131					
Scania	3167	3169	3170					
Bristol VR	5018	5019	5052					
Olympian	5086	5087	5091	5105	5106	5107		

Hemel Hempstead (Whiteleaf Road) - Gade Valley

Mercedes-Benz	2086	2087	2088	2127	2132	2177	2178	2179
	2180	2181	2182	2183	2184	2185	2186	2187
	2188	2189	2190	2191	2192	2193		
Tiger	4002♣	4003♣	4016♣	4017♣	4019♣	4020♣	4023♣	
	4025♣	4026♣						
Volvo	4034♣	4035♣						
DAF coaches	4057	4058						
Dart	3171	3172	3173	3174	3175	3176	3177	3178
Volvo B6	3245	3247						
Scania	3151	3152	3153	3154	3155	3156	3157	3158
	3159	3160	3161	3162				
Olympian	5069	5084	5092					

High Wycombe (Lincoln Road, Cressex Industrial Estate)

Outstation - Old Amersham

Mercedes-Benz	2138	2139	2140	2141	2142	2143	2197	2198
National	3014	3033	3899					
Greenway	3046	3050	3053	3055	3056	3057		
Volvo B6	3110	3115	3116	3126	3127	3138	3139	
Tiger	4007♣	4046♣						
Atlantean	5039	5040						
Olympian	5066	5067	5068	5070	5071	5075	5076	5108
	5109	5110	5134	5135				

Hitchin (Fishponds Road) - Hitchin & District - The Stevenage Line

Outstation - Stevenage

Mercedes-Benz	2055	2056	2057	2059	2060	2063	2071	2080
	2108	2109	2111	2112	2144	2146	2147	2148
	2149	2150	2151	2152	2153	2154	2155	2156
	2157	2160	2161	2162	2176	2194	2195	2199
	2200							
Volvo B6	3105	3106	3107	3108	3109	3111	3112	3113
	3114	3120	3128	3129				
Volvo B10B	3089							
Lynx	3061	3062	3063	3064	3070	3071	3074	3076
Scania	3196	3197	3198	3199	3201	3202		

Leagrave (Sedgwick Road) - Lutonian

Sherpa/DAF	2204	2205	2211	2212				
Iveco	2206	2207	2208	2210	2213	2214	2215	2216
	2217	2218	2219	2220	2221	2222		

Luton (Castle Street) - Luton & Dunstable

Mercedes-Benz	2050	2058	2066	2072	2074	2075	2076	2077
	2078	2079	2081	2082	2120	2123	2125	2158
	2159							
Iveco	2084	2085	2090	2091	2092	2093	2094	2096
	2097	2098	2099	2100				
Iveco coach	4036							
Tiger	4021♣	4022♣						
Volvo Coach	4015♣	4027♣						
DAF coach	4047	4048	4049	4050	4051	4052	4053	4054
	4055	4056						
National	3031	3037	3038	3039	3041	3042	3043	
Volvo B10M	3077	3078	3079	3080	3081			
Volvo B6	3117	3118	3119	3121	3122	3124	3125	3132
	3133	3134	3135	3136	3137			
Scania	3143	3144	3145	3146	3147	3148	3149	3168
	3192	3193	3194	3195				
Bristol VR	5000	5011	5013	5015	5016	5022	5023	5024
	5025	5026	5028	5029	5030	5032	5033	5034
	5035	5036	5038	5046	5047	5049	5050	5866
Olympian	5089	5090	5093	5094	5095	5096	5098	5136
	5137	5138	5139	5140	5141	5142	5143	5144
	5145							
Heritage	1178							

Recent additions to the Watford allocation are a further batch of Plaxton-bodied Dennis Dart low-floor buses. Some of these carry route-branding. Pictured here is 3211, R211GMJ, which is lettered with a vertical illustration of service 10. *Colin Lloyd*

Watford (St Albans Road, Garston) -

Mercedes-Benz	2070	2100	2114	2115	2128	2129	2130	2131
	2133	2134	2135	2136	2137	2144	2165	2166
	2171	2172	2173	2174	2175	2177	2178	2179
	2180	2196						
Iveco	2031							
Transit	2167	2168	2169	2170				
MetroRider	2020	2102	2103	2104	2110			
Dart	3091	3092	3093	3094	3098	3099	3100	3101
	3102	3103	3104	3179	3180	3181	3182	3183
	3184	3185	3186	3187	3188	3189	3190	3206
	3207	3208	3209	3210	3211	3212	3213	3214
	3215							
National	3052							
Lynx	3065	3066	3068	3069	3073	3075		
Volvo B10M	3058è	4009	4039è	4040è				
Javelin	4028	4037=						
Bristol VR	5016							
Olympian	5065	5072	5073	5074	5077	5080	5081	5082
	5111	5112	5113	5114	5115	5116	5117	5118
	5119	5120	5121	5122	5123	5124	5125	5126
	5127	5128	5129	5130	5132	5133	5146	5147
	5148	5149	5150	5151	5152	5153	5154	

Withdrawn

MetroRider	2025	2033				
Iveco	2041	2045	2051	2052	2053	2209
National	3015	3027				
Bristol VR	5027	5051				
Atlantean	5037	5043				

BALMORAL COACHES

R G Bason, 132 Balmoral Road, Queens Park, Northampton, NN2 6JZ

RBP847S	Bristol LHS6L	Plaxton Supreme III	C30F	1978	P C Coaches, Lincoln, 1996
E148RNY	Freight-Rover Sherpa	Carlyle Citybus 2	B20F	1987	Red & White, 1993
F115OVL	Freight-Rover Sherpa	Freight-Rover	M16	1989	private owner, 1991
G947VBC	Toyota Coaster HB31R	Caetano Optimo	C21F	1989	Hill, Hersham, 1996
JBZ8933	Ford Transit	Jubilee	M16	1990	private owner, 1994

Previous Registration:-

JBZ8933   H390XGE

Livery:-Red and cream.

The Bristol LHS was supplied to the National Bus Company (233), the private sector (131), municipals etc (43), to fulfill the role now undertaken by the midibus. The narrow body proved suitable in country lanes with bus bodywork being supplied by Eastern Coach Works while Plaxton provided bodies for most of the coaches. Pictured in the livery of Balmoral Coaches is Plaxton-bodied example RBP847S which originated with Buddens. *Keith Grimes*

BARFORDIAN

Barfordian Coaches Ltd, 16 Roxton Road, Great Barford, Bedfordshire, MK44 3LS

1774RU	Volvo B58-61	Plaxton Supreme IV	C57F	1980	Park's, Hamilton, 1982
HJB451W	Bristol VRT/SL3/6LXB	Eastern Coach Works	H43/31F	1980	City Line, 1997
YAY81	Bova EL26/581	Bova Europa	C49FT	1983	
DBJ969Y	Bedford YNT	Duple Dominant	B63F	1983	Chambers, Bures, 1990
489SYB	Bedford Venturer YNV	Duple 320	C57F	1987	
E94OUH	Freight-Rover Sherpa	Carlyle Citybus 2	B20F	1987	Stephenson, Rochford, 1996
SIW1936	DAF SB2300DHS585	Jonckheere Jubilee P50	C51FT	1988	
224ASV	Leyland Tiger TRCTL11/3ARZ	Duple320	C57F	1989	IOW Tours, Lake, 1997
SIW1931	Bova FHD12-290	Bova Futura	C51FT	1989	
RBZ4224	Toyota Coaster HB31R	Caetano Optimo	C18F	1989	Style Conferences, Newport Pagnell, 1996
SIW1932	Bova FHD12-290	Bova Futura	C51FT	1989	
IAZ3915	Toyota Coaster HB31R	Caetano Optimo	C21F	1990	Owen, Oswestry, 1993
VJI2779	Leyland Tiger TR2R62C18Z6/8	Plaxton Paramount 3200 III	C57F	1991	
VJI3982	Leyland Tiger TR2R62C18Z6/8	Plaxton Paramount 3200 III	C57F	1991	
SIW1937	Neoplan N122/3	Neoplan Skyliner	CH57/22CT	1991	Durham Travel Services, 1997
TFX663	Mercedes-Benz 0303/15R	Plaxton Paramount 3500 III	C51FT	1992	
K221CBD	MAN 16.290HOCL	Jonckheere Deauville P599	C51FT	1993	
L945JFU	Mercedes-Benz 609D	Autobus Classique	DP23F	1994	Mullover, Bedford, 1995
L946JFU	Mercedes-Benz 711D	Autobus Classique	DP24F	1994	Mullover, Bedford, 1995
N660EWJ	Volvo B10M-46	Van Hool Alizée HE	C36FT	1996	

Previous Registrations:-

224ASV	F792GNA	SIW1932	G98VFP
489SYB	D673DVV	SIW1936	E500KNV
1774RU	MDS233V	SIW1937	J1DTS, J118NJR
IAZ3915	G634UBB	TFX663	J60PJB
RBZ4224	G953VBC	VJI2779	H267GRY
SIW1931	F692ONR	VJI3982	J717KBC
		YAY81	From new

Livery:- Orange and yellow

Representing the Barfordian fleet is VJI3982, a Leyland Tiger with Plaxton Paramount 3200 bodywork, unusual in that the Leyland Tiger badge is displayed.
Geoff Rixon

BEESLY ENTERPRISES

A R Langham-Dobson, 3 Rock Street, Wellingborough, Northamptonshire, NN18 4LW

PMR361M	Bedford YRT	Plaxton Elite Express III	C53F	1974	M D Travel, Little Addington, 1998
SHP689R	Bedford YMT	Plaxton Supreme III	C53F	1977	M D Travel, Little Addington, 1998
ODO837Y	Leyland Tiger TRCTL11/3R	Plaxton Paramount 3500	C49FT	1983	M D Travel, Little Addington, 1998
D864PYS	Volkswagen LT55	Optare City Pacer	B25F	1987	M D Travel, Little Addington, 1998
E351UOH	Freight-Rover Sherpa	Carlyle Citybus 2	B20F	1988	M D Travel, Little Addington, 1998
N499ADC	?	?			

Previous Registration:-
ODO837Y   FNM857Y, JEF61, WWE96Y, HIL8405, WWE283Y, WCT502

Depot:- 80 Laurence Leyland Complex, Irthlingborough Road, Wellingborough.

BERKELEYS

Berkeley's Coach Services Ltd, TDS Buildings, Mark Road, Hemel Hempstead, Hertfordshire, HP2 7DN

J781KHD	DAF MB230LB615	Van Hool Alizée HE	C53F	1992	Wilson, Newtongrange, 1998
M633RCP	DAF DE33WSSB3000	Van Hool Alizée HE	C51FT	1995	Lowland, 1997
N63FWU	EOS E180Z	EOS 90	C49FT	1996	Happy Days, Woodseaves, 1998
P890PWW	DAF DE33WSSB3000	Van Hool Alizée HE	C51FT	1997	Cronin, Rossall, 1997
P215RWR	Mercedes-Benz 814D	Autobus Classique Nouvelle 2	C29F	1997	AR Travel, Hemel Hempstead, 1997
P216RWR	Mercedes-Benz 814D	Autobus Classique Nouvelle 2	C29F	1997	AR Travel, Hemel Hempstead, 1997
P859ADO	Mercedes-Benz 814D	Autobus Classique Nouvelle 2	C29F	1997	
R75GNW	EOS E180Z	EOS 90	C48FT	1998	

Livery:- White.

The BERKO BUS

N J Taylor, 1 Castle Street, Berkhamstead, Hertfordshire, HP4 2BQ

	C317URF	Ford Transit 190D	Dormobile	B16F	1985	Ferriday, Allestree, 1996
	D381JUM	Volkswagen LT55	Optare City Pacer	B25F	1987	Moden, Sound, 1993
AMR1	F737KGJ	MCW Metrorider MF154/7	MCW	B33F	1988	Croydon, Leicester, 1994

Previous Registrations:-
F737KGJ   DY6050 (Hong Kong)

Liveries:- *Berko Bus* - Green and Yellow - D381JUM, *Little Jim's* - Red and White - F737KGJ

Depots:-Castle Street and Railway Station Yard, Berkhamstead

Named vehicles:- C317URF *Katie Elizabeth*; D381JUM *Lady Penelope*

The number of Plaxton Elite Express coaches that remain in service is diminishing. Now the oldest vehicle in the Beesley fleet, PMR361M was photographed heading for Wembley with a party of football supporters.
Colin Lloyd

Berkeleys operate three Autobus Classique Nouvelle 2 models of which P215RWR is shown here passing by Marble Arch. The model is based on a Mercedes-Benz 814D chassis though, as can be seen, Autobus produce their own design of coachwork for the front of the vehicle.
Colin Lloyd

Minibus operator, The Berko Bus, provides service in Berkhampstead. Originally with London Buses, D381JUM, a Volkswagen LT55 with Optare CityPacer bodywork is seen preparing to leave for St Albans.

BRYANS OF ENFIELD
FALCON COACHES

B R J Nash, 19 Wetherby Road, Enfield, EN2 0NS
D J Nash, 64 Tynemouth Drive, Enfield, EN1 4LS

	MXX481	AEC Regal IV 9821LT	Metro-Cammell	B41F	1953	Shaftesbury & District, 1998
MB641	AML641H	AEC Merlin 4P2R	MCW	B50F	1969	R&H Wale, 1981
DM1070	GHV70N	Daimler Fleetline CRL6	Park Royal	H44/27D	1975	Grimsby-Cleethorpes, 1989
	THX509S	Leyland Fleetline FE30ALR	Park Royal	H44/27D	1978	See More, East Finchley, 1995
MCW495	MNC495W	MCW Metrobus DR102/10	MCW	H43/30F	1980	Stagecoach Manchester, 1998
	FIL4892	DAF MB200DKFL600	Van Hool Alizée H	C53F	1983	Prentice, West Calder, 1993
	DSU296	Leyland Royal Tiger RT	Van Hool Alizée H	C49F	1986	Glenn Miller Orchestra UK, 1998
	C101OTW	Leyland Olympian ONTL11/2Rsp Eastern Coach Works	CH43/18FT	1986	Brentwood Coaches, 1997

Named Vehicles:- GHV70N *Wild Swan*, FIL4892 *The Hearts Content*. THX509S *Chiswick Works*, MNC495W *The Boy's Brigade*, DSU296 *Glenn Miller*, C101OTW *The Olympic Torch*

Previous Registrations:-

C101OTW	4475WE, C259MWJ, 253DAF, C259MWJ, 823NMC	DSU296	C757FMC
FIL4892	SV2923, WSC903Y	MXX481	MXX481, KSJ622,
THX509S	THX633S, WLT916, DGJ415S		

Livery:- Red (buses); brown (Falcon coaches) DSU296, FIL4892

Depot:-South Mimms Service Area, St Albans Road, Potters Bar, Hertfordshire

Bryans of Enfield operate an interesting collection of vehicles carefully maintained in red livery. Representing the fleet is MB641, an AEC Merlin single-door example. The associated operation, Falcon Coaches, uses two Van Hool-bodied coaches, one based on a DAF chassis and the other, the rear-engined Leyland Royal Tiger.

BUCKBY'S / COOPERS

H F Cooper, 3 Fox Street, Rothwell, Northamptonshire, NN14 6AN
H F Cooper & J M Hochrath, Fox Street Garage, Rothwell, Northamptonshire, NN14 2AN
Avondale Regency Travel Ltd, 1 Bridge Street, Rothwell, Northamptonshire, NN14 2EW

FTO560V	Bedford YMT	Plaxton Supreme IV Express	C53F	1979	Barton, 1988
EBD188X	Bedford YNT	Plaxton Supreme V Express	C53F	1982	
OBX453Y	Bedford YNT	Duple Dominant	B59F	1983	Rodger's, Weldon, 1995
A94GLD	Bedford YMQ	Plaxton Paramount 3200	C35F	1983	Capital, West Drayton, 1990
RIW9473	Bedford YMP	Plaxton Paramount 3200 II	C35F	1985	Capital, West Drayton, 1991
C756OVV	Bedford YNT	Plaxton Paramount 3200 II	C55F	1986	
HIL7749	Bedford YNT	Plaxton Paramount 3200 II	C57F	1986	Midland Fox, 1992
G156UYK	Toyota Coaster HB31R	Caetano Optimo	C18F	1989	Carter, Maida Vale, 1995
H941WNH	Volvo B10M-60	Plaxton Paramount 3200 III	C57F	1990	
L579MVV	Ford Transit VE 6	Dormobile	B20F	1993	
P512MBD	Dennis Javelin	Plaxton Premiére 320	C57F	1997	

Previous Registrations:-

HIL7749	D735XBC, FIL9378, D836DJU	RIW9473	B873MLN

Livery:- Cream or white, blue and red (Buckby's); white and blue (Coopers).

Depot:- Desborough Road Garage, Rothwell.

Photographed at Wellingborough while operating route 15, is Buckby's L579MVV, a Ford Transit prepared for PCV use by Dormobile. The three associated operators in this group are all based in Rothwell. *Keith Grimes*

BUFFALO TRAVEL
CHILTERN EUROPEAN

Grouptravs Ltd; Bornyard Ltd, Enterprise Way, Flitwick, Bedfordshire, MK45 5BW

2	2583KP	Volvo B10M-61	Caetano Algarve	C55F	1986	Skills, Nottingham, 1988
7	9349KP	Volvo B58-61	Plaxton Supreme III	C57F	1978	Fountain, Twickenham, 1981
9	LXI2743	Volvo B58-61	Plaxton Supreme III	C57F	1978	Silver Fox, Renfrew, 1984
10	RNK749M	Bedford YRT	Plaxton Panorama Elite III	C49F	1973	Fountain, Isleworth, 1982
15	WXI4357	Volvo B58-56	Plaxton Supreme III Express	C44F	1975	Harris, High Wycombe, 1990
17	7178KP	Dennis Javelin 8.5SDL1903	Duple 320	C35F	1988	Brook, Werneth, 1995
18	KAZ6898	Volvo B10M-61	Plaxton Paramount 3500 II	C49FT	1985	McCormick, Airdrie, 1996
21	LIL5379	Toyota Coaster HB31R	Caetano Optimo	C21F	1990	Golden Boy, Roydon, 1995
24	JIL7424	Volvo B10M-61	Caetano Algarve	C51FT	1987	Catteralls, Southam, 1995
29	LAZ4364	Ford Transit VE6	Adams	M14	1987	Barrett, Basildon, 1996
30	URY598	Neoplan N722/3	Plaxton Paramount 4000 II	CH53/18CT	1986	Amberline, Speke, 1995
31	RJI6616	Scania K113TRB	Plaxton Paramount 4000 III	CH55/18CT	1990	Movers, Harrogate, 1996
32	TIW3902	Scania K113TRS	Plaxton Paramount 4000 II	CH55/16CT	1986	Grierson, Fishburn, 1996
35	KIW8800	Van Hool TD824	Van Hool Astromega	CH57/27F	1983	Ashall, Manchester, 1996
38	A8KRT	Ford Transit VE6	Mellor	M12	1995	West Riding Stage Coach, Bradford, 1996
39	N539DNW	Ford Transit VE6	Mellor	M12	1995	West Riding Stage Coach, Bradford, 1996
41	2997HL	Renault-Dodge S56	Alexander AM	B25F	1987	Evans, Prenton, 1995
42	NIL2883	Renault-Dodge S56	Alexander AM	B19F	1987	Traction Motors, Smethwick, 1997
43	MIL4418	Renault-Dodge S56	Alexander AM	B25F	1987	Manning, Challow, 1996
55	L555GSM	Dennis Javelin 12SDA2117	Berkhof Excellence 1000L	C51F	1994	Mayne, Buckie, 1995
57	L777GSM	Dennis Javelin 12SDA2131	Berkhof Excellence 1000L	C51F	1994	Mayne, Buckie, 1995
58	UJI1758	Hestair-Duple 425 SDA1510	Duple 425	C57F	1987	Swanbrook, Cheltenham, 1996
62	GSL898N	Daimler Fleetline CRG6LXB	Alexander AL	H49/34D	1975	Independent, Horsforth, 1987
63	GHV979N	Daimler Fleetline CRL6	Park Royal	H45/32F	1974	Ementon, Cranfield, 1988
64	THX493S	Leyland Fleetline FE30ALR	Park Royal	H44/27D	1977	Morgan, Staplehurst, 1994
65	THX533S	Leyland Fleetline FE30ALR	Park Royal	H44/27D	1978	Morgan, Staplehurst, 1994
66	THX605S	Leyland Fleetline FE30ALR	Park Royal	H44/27D	1978	Midland Fox, 1995
67	OJD414R	Leyland Fleetline FE30ALR	Park Royal	H44/27D	1977	Midland Fox, 1995
68	TFU62T	Leyland Fleetline FE30AGR	Roe	H45/29D	1979	Myall & Walsh, Hyde, 1996
68	OJD414R	Leyland Fleetline FE30ALR	Park Royal	H44/24D	1977	London Buses, 1991
71	OJD141R	Leyland Fleetline FE30AGR	Park Royal	H45/32F	1976	Taylor, Sutton Scotney, 1994
72	OUC49R	Leyland Fleetline FE30AGR	MCW	H45/32F	1976	Taylor, Sutton Scotney, 1994
77	K777KGM	Scania K93CRB	Plaxton Premiére 320	C53F	1993	Mayne's, Buckie, 1995
88	RND617X	MCW Metrobus DR102/28	Alexander RL	H45/33F	1982	Bullock, Cheadle, 1997
	OJI2830	Bova EL26/581	Bova Europa	C49FT	1981	Stephenson, Rochford, 1998
	XCP144X	Bova EL26/581	Bova Europa	C51F	1982	Stephenson, Rochford, 1997

Previous Registrations:-

2583KP	C45OTV	MIL4418	D316SDS
2997HL	D314SDS	NIL2883	E277BRG
7178KP	E149AGG	OJI2830	PNT605X, 3572NT, SUJ239X
9349KP	CLC764T	RJI6616	G704LKW
JIL7424	D507WNV, 24PAE, D184DWP	RND617X	ULS617X, JIL8216
KAZ6898	UDX921, A8KRT	TIW3902	C214BOS, LIB601, C214BOS
KIW8800	NDS841Y	UJI1758	E207EPB
LAZ4364	E629YRC	URY598	C180KHG
LIL5379	H170DJF	WXI4357	LUB506P
LXI2743	DGD88T, 7178KP, HKX319T	XCP144X	VWX322X, FSU359

Livery:- White, blue and red; yellow and red (contract buses)

Opposite, top:- **Buffalo Bus operate contract services in Bedfordshire and frequently undertake rail replacement services at weekends. Pictured outside Wembley Park rail station is 72, OUC49R in the red and yellow bus livery.** *David Heath*
Opposite, bottom:- **Photographed while on Park & Ride duties is Renault-Dodge S56 42, NIL2883, one of three with Alexander bodywork. Buffalo had previously sold its commercial bus operation to The Shires in 1995 but retains an extensive contract business.** *Keith Grimes*

CANTABRICA

Cantabrica Coach Holdings Ltd, 146-148 London Road, St Albans, Hertfordshire, AL1 1PQ

J100CCH	Volvo B10M-60	Berkhof Excellence 2000HL	C50FT	1992	
J200CCH	Volvo B10M-60	Berkhof Excellence 2000HL	C50FT	1992	
J200CCH	Volvo B10M-60	Berkhof Excellence 2000HL	C50FT	1992	
G843HRN	Mercedes-Benz 609D	Reeve Burgess Beaver	DP23F	1990	Empire Goldstar, Llandudno Jct, 1996
K600CCH	Volvo B10M-60	Berkhof Excellence 2000HL	C50FT	1992	
K700CCH	Volvo B10M-60	Berkhof Excellence 2000HL	C50FT	1993	
K800CCH	Volvo B10M-60	Berkhof Excellence 2000HL	C50FT	1993	
K900CCH	Volvo B10M-60	Berkhof Excellence 2000HL	C50FT	1993	
K999CCH	Volvo B10M-60	Berkhof Excellence 2000HL	C48FT	1993	
K318FYG	Mercedes-Benz 811D	Optare StarRider	C29F	1993	Metroline (Brents), 1998
L671PWT	Mercedes-Benz 814D	Optare StarRider	C29F	1994	Metroline (Brents), 1998
7804PP	Mercedes-Benz 811D	Autobus Classique	C23F	1994	Metroline (Brents), 1998
L7CCH	Volvo B10M-62	Berkhof Excellence 2000HL	C50FT	1994	
L8CCH	Volvo B10M-62	Berkhof Excellence 2000HL	C50FT	1994	
L9CCH	Volvo B10M-62	Berkhof Excellence 2000HL	C50FT	1994	
L10CCH	Volvo B10M-62	Berkhof Excellence 2000HL	C46FT	1994	
M7CCH	Volvo B10M-62	Berkhof Excellence 2000HL	C50FT	1995	
M8CCH	Volvo B10M-62	Berkhof Excellence 2000HL	C50FT	1995	
M9CCH	Volvo B10M-62	Berkhof Excellence 2000HL	C50FT	1995	
M10CCH	Volvo B10M-62	Berkhof Excellence 2000HL	C50FT	1995	
N20CCH	Peugeot Boxer	Cymric	M15	1996	

Ancillary vehicle

NPD108L	Leyland National 1151/2R/0402		B-D	1972	Courtesy bus.

Previous Registrations:-

7804PP	L959JFU	K600CCH	K771XRO	
			N20CCH	N688TBP

Livery:- Navy blue and red

Depot:-Elton Way, Watford

CENTRAL CARS

L D Lewis, 6 Chichester Close, Dunstable, Bedfordshire, LU5 4AG

WDA999T	Leyland Fleetline FE30AGR	MCW	H43/33F	1979	Travel West Midlands, 1997
MNH572V	Leyland National 11351A/1R		B49F	1979	Arriva The Shires, 1998
B638XJX	DAF MB200DKFL600	Caetano Algarve	C53F	1985	Folds, Kensworth, 1997
261HTF	Volvo B10M-61	Jonckheere Jubilee	C49FT	1986	Dereham Coachways, 1995
F331NLN	Freight-Rover Sherpa	Optare	M16	1988	Folds, Kensworth, 1997
G140WPP	Ford Transit VE6	Chassis Developments	M15	1990	
L140BPH	Mercedes-Benz 609D	Crystals	M16	1994	

Previous Registrations:-

261HTF	C420LRP, LVR956

Depots:- Matthew Street, Dunstable and Jockey Farm, Kensworth.

Cantabrica operate a modern coach fleet that mostly comprises Berkhof-bodied Volvo B10Ms. Typical of the type is K999CCH, pictured at Scratchwood Services on the M1. An interesting feature is the provision of windscreen wipers on the top window for the passengers benefit. *Colin Lloyd*

Ancillary vehicles are not often pictured in these publications, but as an exception we see neatly liveried NPD108L of Cantabrica. This Leyland National was one of the early models delivered to London Country, though initially used by Nottingham City Transport. It now provides transfer facilities as the Cantabrica fleet exchange passengers at Scratchwood Services. *Colin Lloyd*

CEDAR COACHES

E J Reid, Arkwright Road, Bedford, MK42 0LE

1	WRR396Y	Dennis Falcon V DDA403	East Lancashire	H50/38D	1982	City of Nottingham, 1992
2	UFW38W	Bristol VRT/LL3/6LXB	East Lancashire	H50/36F	1981	RoadCar, 1996
3	NFW37V	Bristol VRT/LL3/6LXB	East Lancashire	H50/36F	1980	RoadCar, 1995
4	VRS152L	Daimler Fleetline CRL6	Alexander AL	H45/29F	1973	Grampian, 1983
5	WUM106S	Leyland Fleetline FE30AGR	Roe	H43/33F	1978	Yorkshire Rider, 1995
6	GSL908N	Daimler Fleetline CRG6LXB	Alexander AL	H49/34D	1975	Tayside, 1984
7	PYJ458L	Daimler Fleetline CRG6LXB	Alexander AL	H49/34D	1972	Enterprise & Silver Dawn, Lincoln, 1987
8	BTV659T	Leyland Atlantean AN68A/1R	East Lancashire	H47/31D	1979	City of Nottingham, 1996
9	BTV661T	Leyland Atlantean AN68A/1R	East Lancashire	H47/31D	1979	City of Nottingham, 1996
10	OCU801R	Leyland Fleetline FE30AGR	Alexander AL	H44/29F	1977	Stagecoach United Counties, 1996
12	GAJ126V	Leyland Fleetline FE30AGR	Northern Counties	H43/31F	1980	Reay, Fletchertown, 1997
13	SCN255S	Leyland Atlantean AN68A/2R	Alexander AL	H49/37F	1978	Stagecoach Chltenham (CL), 1998
	OSR204R	Bristol VRT/LL3/6LXB	Alexander AL	H49/32D	1977	Happy Days, Woodseaves, 1996
	OCU804R	Leyland Fleetline FE30AGR	Alexander AL	H44/30F	1977	Stagecoach United Counties, 1998
	OCU808R	Leyland Fleetline FE30AGR	Alexander AL	H44/27F	1977	Stagecoach United Counties, 1998
	VDV104S	Bristol LH6L	Eastern Coach Works	B43F	1978	Barwick & Aspinall, Cawood, 1996
	OUF65W	Leyland Leopard PSU3F/4R	Plaxton Supreme IV Express	C53F	1981	Andy James, Tetbury, 1997
	512AUO	Leyland Tiger TRCTL11/2R	Duple Dominant IV Express	C53F	1983	The Delaine, Bourne, 1996
	WSU368	Kässbohrer Setra S228DT	Kässbohrer Imperial	CH54/20DT	1984	DeCourcey, Coventry, 1989
	C148SPB	Leyland Tiger TRCTL11/3RH	Berkhof Everest 370	C53F	1986	Arriva The Shires, 1998
	TXI2898	Neoplan N122/3	Neoplan Skyliner	CH57/20CT	1987	Priory, Gosport, 1996
	F164SMT	Leyland Swift LBM6T/2RS	Reeve Burgess Harrier	B37F	1989	Reay, Fletchertown, 1997
	G411PGG	Mercedes-Benz 811D	Reeve Burgess Beaver	B33F	1989	Timeline, Bolton, 1995
	G830RDS	Mercedes-Benz 811D	Reeve Burgess Beaver	B33F	1990	Timeline, Bolton, 1995
	G103YNK	Leyland Swift ST2R44C97T5	Elme	DP39F	1990	
	713WAF	EOS E180Z	EOS 100	C53FT	1992	Executive Travel, Wednesfield, 1997
	R9CCC	Scania L94 IB	Irizar Intercentury 12.32	C55F	1998	

Heritage vehicles:-

	HOD55	Bedford OB	Duple Vista	C29F	1949	Porter, Dummer, 1985
	MPP747	Dennis Lancet III	Yeates	C35F	1950	preservation, 1977

Previous Registrations:-

512AUO	YPD107Y	OUF65W	MAP343W, DSV943
713WAF	J100CGC, DXI92	TXI2898	D444SET
		WSU368	A263TYC

Livery:- Red and cream, or green and yellow.

Cedar Coaches operate local services and high-specification coaches. Lincoln City purchased East Lancashire-bodied Bristol VRs in the early 1980s. Now numbered 3, with Cedar Coaches NFW37V is seen in Stevenage.
Malcolm King

CHAMBERS

Chambers Coaches (Stevenage) Ltd, 38 Trent Close, Stevenage, SG1 3RT

YNF333Y	Mercedes-Benz L207D	Devon Conversions	M12	1982	Houghton, Goosnargh, 1993
FNM850Y	Leyland Tiger TRCTL11/2R	Plaxton Supreme V	C53F	1983	
A355YOX	Leyland Tiger TRCTL11/3R	Marshall Campaigner	DP52F	1984	MoD, 1994
B248RHP	Ford Transit 190D	Mellor	M16	1984	Bettison, Jacksdale, 1995
B274VRO	Ford Transit 190D	Dormobile	M5L	1985	private owner, 1990
C820FMC	Leyland Tiger TRCTL11/3RZ	Plaxton Paramount 3200 II	C57F	1986	
C106KVS	Leyland Tiger TRCTL11/3RZ	Plaxton Paramount 3200 II	C57F	1986	British Airways, Heathrow, 1988
D138HML	Leyland Tiger TRCTL11/3RZ	Plaxton Paramount 3200 II	C57F	1986	
781CRC	Dennis Javelin 12SDA1919	Plaxton Paramount 3200 III	C57F	1989	
38CRC	Dennis Javelin 8.5SDA1915	Plaxton Paramount 3200 III	C35F	1989	Wrays, Harrogate, 1993
F999UME	Leyland Swift LBM6T/2RS	Wadham Stringer Vanguard II	B39F	1989	
G838VAY	Dennis Javelin 12SDA1916	Plaxton Paramount 3200 III	C49FT	1989	
G421YAY	Dennis Javelin 12SDA1907	Duple 320	C57F	1990	Dent, North Kelsey, 1994
H5CRC	Scania K113CRB	Plaxton Paramount 3500 III	C49FT	1990	
H3CRC	Mercedes-Benz 609D	Reeve Burgess	C23F	1991	
H6CRC	Mercedes-Benz 609D	Walsall Motor Bodies	C24FL	1991	van, 1994
J4CRC	Dennis Javelin 12SDA1929	Plaxton Paramount 3200 III	C57F	1991	
K2CRC	Dennis Javelin 11SDL1921	Plaxton Paramount 3200 III	C53F	1992	
K265FUV	Dennis Javelin 12SDA2115	Plaxton Première 350	C57F	1993	Redwing, Camberwell, 1996
L1CRC	Dennis Javelin 12SDA2131	Plaxton Première 320	C57F	1994	
M1CRC	Toyota Coaster HZB50R	Caetano Optimo III	C21F	1995	
N4CRC	Mercedes-Benz 412D	Autobus Classique	M16	1996	
P4CRC	Dennis Javelin 12SDA2136	Plaxton Première 320	C57F	1996	
R2CRC	Dennis Javelin	Plaxton Première 320	C57F	1997	
S1CRC	Dennis Javelin (10m)	Plaxton Première 320	C39F	1998	

Previous Registrations:-

38CRC	F374MUT	H3CRC	H778FMJ
781CRC	F638SAY	H5CRC	H801RWJ
A355YOX	20KB63	H6CRC	H199MSX
C106KVS	C751FMC, 781CRC	L1CRC	M698HBC

Livery:- White, red and blue

Depot:-Jacks Hill Garage, Graveley

Opposite:- **Chambers operate private hire and contracts from their base in Stevenage. Representing the fleet are D138HML, a Leyland Tiger with Plaxton Paramount bodywork, and K265FUV, a Dennis Javelin with Plaxton Première 350 bodywork. The Dennis product has regularly been purchased by Chambers since their first example arrived in 1989.** *Tony Wilson*

Previous page:- **Two of the executive vehicles operate by Cedar Coaches are shown here. R9CCC, a Scania-Irizar combination is seen at the 1998 UK Coach Rally at Brighton and 713WAF, an integral EOS 100, is seen attending the Hampton Court flower show.** *Geoff Rixon*

CLASSIC COACHES

D H Crowther, 1a Barbers Wood Close, Booker, High Wycombe, Buckinghamshire, HP12 4EW

GWT630	Albion Valkyrie CX13	Burlingham	C33F	1947	preservation, 1993
NHU2	Bristol LSX5G	Eastern Coach Works	B44F	1952	preservation, 1993
EHL336	Leyland Tiger PS2/13A	Roe	C35F	1952	preservation, 1993
JCY870	AEC Regal IV 9822E	Burlingham Seagull	C39C	1955	preservation, 1993
JVH378	AEC Regent III 9613E	East Lancashire	H33/28R	1955	preservation, 1993
JHL983	AEC Reliance MU3RV	Roe Dalesman	C41C	1957	preservation, 1993
NDL869	AEC Reliance MU3RV	Duple Britannia	C41F	1957	preservation, 1995
NVS707	Leyland Titan PD2/30	Park Royal	L27/26R	1957	preservation, 1993
5228NW	Leyland Titan PD3/5	Roe	H38/32R	1959	preservation, 1993
5280NW	Leyland Titan PD3/5	Roe	H38/32R	1959	preservation, 1993
LJX198	AEC Regent V 2D3RA	Weymann	H39/32F	1959	preservation, 1996
WWN191	AEC Reliance 2MU3RV	Harrington Cavalier	C41F	1960	preservation, 1993
572CNW	Daimler CVG6LX	Roe	H39/31F	1962	preservation, 1995
574CNW	Daimler CVG6LX	Roe	H39/31F	1962	preservation, 1993
570EFJ	AEC Reliance 2MU4RA	Harrington Cavalier	C40F	1962	preservation, 1993
264KTA	Bristol MW6G	Eastern Coach Works	C39F	1962	Bushey Meads Youth Club, 1994
ABD253B	Bristol RELH6G	Eastern Coach Works	DP47F	1964	preservation, 1993
ANW710C	AEC Reliance 2MU2RA	Roe	C37F	1965	preservation, 1993
HLP10C	AEC Reliance 2U3RA	Harrington Grenadier	C51F	1965	preservation, 1995
CUV198C	AEC Routemaster R2RH	Park Royal	H36/28R	1965	preservation, 1998
EDV505D	Bristol MW6G	Eastern Coach Works	C39F	1966	preservation, 1994
EDV546D	Bristol MW6G	Eastern Coach Works	C39F	1966	Juniper Hill School, 1996
HNW366D	Leyland Titan PD3A/2	Roe	H41/32R	1966	preservation, 1995
LDV469F	Bristol RELH6G	Eastern Coach Works	C45F	1966	Stoke Poges School, 1995
LDV847F	Bristol RELH6G	Eastern Coach Works	C45F	1966	Spinfield School, Marlow, 1995
PBC98G	Leyland Atlantean PDR1A/1	Eastern Coach Works	H43/31F	1968	Peakbus, Chesterfield, 1996
PBC113G	Leyland Atlantean PDR1A/1	Park Royal	H43/31F	1968	D Coaches, Morriston, 1996
TBU30G	AEC Reliance 6MU3R	Plaxton Panorama Elite	C51F	1969	preservation, 1993
BWU691H	Leyland Leopard PSU4A/2R	Pennine	B43F	1969	Blue Bus, Horwich, 1995
GUP647H	AEC Reliance 6MU3R	Plaxton Derwent	B55F	1969	Calvary, Washington, 1996
RDV424H	Bristol RELH6G	Eastern Coach Works	C45F	1970	Western National, 1995
TCD375J	Daimler Fleetline CRG6LX	Northern Counties	O40/31F	1970	Northern Bus, Anston, 1998
TCD376J	Daimler Fleetline CRG6LX	Northern Counties	O40/31F	1970	Northern Bus, Anston, 1998
YOX69K	Daimler Fleetline CRG6LX	Park Royal	O43/30F	1971	Travel West Midlands, 1998
SWC24K	Bristol RELL6L	Eastern Coach Works	B53F	1972	preservation, 1995
KHD921K	Leyland Leopard PSU3B/4R	Marshall	B53F	1972	preservation, 1996
OCK367K	Bristol RESL6L	Eastern Coach Works	B47F	1972	preservation, 1997
MHW285K	Bristol RELL6L	Eastern Coach Works	B53F	1972	Dunn-Line, Nottingham, 1996
PHN178L	Bristol RELL6G	Eastern Coach Works	OB53F	1973	East Yorkshire, 1997
KCG627L	Leyland National 1151/1R/0402		B49F	1973	preservation, 1997
NDL637M	Bristol VRT/SL2/6G	Eastern Coach Works	H39/31F	1973	Home James, Totton, 1996
RTA693M	Bedford YRQ	Duple Dominant	C45F	1973	Harris, Slough, 1996
GPD304N	Bristol LHS6L	Eastern Coach Works	B37F	1974	Guernseybus, 1996
UMO180N	Leyland National 11351/1R		B49F	1974	Stagecoach South, 1998
JUG356N	Bristol LHS6L	Eastern Coach Works	B29F	1975	Guernseybus, 1996
JUG357N	Bristol LHS6L	Eastern Coach Works	B29F	1975	Guernseybus, 1996
KPM429P	Bristol LH6L	Plaxton Elite III	C45F	1975	Safeguard, Guildford, 1996
MGR671P	Bristol VRT/SL3/6LG	Eastern Coach Works	H43/31F	1975	Home James, Totton, 1996
IIL6441	Leyland Leopard PSU5A/4R	Duple Dominant	C53F	1976	Smith, High Wycombe, 1996
NSP323R	Ailsa B55-10	Alexander AV	H44/31D	1976	Crosskeys, Newingreen, 1998
NSP324R	Ailsa B55-10	Alexander AV	H44/31D	1976	Crosskeys, Newingreen, 1998
OHR185R	Leyland Fleetline FE30AGR	Eastern Coach Works	H43/31F	1977	Jacobs, Fair Oak, 1996
OHR186R	Leyland Fleetline FE30AGR	Eastern Coach Works	H43/31F	1977	Jacobs, Fair Oak, 1996
TMJ637R	Bristol LH6L	Plaxton Supreme III	C53F	1977	Safeguard, Guildford, 1996

Opposite, top:- **Roe-bodied AEC Reliance ANW710C is pictured in Claydon in preserved condition, liveried in the Leeds City Transport colours in which it originally operated.** *Tony Wilson*
Opposite, bottom:- **Fleet livery on Classic Coaches is shown on XPC14S, pictured on arrival in High Wycombe.** *David Heath*

PUK641R	Leyland National 11351A/1R		B49F	1977	London & Country, 1997
SOA663S	Leyland National 11351A/1R		B49F	1977	London & Country, 1997
TWN803S	Leyland National 11351A/1R		B49F	1977	
UPB307S	Leyland National 10351A/1R		B41F	1977	Central Parking, Heathrow, 1998
UPB340S	Leyland National 10351A/1R		B41F	1977	London & Country, 1997
PJJ345S	Leyland National 10351A/1R		B41F	1977	Stagecoach South (East Kent), 1998
XPC14S	Leyland National 10351A/1R		B41F	1978	London & Country, 1997
XEU858T	Leyland National 10351B/1R		B49F	1979	AJC, Leeds, 1997
CRP120T	AEC Reliance 6UZR	Duple Dominant Express	C53F	1978	Amos, Daventry, 1998
XAK911T	Bristol VRT/SL3/501	Eastern Coach Works	H43/31F	1979	RoadCar, 1996
XAK909T	Bristol VRT/SL3/501	Eastern Coach Works	H43/31F	1979	RoadCar, 1996
TFN980T	Bristol VRT/SL3/6LXB	Willowbrook	H43/31F	1978	Altonian, Alton, 1998
EPC900V	Bedford YMT	Duple Dominant II	C53F	1979	Martin Baker, Denham, 1998
DKG270V	Bedford YMT	Plaxton Supreme III	C53F	1979	Vicary, Battle, 1996
DWF195V	Bristol VRT/SL3/501	Eastern Coach Works	H43/31F	1979	Stagecoach Midland Red, 1998
HPB814V	Bedford YMT	Plaxton Supreme IV	C53F	1980	Safeguard, Guildford, 1996
XPT569V	Bedford YMT	Plaxton Supreme IV	C53F	1980	Roberts, South Littleton, 1997
KPC405W	Bedford YMT	Duple Dominant II	C53F	1980	Safeguard, Guildford, 1996
GGM86W	Bristol VRT/SL3/6LXB	Eastern Coach Works	H43/31F	1980	Stagecoach South, 1998
JWV267W	Bristol VRT/SL3/6LXB	Eastern Coach Works	H43/31F	1980	Stagecoach South, 1998
JRV416X	DAF MB200DKTL600	Jonckheere Bermuda	C57F	1982	Sea View Services, Sandown, 1998
D461PON	MCW MetroRider MF150/14	MCW	B28F	1987	Westlink, 1998
D462PON	MCW MetroRider MF150/14	MCW	B28F	1987	Westlink, 1998

Previous Registrations:-

264KTA	From new	JRV416X	WRK16X, EUI4376, YJO809X, ODL678
570EFJ	From new	JUG356N	JUG356N, 31914, 12723
572CNW	From new	JUG357N	JUG357N, 31915, 12727
574CNW	From new	JVH378	From new
5228NW	From new	LJX198	From new
5280NW	From new	NDL869	From new
EHL336	From new	NHU2	From new
GPD304N	GPD304N, 19678, 2972	NVS707	TWY7, NNW985A
GWT630	From new	RTA693M	SNK246M, 645CJD
IIL6441	MWG497P	TCD375J	TCD375J, 222WFM
JCY870	From new	TCD376J	TCD376J, 223FWW
JHL983	From new	WWN191	From new

Livery:- Blue and cream (buses); red and cream (coaches), or original operator's livery. Some of the older vehicles are on display at the Dewsbury Bus Museum.

Depot:- Binders Industrial Estate, Cryers Hill, High Wycombe; Bletchley Park, Wilton Avenue, Bletchley; Tame Road, Kingsey.

**The newer of the double-deck fleet operated by Classic coaches are Bristol VRs with Eastern Coach Works bodies.
Pictured at Putney Bridge is XAK911T, an example purchased from RoadCar in 1996.**
Colin Lloyd

CLIFFS COACHES

C C & J D Neighbour, 150 Wrights Lane, Prestwood, Buckinghamshire, HP16 0LG

F540OEB	DAF SB2305DHS585	Caetano Algarve	C53F	1988	Norman, Parson Grove, 1997
G42HKY	Scania K93CRB	Duple 320	C55F	1990	
K647SBX	Renault Master	Cymric	M16	1993	
M9CJN	Volkswagen Caravelle	Volkswagen	M8	1995	
M95BPX	Iveco Daily 49.10	European Coach Conversions	C18FL	1995	
M495XWF	Scania K113CRB	Irizar Century 12.35	C49FT	1995	
P56BTF	LDV Convoy	LDV	M12L	1996	
R650RKX	Mercedes-Benz Sprinter 412D	Mercedes-Benz	M16	1997	

Previous Registration:-
F540OEB   F771RHP, A13WMT

Livery:- Blue and white.

Depot:- Binders Industrial Estate, Cryers Hill, High Wycombe.

Cliff's Coaches operate from High Wycombe and all bar one of the current fleet has been delivered new. Included are two Scania coaches, a K113 model with Irizar bodywork and K93 G42HKY, one of the Duple-bodied examples featuring the 320 design. This latter vehicle is seen on an excursion to Chessington World of Adventures. *David Heath*

COUNTRY LION / BRITTAIN'S

Country Lion (Northampton) Ltd, St. James Mill Road, Northampton, NN5 5JP

PVV888J	Bedford J2SZ10	Plaxton Embassy	C20F	1971	
PBD42R	Bristol VRT/SL3/6LXB	Alexander AL	H45/27D	1977	Brittain's, Northampton, 1995
VVV61S	Bristol VRT/SL3/6LXB	Alexander AL	H45/27D	1977	Brittain's, Northampton, 1995
CNH56T	Bristol VRT/SL3/6LXB	Alexander AL	H45/27D	1978	Brittain's, Northampton, 1995
MJU797W	Volvo B58-61	Plaxton Supreme IV	C55F	1980	Brittain's, Northampton, 1995
C121MAK	Neoplan N722/3	Plaxton Paramount 4000 II	CH53/18DT	1986	Yorkshire Traction, 1997
C122MAK	Neoplan N722/3	Plaxton Paramount 4000 II	CH53/18DT	1986	Yorkshire Traction, 1997
C114MAK	Neoplan N722/3	Plaxton Paramount 4000 II	CH53/18DT	1986	Yorkshire Traction, 1997
F41YNH	Ford Transit VE6	Chassis Developments	C16F	1989	
A19CLN	Scania K93CRB	Van Hool Alizée H	C55F	1990	Brittain's, Northampton, 1995
A15CLC	Volvo B10M-60	Plaxton Paramount 3500 III	C53F	1991	Park's, Hamilton, 1993
PRP3V	DAF SB3000KS601	Caetano Algarve II	C55F	1993	Brittain's, Northampton, 1995
YNH1W	Scania K113CRB	Van Hool Alizée HE	C55F	1994	Brittain's, Northampton, 1995
A14CLC	Dennis Javelin 10SDA2139	Plaxton Première 320	C43F	1995	
A16CLC	Ford Transit VE 6	Devon Conversions	C16F	1995	
N937FLE	Fiat Ducato	Devon Conversions	M14	1995	GN, Greenford, 1997
L10NBB	Mercedes-Benz 814D	Autobus Classique Nouvelle	C25F	1995	
A18CLN	Volvo B10M-62	Plaxton Excalibur	C49FT	1995	
N305DHE	Dennis Dart SLF	Plaxton Pointer	N40F	1996	Plaxton demonstrator, 1997
L10NCC	Mercedes-Benz 811D	Autobus Classique Nouvelle	C29F	1996	
A15CLN	Volvo B10M-62	Plaxton Première 320	C57F	1996	
L1ONC	Volvo B10M-62	Van Hool Alizée HE	C43FT	1996	
L1ONB	Volvo B10M-62	Plaxton Excalibur	C..F	1996	
A10CLC	Volvo B10M-62	Plaxton Première 350	C53F	1997	
P4CLN	Dennis Dart SLF	Marshall C39	N43F	1997	
P5CLN	Dennis Dart SLF	East Lancashire Spryte	N47F	1997	
L1OND	Mercedes-Benz Vario 0814	Autobus Classique Nouvelle 2	C25F	1997	
A9CLN	Mercedes-Benz Vario 0814	Plaxton Cheetah	C29F	1998	
A12CLN	Volvo B10M-62	Plaxton Première 320	C57F	1998	
A17CLN	Volvo B10M-62	Plaxton Première 350	C53F	1998	
A20CLC	Volvo B10M-62	Plaxton Première 350	C53F	1998	
A8CLN	Scania L94IB	Irizar Intercentury 12.32	C55F	1998	
A15NFC	Volvo B10M-62	Van Hool Alizée 2	C53F	1996	
L10NKK	Mercedes-Benz O1120L	Ferqui Solera	C35F	1998	
L10N..	Mercedes-Benz O1120L	Ferqui Solera	C35F	1998	

Previous Registrations:-

A15CLC	H825AHS	C121MAK	C91KET, YTC838
A15CLN	N647CVV	C122MAK	C93KET, 3880HE
A19CLN	G798FJX	PRP3V	K589VBC
C114MAK	C94KET, 2316HE	YNH1W	L420LHE

Livery:- White, yellow and brown

The Northampton-based operator, Country Lion operate services in the town. Shown here are three of the fleet on active service. The upper picture shows L10NHH, A Mercedes-Benz with Autobus bodywork which has just been replaced by a new Ferqui Solera. The other pictures show a pair of Dennis Darts delivered in 1997. P4CLN carries bodywork by Marshall, while that on P5CLN was constructed by East Lancashire Coachbuilders. The business expanded in 1995 with the purchase of local competitor, Brittans.
Tony Wilson/ Keith Grimes

DRURY

A S Drury, 22 Gravel Walk, Emberton, Olney, Buckinghamshire, MK46 5JA

XWG639T	Leyland Atlantean AN68A/1R	Roe	H45/29D	1978	Poynter, Wye, 1996
XEL587	Neoplan N122/3	Neoplan Skyliner	CH53/20CT	1982	Inland Travel, Flimwell, 1995
FIL6282	Kässbohrer Setra S215HD	Kässbohrer Tornado	C49FT	1983	Kentishman, Swanley, 1997
993HNW	Kässbohrer Setra S228DT	Setra Imperial	CH51/20DT	1985	Irvine, Carlisle, 1998

Previous Registrations:-

FIL6282	A321FPA	XEL587	EFW855X, XEL587, MAN111J

ENFIELDIAN

Oakfield Tours Ltd, Unit 3, 48 London Road, Enfield, EN2 6EZ

VJD44S	Leyland Leopard PSU3E/4R	Plaxton Supreme III	C53F	1977	Heaney, Enfield, 1991
WRY216X	DAF MB200DKTL600	Plaxton Supreme V	C55F	1982	Wilfreda-Beehive, Adwick le Street, 1990
A520NCL	Volvo B10M-61	Plaxton Paramount 3500	C53F	1984	Ralph's, Langley, 1994
GIL5979	Volvo B10M-61	Van Hool Alizée H	C53F	1985	Amport & District, 1998
C513DND	Volvo B10M-61	Plaxton Paramount 3200 II	C53F	1986	Metroline (Brents), 1997
C42MAK	Volvo B10M-61	Duple Caribbean 2	C53F	1986	?,1997

Previous registration:-

C42MAK	?	GIL5979	B478UNB

Livery:- White with two tone blue and yellow

Depot:- Paradise Wildlife Park, Broxbourne, Hertfordshire

EXODUS

Exodus Coach Company Ltd, PO Box 578, Bedford, MK44 2ZH

YSV306	Bedford YRQ	Caetano Cascais II	C17F	1976	Team Thrust, Bedford, 1998
910OCV	Bedford YMT	Duple Dominant III	C53F	1977	Rambler, Hastings, 1998
YEB105T	Bedford YMT	Plaxton Supreme IV	C53F	1979	Rambler, Hastings, 1998
RIB6838	Volvo B58-61	Duple Dominant III	C53F	1980	Floyd, Orpington, 1997
YSV727	Volvo B58-61	Plaxton Viewmaster IV	C14FT	1980	Midnight Express, Hastings, 1997
YSV375	DAF MB200DKFL600	LAG Galaxy	C49FT	1984	Thomas, Portchester, 1997
YSV994	Hestair-Duple SDA1913	Duple 425	C53FT	1990	Jennings, Bude, 1998
K1OLE	Scania K113CRB	Plaxton Excalibur	C36FT	1993	Blueways, Battersea, 1997

Previous Registrations:-

910OCV	OTR412S	YSV375	A338HNR
RIB6838	KPC393W, 149GJF, LJH171W	YSV727	DMT776V
YEB105T	YEB105T, NCF715	YSV994	G631CRL
YSV306	LYL322P		

Livery:- Blue and red.

Depot:- Willow Farm, Ravensden.

Pictured in Victoria Street, London, is Volvo A520NCL of Enfieldian. The vehicle carries Plaxton Paramount 3500 bodywork . *Colin Lloyd*

The Exodus fleet includes YSV375, a DAF MB200 with a LAG Galaxy body. The vehicle was photographed arriving at Wembley for a football match. Recent arrival K1OLE, the former England Football Team coach, is now serving Dr Martens League members Rushden and Diamonds. *Colin Lloyd*

EXPRESSLINES

Expresslines Ltd, Unit 10 Fenlake Industrial Estate, Bedford, MK42 0HB

C140KVV	Mercedes-Benz L608D	Reeve Burgess	C24F	1985	Gibbs, Calverton, 1989
D351JUM	Volkswagen LT55	Optare City Pacer	B25F	1986	Waddon, Bedwas, 1993
F724SML	Leyland Swift LBM6T/2RSO	Reeve Burgess Harrier	C37F	1989	Castle, Clanfield, 1996
F997MTM	Ford Transit VE6	Chassis Developments	M16	1989	O'Brien, Queensbury, 1997
G820LAT	Mercedes-Benz 408D	Coachcraft	M16	1989	Weyland's, Stockton, 1992
G775WBE	Mercedes-Benz 408D	Coachcraft	M15	1989	Regan, Ware, 1992
G283ANK	Ford Transit VE6	Chassis Developments	M16	1990	Cavalier, Long Sutton, 1996
G441ETW	Ford Transit VE6	Crystals	C20F	1990	Bexhill Community Bus, 1997
H187GKM	Ford Transit VE6	Crystals	B20F	1991	Kent CC ,1997
H189GKM	Ford Transit VE6	Crystals	B20F	1991	Kent CC, 1996
H951LSF	Mercedes-Benz 811D	PMT Ami	C33F	1991	Rainham Coach Co, Gillingham, 1995
H125JTW	Ford Transit VE6	Ford	M14	1991	Ford, Dagenham, 1991
N715FLN	Mercedes-Benz 814D	Cacciamali Ibis	C25F	1995	MTL London, 1997

Livery:- Maroon, grey and white

Note:- Several 8-seat Ford Transits are operated as non-PCVs

The Reeve Burgess Harrier body, as built on Leyland Swift F724SML, had both bus and coach variants. The vehicle is seen with the coach door swung to the open position. This vehicle took part in Showbus 97 and, as shown on the vehicle, gained awards. *Colin Lloyd*

FIRST NORTHAMPTON

Northampton Transport Ltd, The Bus Depot, St James Road, Northampton, NN5 5JD

9	PSU630	Volvo B10M-61	Plaxton Paramount 3500 III	C49FT	1987	Rider Group, 1997
10	LSK527	Dennis Javelin 8.5SDL1903	Duple 320	C35F	1988	Grampian (Kirkpatrick), 1997
11	G427PWW	Volvo B10M-60	Plaxton Paramount 3500 III	C53F	1990	First Leeds, 1998
17	FFK312	Leyland Tiger TRCTL11/2R	Plaxton Paramount 3200 E	C49F	1983	Leicester Citybus, 1997
18	BUT18Y	Leyland Tiger TRCTL11/2R	Plaxton Paramount 3200 E	C53F	1983	Leicester Citybus, 1996
19	PXI8935	Leyland Tiger TRCL10/3RZA	Duple 340	C53F	1987	SMT, 1996
20	NTL655	Leyland Tiger TRCL10/3RZA	Duple 340	C53F	1987	SMT, 1996
41	N41RRP	Volvo B10L	Alexander Ultra	B45F	1995	
42	N42RRP	Volvo B10L	Alexander Ultra	B45F	1995	
43	N43RRP	Volvo B10L	Alexander Ultra	B45F	1995	
46	UFW40W	Bristol VRT/LL3/6LXB	East Lancashire	H50/38F	1981	RoadCar, 1997
47	UFW41W	Bristol VRT/LL3/6LXB	East Lancashire	H50/38F	1981	RoadCar, 1997

48-58		Bristol VRT/SL3/6LXB	Alexander AL	H45/27D	1978

48	CNH48T	50	CNH50T	53	CNH53T	57	CNH57T	58	CNH58T
49	CNH49T	52	CNH52T	54	CNH54T				

70	VVV70S	Bristol VRT/SL3/6LXB	Alexander AL	H45/27D	1977
74	ABD74X	Bristol VRT/SL3/6LXB	East Lancashire	H44/27D	1982
75	ABD75X	Bristol VRT/SL3/6LXB	East Lancashire	DPH43/27D	1982
76	ABD76X	Bristol VRT/SL3/6LXB	East Lancashire	DPH43/27D	1982

First Northampton was one of the first English operators to take the Alexander Ultra body after it was announced in 1994. Based on the Säffle design for the Volvo B10L, only one of the Säffle products is in service in Britain, Alexander building the remainder under licence using System 2000 structure. The attractive design has received much acclaim and 43, N43RRP is shown here. *Tony Wilson*

83-88

Volvo Citybus B10M-50 — Alexander RV — DPH47/35F 1989

| 83 | F83XBD | 84 | F84XBD | 85 | F85XBD | 86 | F86DVV | 88 | F88DVV |

89-94

Volvo Citybus B10M-55 — Alexander RV — DPH47/35F 1990

| 89 | H289VRP | 91 | H291VRP | 92 | H292VRP | 93 | H293VRP | 94 | H294VRP |
| 90 | H290VRP | | | | | | | | |

95-100

Volvo Citybus B10M-50 — Alexander RV — DPH47/35F 1991

| 95 | J295GNV | 97 | J297GNV | 98 | J298GNV | 99 | J299GNV | 100 | J210GNV |
| 96 | J296GNV | | | | | | | | |

101	D101XNV	Volvo Citybus B10M-50	East Lancashire	DPH47/31F	1986
102	D102XNV	Volvo Citybus B10M-50	East Lancashire	DPH47/31F	1986
111	E111NNV	Volvo Citybus B10M-50	Duple 300	DP49F	1988
112	G112ENV	Volvo Citybus B10M-55	Duple 300	DP49F	1989
113	G113ENV	Volvo Citybus B10M-55	Duple 300	DP51F	1989
114	G114ENV	Volvo Citybus B10M-55	Duple 300	DP51F	1989
115	J115MRP	Volvo Citybus B10M-55	East Lancashire EL2000	DP47F	1992

121-132

Volvo Citybus B10M-50 — Alexander RV * — DPH47/35F 1992-93 — *122 East Lancashire Pyoneer, 1998

121	K121URP	124	K124URP	127	K127GNH	129	K129GNH	131	K131GNH
122	WSU481	125	K125URP	128	K128GNH	130	K130GNH	132	K132GNH
123	K123URP	126	K126URP						

341	R341SUT	Scania L113CRL	Wright Axcess-ultralow	N37F	1998	
342	R342SUT	Scania L113CRL	Wright Axcess-ultralow	N37F	1998	
343	R343SUT	Scania L113CRL	Wright Axcess-ultralow	N37F	1998	
401	F50ENF	Leyland Tiger TRBL10/3ARZA	Alexander N	B55F	1989	First Leicester, 1998
407	F37ENF	Leyland Tiger TRBL10/3ARZA	Alexander N	B55F	1988	Leicester Citybus, 1997
408	EWR652Y	Leyland Tiger TRBTL11/2R	Duple Dominant	DP47F	1983	Essex Buses (Eastern National), 1998
409	EWR651Y	Leyland Tiger TRBTL11/2R	Duple Dominant	DP47F	1983	Essex Buses (Eastern National), 1998
410	A660KUM	Leyland Tiger TRBTL11/2R	Duple Dominant	DP47F	1983	Essex Buses (Eastern National), 1998
411	EWR653Y	Leyland Tiger TRBTL11/2R	Duple Dominant	DP47F	1983	Essex Buses (Eastern National), 1998

501-506

Volvo B10L(CNG) — Alexander Ultra — B41F 1997

| 501 | P501MVV | 503 | P503MVV | 504 | P504MVV | 505 | P505MVV | 506 | P506MVV |
| 502 | P502MVV | | | | | | | | |

628	C108SDX	Dennis Falcon HC SDA416	Northern Counties	B45F	1985	Leicester Citybus, 1997
629	C109SDX	Dennis Falcon HC SDA416	Northern Counties	B45F	1986	Leicester Citybus, 1997
631	YDX100Y	Dennis Falcon HC SDA408	East Lancashire	B44D	1983	Leicester Citybus, 1997

707-714

Renault S75 — Wright — B28F 1990

| 707 | HDZ5466 | 710 | HDZ5471 | 711 | HDZ5472 | 712 | HDZ5473 | 714 | HDZ5478 |
| 708 | HDZ5488 | | | | | | | | |

Previous Registrations:

FFK312	BUT19Y		NTL655	E353KSF, A13SMT, WSV144
			PSU630	D783SGB
G427PWW	G73RGG, 8995WY		PXI8935	E352KSF, A12SMT
LSK527	E151XHS		WSU481	K122URP

Local livery:- Cream, red and maroon

Opposite, top:- **Northampton was a keen user of the Volvo B10M double-deck chassis, sometimes referred to as the D10M. Photographed in the town is 101, D101XNG is one of two East Lancashire bodied examples delivered in 1986 and fitted with high-back seating. During 1998 the fleet names have been changed to show First on the front of the vehicle and First Northampton on the vehicle sides. Previous policy on naming vehicles after local dignitaries has been recinded and the names will be removed from vehicles on repaint.** *Tony Wilson*

Opposite, bottom:- **FirstGroup have been at the forefront of alternative fuel development with several experiments underway across the group. In 1997, First Northampton took six Volvo B10L's with Alexander Ultra bodywork and powered by CNG. These carry the green livery first seen on City Line's example.** *Tony Wilson*

Allocation:

Northampton (St James Road)

Tiger coach	17	18	19	20			
Volvo B10M coach	9	11					
Javelin coach	10						
Tiger bus	401	407	408				
Renault S75	707	708	710	711	712	714	
Falcon	628	629	631				
Volvo B10M Bus	111	112	113	114	115		
Volvo B10L	41	42	43	501	502	503	504	505
	506						
Scania L113	341	342	343				
Bristol VR	46	47	48	49	50	52	53	54
	57	58	70	74	75	76	
Volvo Citybus	83	84	85	86	88	89	90	91
	92	93	94	95	96	97	98	99
	100	101	102	121	122	123	124	125
	126	127	128	129	130	131	132	

Reserve

Tiger bus	409	410	411

Prior to the Volvo B10M double-deck, Northampton purchased the Bristol VR chassis with bodywork by Alexander. Three East Lancashire-bodied examples delivered in 1982 remain in the fleet, with 75, ABD75X, seen here in the town centre, being one of a pair with high-back seating. *Phillip Stephenson*

GEOFF AMOS

Geoff Amos Coaches Ltd, Woodford Road Service Station, Eydon, Daventry,
Northamptonshire, NN11 6PL

47	TVV170W	Bedford YMT	Duple Dominant	B63F	1980	
48	XAM116A	Bova EL26/581	Bova Europa	C53F	1982	
49	XAM118A	Bova EL26/581	Bova Europa	C53F	1982	
50	A140TNV	Bedford YNT	Duple Dominant	B63F	1983	
51	B368KNH	Dennis Dorchester SDA807	Reeve Burgess	B71F	1984	
52	XAM109A	Bova FLD12.250	Bova Futura	C53F	1986	
53	XAM730A	Bova FHD12.280	Bova Futura	C49F	1986	
54	D957ENH	Dennis Dorchester SDA801	Wadham Stringer Vanguard II	B71F	1987	
55	E913PNV	Dennis Dorchester SDA812	Wadham Stringer Vangaurd II	B71F	1988	
56	SJI3928	Dennis Dorchester SDA813	Caetano Algarve	C53F	1988	
57	SJI3929	Dennis Dorchester SDA813	Caetano Algarve	C49FT	1988	
59	TBZ5791	DAF SB3000DKV601	Caetano Algarve	C49F	1990	
62	XAM731A	Leyland Tiger TRCTL11/3R	Plaxton Supreme IV	C50F	1982	
64	XAM124A	DAF SBR3000DKS570	Plaxton Paramount 4000 II	CH55/17CT	1988	Tourswift, Chester-le-Street, 1992
79	TBZ5793	DAF SB3000DKV601	Caetano Algarve	C51F	1990	Brittain's, Northampton, 1994
80	UJI2463	Neoplan N216H	Neoplan Jetliner	C49FT	1984	Elite, Stockport, 1996
81	KPJ256W	Leyland Atlantean AN68B/1R	Roe	H43/30F	1980	County, 1996
82	JWF47W	Leyland Atlantean AN68B/1R	Roe	H43/31F	1980	Eastbourne Buses, 1997
83	KPJ238W	Leyland Atlantean AN68B/1R	Roe	H43/30F	1980	County, 1997
84	KPJ244W	Leyland Atlantean AN68B/1R	Roe	H43/30F	1980	County, 1997
85	TBZ5873	DAF SB2300DHS585	Smit Euroliner	C53F	1985	Adkins, Upper Boddington, 1997
86	CPO351W	Leyland Atlantean AN68A/1R	East Lancashire	H46/27F	1980	Driver Express, South Godstone, 1998
87	KPJ271W	Leyland Atlantean AN68B/1R	Roe	H43/30F	1980	Arriva Kent Thameside, 1998

Previous Registrations:-

B368KNH	XAM124A	TBZ5791	H169EJF	XAM116A	ENH44X
D957ENH	XAM731A	TBZ5793	H403CJF	XAM118A	ENH45X
SJI3928	F875TNH	UJI2463	B178BFE	XAM124A	E420LOU
SJI3929	F876TNH	XAM730A	From new	XAM731A	GGJ347X
TBZ5873	B88MUT	XAM109A	From new		

Livery:- White, lilac and purple

A rare combination of service vehicle is D957ENH, one of a pair of type operated by Geoff Amos. This vehicle has a Dennis Dorchester chassis with Wadham Stringer Vanguard bodywork. The majority of Dorchester chassis were built for coach use in the early 1980s. Even rarer is the Reeve Burgess-bodied example, B368KNH.
David Heath

FUNSTONS

Funstons Transport Services Ltd, The Depot, Chrishall, Royston, Hertfordshire, SG8 5QS

KAZ6904	AEC Reliance 6U3ZR	Plaxton Supreme IV	C55F	1979	Blue Diamond, Harlow, 1992
KAZ6903	Leyland Leopard PSU5C/4R	Duple Dominant II	C53F	1979	Brighton & Hove, 1988
PSU353	DAF MB200DKFL600	Caetano Algarve	C53F	1984	Thomas, Tonypandy, 1987
KAZ6901	Bedford Venturer YNV	Van Hool Alizée	C53F	1987	Reid, Islington, 1991
HIL9273	Bedford YMP	Plaxton Paramount 3200 III	C35F	1987	Brentwood Coaches, 1997
MIL9599	Scania K112CRB	Jonckheere Jubilee P599	C31FT	1988	Scancoaches, North Acton, 1997
KAZ6900	Scania K112CRB	Jonckheere Jubilee P599	C51F	1988	Scancoaches, North Acton, 1997
KAZ6902	Iveco Daily 49.10	Robin Hood City Nippy	DP19F	1988	Biss Brothers, Stansted, 1996
P235MBM	Dennis Javelin	Neoplan Transliner	C49FT	1997	

Previous Registrations:-

HIL9273	D801ALR		KAZ6903	EAP939V
KAZ6900	E512KNV		KAZ6904	BGY587T
KAZ6901	C413DML		MIL9599	E509KNV
KAZ6902	E357NEG		PSU353	A336VHB

Livery:- White and red; light and dark blue (Trans Europe) PSU353.

Depot:- The Depot, Chrishall and York Way, Royston

GOODE

D W L Goode, 47 Burford Road, Boothville, Northampton, NN3 1AF

CGF312S	Leyland Leopard PSU5C/4R	Plaxton Supreme III	C55F	1978	Epsom Coaches, 1988
BGP345X	Leyland Tiger TRCTL11/3R	Plaxton Supreme IV	C50F	1981	Epsom Coaches, 1989

Livery:- Maroon and cream

Depot:- Vale Farm, Ashton

GREENWAY TRAVEL

B L C Turner, North End, Bury Mead Road, Hitchin, Hertfordshire, SG5 1RT

OGS1V	Ford R1114	Plaxton Supreme IV	C53F	1980	
NRO265V	Ford R1014	Duple Dominant IV	C35F	1980	Tyler, Hitchin, 1993
RBM2W	Ford R1114	Plaxton Supreme IV	C53F	1980	
FNM5Y	Bova EL26/581	Bova Europa	C53F	1982	
BLJ714Y	Ford R1115	Plaxton Paramount 3200	C49F	1983	Excelsior, Bournemouth, 1985
A104EBC	Ford R1115	Plaxton Paramount 3200	C53F	1983	Simons, Hanslope, 1989
C681KFW	Mercedes-Benz L608D	Coachcraft	C21F	1986	

Named Vehicles:- FNM5Y *Ray*, A104EBC *Super Cruiser*.

Livery:- Yellow and two tone blue.

A140TNV from the Geoff Amos fleet is a Bedford YNT with Duple Dominant bus bodywork, now one of only two Bedfords that remain in the fleet.
Phillip Stephenson

Goode's small operation contains just two Plaxton-bodied Leylands, both purchased from Epsom Coaches. Pictured entering Northampton bus station on a Saturday service is Leopard CGF312S.
Keith Grimes

Ford coaches are fast becoming a rare breed on the British coach scene. The last model from the company was the R1115 and Greenway Travel operate two of the type with Plaxton Paramount bodywork. Seen here is BLJ714Y which was new to Excelsior of Bournemouth.

HALLMARK

Hallmark Cars Ltd, 5-7 Newtown Trading Estate, Chase Street, Luton, LU1 3QZ

MSK287	MAN 16.290HOCL	Jonckheere Deauville P599	C23FT	1989	
G167XJF	Toyota Coaster HB31R	Caetano Optimo	C18F	1990	
HC6422	DAF SB3000DKV601	Van Hool Alizée	C51FT	1992	
K17FTG	Volvo B10M-60	Plaxton Excalibur	C50F	1992	Flight, Birmingham, 1996
K226WNH	MAN 16.290HOCL	Jonckheere Deauville P599	C51F	1993	
K227WNH	MAN 16.290HOCL	Jonckheere Deauville P599	C51F	1993	
K525RJX	DAF SB3000DKV601	Van Hool Alizée HE	C51FT	1993	
L530EHD	EOS E180Z	EOS 100	C49FT	1994	
L531EHD	EOS E180Z	EOS 100	C49FT	1994	
L128GBA	Leyland-DAF 200	Leyland-DAF	M12	1994	
L129GBA	LDV 400	Concept	M16	1994	
L130GBA	LDV 400	Concept	M16	1994	
M6CLS	Toyota Coaster HZB50R	Caetano Optimo III	C18F	1994	Chauffeurline, Melbourne, 1997
M601RCP	EOS E180Z	EOS 100	C49FT	1995	
M602RCP	EOS E180Z	EOS 100	C49FT	1995	
M603RCP	EOS E180Z	EOS 100	C51FT	1995	
M604RCP	EOS E180Z	EOS 100	C49FT	1995	
M612RCP	DAF SB220LT550	Ikarus Citibus	B48F	1995	
M15HMC	Neoplan N116/3	Neoplan Cityliner	C48FT	1995	
M16HMC	Neoplan N116/3	Neoplan Cityliner	C48FT	1995	
M839RCP	Mercedes-Benz 711D	Autobus Classique	C..F	1995	
M521FAC	Volkswagen Caravelle	Volkswagen	M7	1995	
M527FAC	Volkswagen Caravelle	Volkswagen	M7	1995	
M752UKX	Volkswagen Caravelle	Volkswagen	M7	1995	
M754UKX	Volkswagen Caravelle	Volkswagen	M7	1995	
M759UKX	Volkswagen Caravelle	Volkswagen	M7	1995	
M685UUR	Volkswagen Caravelle	Volkswagen	M7	1995	
M687UUR	Volkswagen Caravelle	Volkswagen	M7	1995	
N506FVS	Volkswagen Caravelle	Volkswagen	M7	1996	
N507FVS	Volkswagen Caravelle	Volkswagen	M7	1996	
N508FVS	Volkswagen Caravelle	Volkswagen	M7	1996	
N509FVS	Volkswagen Caravelle	Volkswagen	M7	1996	
N770EOD	Ford Transit	Ford	M8	1996	
N359EAR	Ford Transit	Ford	M8	1996	
N15CAN	Scania K113TRB	Irizar Century 12.37	C41FT	1996	Chauffeurline, Melbourne, 1997
N244NNR	Toyota Coaster HZB50R	Caetano Optimo III	C18F	1996	
N6HMC	Dennis Javelin 12SDA2171	Neoplan Transliner	C50FT	1996	
N7HMC	Dennis Javelin 12SDA2171	Neoplan Transliner	C50FT	1996	
N8HMC	Dennis Javelin 12SDA2171	Neoplan Transliner	C50FT	1996	
N9HMC	Dennis Javelin 12SDA2171	Neoplan Transliner	C50FT	1996	
N1HMC	Neoplan N116/3	Neoplan Cityliner	C28FT	1996	
N3HMC	Neoplan N116/3	Neoplan Cityliner	C48FT	1996	
N4HMC	Neoplan N116/3	Neoplan Cityliner	C48FT	1996	
N5HMC	Neoplan N116/3	Neoplan Cityliner	C48FT	1996	
N10HMC	Dennis Javelin	Plaxton Première 350	C49FT	1996	
P960DNR	Toyota Coaster BB50R	Caetano Optimo IV	C18F	1997	
P961DNR	Toyota Coaster BB50R	Caetano Optimo IV	C18F	1997	
P970DNR	Toyota Coaster BB50R	Caetano Optimo IV	C18F	1997	
P975HWF	Dennis Javelin	Neoplan Transliner	C49FT	1997	
P982HWF	Dennis Javelin	Neoplan Transliner	C49FT	1997	
P983HWF	Dennis Javelin	Neoplan Transliner	C49FT	1997	
P984HWF	Dennis Javelin	Neoplan Transliner	C49FT	1997	
P17HMC	Volvo B10M-62	Plaxton Première 350	C49FT	1997	
P18HMC	Volvo B10M-62	Plaxton Première 350	C49FT	1997	
P19HMC	Volvo B10M-62	Plaxton Première 350	C49FT	1997	
P20HMC	Volvo B10M-62	Plaxton Première 350	C49FT	1997	
P22HMC	Volvo B10M-62	Plaxton Première 350	C49FT	1997	
P44HMC	Volvo B10M-62	Plaxton Première 350	C49FT	1997	
P55HMC	Volvo B10M-62	Plaxton Première 350	C49FT	1997	
P88HMC	Volvo B10M-62	Plaxton Première 350	C49FT	1997	

Hallmark operate a large fleet of quality coaches. The latest arrivals in the fleet are examples of the integral EOS which join a batch supplied in 1995. From that delivery M601RCP is shown here in a mostly white livery with gold stripes and lettering. *Geoff Rixon*

P201RUM	DAF DE02GSSB220	Ikarus Citybus	B31D	1997
P202RUM	DAF DE02GSSB220	Ikarus Citybus	B31D	1997
P203RUM	DAF DE02GSSB220	Ikarus Citybus	B31D	1997
P204RUM	DAF DE02GSSB220	Ikarus Citybus	B31D	1997
P205RUM	DAF DE02GSSB220	Ikarus Citybus	B31D	1997
R831COT	Mercedes-Benz Vario 0814	Robin Hood RH2000	C25F	1998
R832COT	Mercedes-Benz Vario 0814	Robin Hood RH2000	C25F	1998
R985KKN	Mercedes-Benz Vario 0814	Robin Hood RH2000	C25F	1998
R986KKN	Mercedes-Benz Vario 0814	Robin Hood RH2000	C25F	1998
R68KFL	Ford Transit VE6	Advanced	M8	1998
R71KFL	Ford Transit VE6	Advanced	M8	1998
R981SKX	Volkswagen Caravelle	Volkswagen	M7	1998
R989SKX	Volkswagen Caravelle	Volkswagen	M7	1998
??	Ford Transit VE6	Advanced	M8	1998
R46GNW	EOS E180Z	EOS 90	C48FT	1998
R47GNW	EOS E180Z	EOS 90	C48FT	1998
R48GNW	EOS E180Z	EOS 90	C48FT	1998
R49GNW	EOS E180Z	EOS 90	C48FT	1998
R50GNW	EOS E180Z	EOS 90	C48FT	1998
R51GNW	EOS E180Z	EOS 90	C48FT	1998
R52GNW	EOS E180Z	EOS 90	C48FT	1998
R53GNW	EOS E180Z	EOS 90	C48FT	1998
R5HMC	EOS E230Z	EOS 230	C28FT	1998
R6HMC	EOS E230Z	EOS 230	C28FT	1998

Previous Registrations:-

HC6422	J63GCX		
		MSK287	G840GNV

Livery:-Brown and gold, or white and gold

Depots:- Chase Street, Luton; Firbank Industrial Estate, Luton; Beehive Ring Road, Gatwick, West Sussex; Grimstock Hill, Coleshill, Warwickshire and Narvik Way, North Shields.

HARRIS COACHWAYS

D A Harris, 7 Dilwyn Court, Abercromby Avenue, High Wycombe,
Buckinghamshire, HP12 3BH

YDK225L	Ford Transit	Williams Deansgate	M12	1973	Bedford, High Wycombe, 1985
HAY201V	Bedford YMT	Caetano Alpha	C53F	1979	Butler, Loughborough, 1986
BRW738Y	DAF SB2005DHU685	Plaxton Supreme IV	C53F	1982	Smith, Wilmcote, 1992
PMB47Y	Leyland Tiger TRCTL11/3R	Jonckheere Jubilee P50	C53F	1983	Vale of Llangollen, Cefn Mawr, 1989
YIJ387	Volvo B10M-61	Plaxton Paramount 3200	C53F	1983	Hunsbury, Northampton, 1998
LFO800Y	Leyland Tiger TRCTL11/3R	Duple Dominant IV Express	C53F	1983	Cunningham, Chelmsley Wood, 1995
UTN3Y	Ford Transit 150D	Dewey	M12	1983	Magpie, High Wycombe, 1992
B45TVR	Freight-Rover Sherpa	Dixon Lomas	M16	1985	Arle, Shipton Oliffe, 1995
C318URF	Ford Transit 190D	Dormobile	B16F	1985	Midland Red North, 1993
C78MAK	Volvo B10M-61	Caetano Algarve	C53F	1986	Green, High Wycombe, 1998
C95NNV	Bedford YNV Venturer	Caetano Algarve	C53F	1986	Garratt, Leicester, 1998
H934JDP	Mercedes-Benz 811D	Reeve Burgess Beaver	C33F	1990	Magpie, High Wycombe, 1993

Previous Registration:-

C78MAK	C199RVV, WIB7193, C145MDS, OIW5800		
PMB47Y	BRN696Y, 9509VT	YIJ387	FUA393Y, TXI6342

Livery:- White and blue.

Depot:- Binders Industrial Estate, Cryers Hill, High Wycombe.

Legoland, near Windsor, has provided another exciting location for operators to add to their excursion menu. It is at this location that Harris' PMB47Y is seen after delivering a party of school children. The vehicle is a Leyland Tiger with Jonckheere Jubilee bodywork. *David Heath*

HERBERTS TRAVEL

M F Herbert, 32 Ivel Road, Shefford, Bedfordshire, SG17 5LA

HXI252	Leyland Leopard PSU3C/4R	Plaxton Supreme III	C53F	1976	Simmonds, Letchworth, 1983
591HNM	Bedford CFL	Plaxton Mini Supreme	C17F	1982	
A969SKK	Mercedes-Benz L307D	Reeve Burgess	M12	1983	The Kings Ferry, 1991
A61NPP	Mercedes-Benz L307D	Reeve Burgess	M12	1983	Aron, Northolt, 1985
A839TOO	Ford R1115	Wright Contour	C41F	1984	Ford, Warley, 1986
554JPP	Neoplan N116	Neoplan Cityliner	C53FT	1985	Golden Travel, North Kensington, 1990
B64APP	Ford Transit	Chassis Developments	C16F	1985	Austin, Milton Keynes, 1990
D220PVS	Ford Transit	Chassis Developments	C16F	1987	
E134MHN	Mercedes-Benz L307D	Whittaker	M12	1988	Turner, Ulleskelf, 1993
E601LBF	Mercedes-Benz 811D	Coachcraft	C24F	1988	Golden Travel, North Kensington, 1990
E976YKO	Ford Transit VE6	Dormobile	M16	1988	Age Concern, Norfolk, 1993
F629FNA	Freight-Rover Sherpa	Made-to-Measure	M14	1988	Smith, Marlow, 1990
F279GNB	Peugeot Talbot Express	Made-to-Measure	M10	1989	
F808LBM	Peugeot Talbot Express	Made-to-Measure	M10	1989	
▸ F936MTM	Ford Transit	Chassis Developments	C16F	1989	
G940EEH	MCW MetroRider MF154/14	MCW	C28F	1990	Thamesroute, Highbury, 1996
L15ALU	Fleur-de-Lys Lincoln 700/50	Fleur-de-Lys	C20F	1994	private owner, 1994

Previous Registrations:-

554JPP	HST11, B830TKV	A969SKK	A949VMH, XIA257
591HNM	From new	HXI252	LCF94P

Livery:- Red, white and black

Neoplan produce integral buses and coaches, both double-deck and single-deck in addition to bodying chassis from other suppliers. Three plants are based in Germany - at Berlin, Pilsing, and Stuttgart - with other subsidiary units in Ghana and the USA. The business is no longer a subsidiary of the Auwarter conglomerate. The Neoplan N116 is built as the Cityliner and is shown here in the livery of Herberts of Hitchin who acquired the vehicle in 1990.

Hyltone operate only one full-size coach, A659MWR, which was pictured at Thorpe Park coachpark. Pictured in rain - or near the water-splash - the vehicle is a Bedford YNT with Plaxton Paramount 3200 bodywork.

Operating with JL Travel when pictured earlier in 1998, NIL7714 is a Leyland Leopard with Duple Dominant bodywork. Since being pictured, the vehicle has been reported as painted into fleet livery.
Keith Grimes

HATS & HERTS COACHES

I P Swinson, The Bungalow, Ryders Avenue, Colney Heath, Hertfordshire, AL4 0RZ

RBY46L	Bedford YRT	Plaxton Panorama Elite III	C53F	1973	Fleet Coaches, 1994
FIL7674	Bedford YMT	Plaxton Supreme III	C53F	1977	Hunsbury, Northampton, 1994
LHK644V	Ford R1114	Plaxton Supreme IV	C53F	1979	Hallums, Southend, 1996
TJI6574	Bedford YMT	Duple Dominant II	C53F	1980	Carters, Litcham, 1995

Previous Registrations:-

FIL7674	SBD57R		TJI6574	JGU939V

Depot:- Ryders Avenue, Colney Heath and Watford Metropolitan Station Approach, Watford

HYLTONE

AW, RC, & A Lockwood, 51 Georges Hill, Widmer End, Buckinghamshire, HP15 6BH

FLJ869V	Volkswagen LT28	Devon Conversions	M12	1980	Davies & Evans, Bodelwyddan, 1985
GPJ640V	Ford Transit	Ford	M9	1980	MoD, 1988
A659MWR	Bedford YNT	Plaxton Paramount 3200	C53F	1983	York Pullman, Elvington, 1995
A58YMH	Fiat 60.10	Robin Hood	C19F	1984	Arsenal FC, 1986
IIL6567	Bedford YMP	Plaxton Paramount 3200 II	C35F	1985	Pilling, Sowerby Bridge, 1992
D778JUB	Freight-Rover Sherpa	Dormobile	B20F	1986	Andrews, Parkgate, 1994

Previous Registrations:-

A58YMH	AFC3		IIL6567	C441WFO

Named Vehicle:- A58YMH *Miss Angela*

Livery:- White, red and maroon.

Depot:- Binders Industrial Estate, Cryers Hill, High Wycombe.

J & L TRAVEL

I G Smith, Mount Pleasant, Taylors Lane, St. Leonards, Buckinghamshire, HP5 6LQ

SXI6397	AEC Reliance 6U2R	Duple Dominant II Express	C53F	1978	Smith-Ivins, High Wycombe, 1995
VDY379	AEC Reliance 6U2R	Plaxton Supreme IV Express	C53F	1979	Magpie, High Wycombe, 1995
NIL7714	Leyland Leopard PSU5/	Duple Dominant II Express	C53F	1978	?
XBC445X	Bedford YMQ	Duple Dominant IV	C35F	1982	Court, Fillongley, 1996
A320HFP	Bova EL28/581	Duple Calypso	C53F	1984	Snell, Newton Abbot, 1991
E903EAY	Bedford YNV Venturer	Duple 320	C53FT	1987	Haywood & Prosser, Bedworth, 1997
ESU939	DAF SB2305DHS585	Caetano Algarve	C53F	1988	D & J, Silvertown, 1994
F87GAO	DAF SB2305DHTD585	Duple 320	C57F	1988	Smiths-Ivins, High Wycombe, 1984

Previous Registrations:-

ESU939	E172KNH		VDY379	EPM139V
NIL7714	?		XBC445X	KJR700X, PSV172
SXI6397	XPK55T			

Livery:- White, black, red and green.

JEFFS / BASFORDS / PAYNES

K R Jeffs; Basford's Coaches Ltd; Payne's Coaches & Car Hire Ltd,
Old Station Yard, Helmdon, Brackley, Northamptonshire, NN13 5QT

MPE772P	Bedford YMT	Duple Dominant II	C53F	1976	Shearer, Mayford, 1996
NFX447P	Bedford YMT	Plaxton Supreme III	C53F	1976	Windrush Valley, Witney, 1990
PJF227R	Bedford YLQ	Plaxton Supreme III	C45F	1976	Ron, Ashington, 1996
647PJO	Leyland Leopard PSU5A/4R	Plaxton Supreme III	C50F	1976	Percivals, Oxford, 1987
AUD465R	Bristol VRT/SL3/6LXB	Eastern Coach Works	H43/31F	1977	South Midland, 1988
PTT106R	Bristol LH6L	Plaxton Supreme III Express	C41F	1977	
RIJ3987	Volvo B58-56	Plaxton Viewmaster III	C53F	1977	Haugh, Muswell Hill, 1997
ADC277A	Bedford YLQ	Plaxton Supreme III	C45F	1977	Windrush Valley, Witney, 1990
279JJO	Leyland Leopard PSU5A/4R	Plaxton Supreme III	C57F	1977	Percivals, Oxford, 1987
CJO466R	Bristol VRT/SL3/6LXB	Eastern Coach Works	H43/31F	1977	South Midland, 1988
VVV66S	Bristol VRT/SL3/6LXB	Alexander AL	H45/27D	1977	Northampton, 1991
WVV827S	Bedford YMT	Duple Dominant II	C53F	1978	
WVV829S	Bedford YMT	Duple Dominant II	C53F	1978	
WVV830S	Bedford YMT	Duple Dominant II	C53F	1978	
VRP45S	Bristol VRT/SL3/6LXB	Alexander AL	H45/27D	1978	Northampton, 1991
VRP51S	Bristol VRT/SL3/6LXB	Alexander AL	H45/27D	1978	Northampton, 1991
VYU758S	Bedford YMT	Duple Dominant II	C53F	1978	Plustrans, Gillingham, 1990
5615RO	Leyland Leopard PSU3E/4R	Duple Dominant II	C53F	1978	Percivals, Oxford, 1987
VBW846	Leyland Leopard PSU5C/4R	Plaxton Supreme III	C55F	1978	Percivals, Oxford, 1987
BNO686T	Bedford YMT	Duple Dominant II Express	C53F	1978	Begent, Fernhurst, 1996
ERP19T	Leyland Leopard PSU5C/4R	Duple Dominant II	C53F	1979	
VNP893	Leyland Leopard PSU3E/4R	Plaxton Supreme III	C53F	1979	Windrush Valley, Witney, 1990
FDF276T	Leyland Leopard PSU5C/4R	Plaxton Supreme IV	C57F	1979	Pulham, Bourton-on-the-Water,1991
GDG442V	Leyland Leopard PSU3E/4R	Plaxton Supreme IV Express	C53F	1979	Pulham, Bourton-on-the-Water,1991
YFC16V	Leyland Leopard PSU3E/4R	Duple Dominant II Express	C49F	1979	Windrush Valley, Witney, 1990
YFC17V	Leyland Leopard PSU3E/4R	Duple Dominant II Express	C49F	1979	Windrush Valley, Witney, 1990
NBD304V	Bedford YMT	Duple Dominant II	C53F	1980	
NBD305V	Bedford YMT	Duple Dominant II	C53F	1980	
NBD306V	Bedford YMT	Duple Dominant II	C53F	1980	
NBD307V	Bedford YMT	Duple Dominant II	C53F	1980	
NBD309V	Bedford YMT	Duple Dominant II	C53F	1980	
NBD310V	Bedford YMT	Duple Dominant II	C53F	1980	
NBD311V	Bedford YMT	Duple Dominant II	C53F	1980	
MDS228V	Volvo B58-61	Duple Dominant II	C57F	1980	Tansey, Woolston, 1991
195JOH	Volvo B58-61	Jonckheere Bermuda	C53F	1980	
938HNM	Volvo B10M-61	Jonckheere Bermuda	C51F	1981	
ESU635	Volvo B10M-61	Jonckheere Bermuda	C51F	1981	
FSV720	Volvo B10M-61	Jonckheere Bermuda	C51F	1981	
TGY698	Volvo B10M-61	Jonckheere Bermuda	C51F	1981	
VKX510	Volvo B10M-61	Jonckheere Bermuda	C53F	1981	
802AOJ	Volvo B10M-61	Jonckheere Bermuda	C49FT	1981	
RHE992X	Volvo B58-56	Duple Dominant IV	C53F	1981	Godson, Crossgates, 1996
872KMY	Volvo B58-61	Jonckheere Bermuda	C51FT	1982	
VXT571	Volvo B10M-61	Jonckheere Jubilee P50	C49FT	1983	
112AXN	Volvo B10M-61	Jonckheere Jubilee P50	C49FT	1983	
A933YOX	Volvo B10M-61	Duple Caribbean	C49FT	1983	Millership, Dudley, 1997
147VKN	Volvo B10M-61	Jonckheere Jubilee P50	C51FT	1984	
XWG254	Volvo B10M-61	Jonckheere Jubilee P50	C53FT	1984	
YSV815	Volvo B10M-61	Jonckheere Jubilee P50	C53FT	1984	
487VYA	Volvo B10M-61	Jonckheere Jubilee P50	C53FT	1984	
3493CD	Volvo B10M-61	Plaxton Paramount 3200 II	C53F	1985	Dore, Leafield, 1993
E741DJO	Volvo B10M-61	Plaxton Paramount 3500 III	C53F	1988	Dore, Leafield, 1993
E81HPG	Mercedes-Benz 811D	Plaxton Mini Supreme	C19F	1988	Bicknell, Godalming, 1989

Opposite:- **The motif used by theJeffs group is a leaping deer embodied within the name. Vehicles from the Jeffs operation and the Paynes fleet are shown here. The upper picture shows Caetano Algarve-bodied Volvo L35CAY while the lower picture shows Optare StarRider service bus F48CVV, one of the examples with high-back seating, preparing to leave Oxford for Milton Keynes.** *P J Stockwell*

In 1981, a batch of Jonckheere Bermuda-bodied Volvo B10Ms joined the group fleet and these vehicles have remained to give sterling service for some seventeen years. Now carrying cherished marks, the type are still active and looking smart as shown by ESU635, seen here with Jeffs names. *Keith Grimes*

F567HPP	Ford Transit VE6	Chassis Developments	C16F	1988	Willoughby & Harris, Freeland, 1993
F480AKC	Mercedes-Benz 609D	North West Coach Sales	C24F	1989	Windrush Valley, Witney, 1990
F47CVV	Mercedes-Benz 811D	Optare StarRider	DP33F	1989	
F48CVV	Mercedes-Benz 811D	Optare StarRider	DP33F	1989	
G933JKY	Leyland-DAF 400	Crystals	C16F	1989	Willoughby & Harris, Freeland, 1993
G907WAY	Volvo B10M-60	Caetano Algarve	C53F	1990	
G908WAY	Volvo B10M-60	Caetano Algarve	C53F	1990	
G909WAY	Volvo B10M-60	Caetano Algarve	C53F	1990	
G910WAY	Volvo B10M-60	Caetano Algarve	C53F	1990	
G911WAY	Volvo B10M-60	Caetano Algarve	C53F	1990	
G912WAY	Volvo B10M-60	Caetano Algarve	C53F	1990	
G913WAY	Volvo B10M-60	Caetano Algarve	C53F	1990	
G914WAY	Volvo B10M-60	Caetano Algarve	C53F	1990	
G956VVR	Ford Transit VE6	Steedrive	C16F	1990	Willoughby & Harris, Freeland, 1990
H409CJF	Toyota Coaster HDB30R	Caetano Optimo II	C21F	1990	
H183EJF	Volvo B10M-61	Caetano Algarve I	C53F	1991	
H184EJF	Volvo B10M-60	Caetano Algarve I	C49FT	1991	
J520LRY	Dennis Javelin 12SDA1919	Caetano Algarve I	C53F	1991	
J521LRY	Dennis Javelin 12SDA1919	Caetano Algarve I	C53F	1991	
J470NJU	Toyota Coaster HDB30R	Caetano Optimo II	C18F	1992	
J471NJU	Toyota Coaster HDB30R	Caetano Optimo II	C18F	1992	
J472NJU	Volvo B10M-60	Caetano Algarve II	C35FT	1992	
J473NJU	Volvo B10M-60	Caetano Algarve II	C49FT	1992	Wilson's, Carnwath, 1998
J474NJU	Volvo B10M-60	Caetano Algarve II	C49FT	1992	
J475NJU	Volvo B10M-60	Caetano Algarve II	C49FT	1992	Wilson's, Carnwath, 1998
J476NJU	Volvo B10M-60	Caetano Algarve II	C49FT	1992	
J477NJU	Volvo B10M-60	Caetano Algarve II	C49FT	1992	
K97UFP	Dennis Javelin 12SDA2101	Caetano Algarve II	C57F	1993	
K98UFP	Dennis Javelin 12SDA2101	Caetano Algarve II	C57F	1993	
L35CAY	Volvo B10M-62	Caetano Algarve II	C53F	1994	
L36CAY	Volvo B10M-62	Caetano Algarve II	C53F	1994	
L37CAY	Volvo B10M-62	Caetano Algarve II	C53F	1994	
L38CAY	Volvo B10M-62	Caetano Algarve II	C53F	1994	
L39CAY	Volvo B10M-62	Caetano Algarve II	C53F	1994	

Pictured on service as it arrives in Milton Keynes, 5615RO, formerly XWX183S, is a Leyland Leopard with Duple Dominant II bodywork. After Stagecoach United Counties, Jeffs is the largest bus and coach operation in terms of vehicle numbers based in Northampton. *Colin Lloyd*

M849LFP	Volvo B10M-62	Caetano Algarve II	C53F	1995
M850LFP	Volvo B10M-62	Caetano Algarve II	C53F	1995
N789SJU	Volvo B10M-62	Caetano Algarve II	C53F	1996
N790SJU	Volvo B10M-62	Caetano Algarve II	C53F	1996
P180ANR	Volvo B10M-62	Caetano Algarve II	C49FT	1997
P181ANR	Volvo B10M-62	Caetano Algarve II	C49FT	1997
R490UFP	Volvo B10M-62	Caetano Algarve II	C49FT	1998

Previous Registrations:-

112AXN	NNV607Y	E741DJO	E665UNE, 6504CD
147VKN	A591XRP	ESU635	XNV142W
195JOH	PBD776V	FSV720	XNV143W
279JJO	SUR286R	RHE992X	JBX694X, 858BXU
487VYA	A594XRP	RIJ3987	TGD996R
5615RO	XWX183S	TGY698	XNV144W
647PJO	SGN331R	VBW846	CGF311S
802AOJ	BBD851X	VKX510	XNV145W
872KMY	DVV528X	VNP893	EWW206T
938HNM	XNV140W	VXT571	NNV606Y
3493CD	B531BML	XWG254	A592XRP
A933YOX	A272GJU, DJI654, A97ODY, MIL2273	YSV815	A593XRP
ADC277A	PKU621R		

Livery:- White, green and red.

Depots:- Supergas Industrial Estate, Downs Road, Curbridge, Oxfordshire; Buckingham Industrial Park, Buckingham; High Street, Greens Norton and Old Station Yard, Helmdon.

KELLYS COACHES

J R Loach, The Old School House, 1 Branch Road, Park Street, St Albans, Hertfordshire, AL2 2LU

NPJ480R	Leyland National 11351A/1R		B49F	1976	Stagecoach South, 1998
RIB1739	Leyland Leopard PSU3E/4R	Plaxton Supreme III	C53F	1977	Riddle, Hounslow, 1997
EPH224V	Leyland Atlantean AN68A/1R	Roe	H43/30F	1980	Kentish Bus, 1997
JKW303W	Leyland Atlantean AN68B/1R	Alexander AL	H45/29D	1981	Pullman, Haddenham, 1997

Previous Registrations:-

RIB1739	TMH702S

Livery:- Black and lilac.

Depot:- South Mimms Service Area, St Albans Road, South Mimms

The Pub to Club express operation of Kelly Coaches was pictured outside Wimbledon during June 1998. The vehicle, EPH224V, is a Leyland Atlantean with Roe bodywork and was new to London Country in 1980.

KEYSTONE

E Allan, Top Close, Thrapston, Northamptonshire, NN14 4PP

OJD216R	Leyland Fleetline FE30AGR	MCW	H44/24D	1977	Davian, Enfield, 1991
BBW141V	Bedford YMT	Plaxton Supreme IV Express	C53F	1979	Rainbow, Westbury, 1987
52GYY	Volvo B58-61	Plaxton Supreme IV	C57F	1980	Brentwood Coaches, 1990
GFE836Y	Bedford YNT	Plaxton Supreme V Express	C53F	1982	Smith, Potterspury, 1991
YPD128Y	Leyland Tiger TRCTL11/2R	Duple Dominant IV Express	C53F	1983	The Delaine, Bourne, 1995
GIL4276	Volvo B10M-61	Berkhof Esprite 350	C57F	1984	Pamray, Littleport, 1996
A847MAC	DAF MB200DKFL600	Caetano Algarve	C53F	1984	Taylor, Widnes, 1993
D393SGS	Freight Rover Sherpa	Dormobile	B16F	1987	Beesly Enterprise, Wellingborough, 1998
E331HNV	Leyland-DAF 400	Chassis Developments	C16F	1988	Woodford Community Bus, 1991
E176KNH	DAF MB230DKFL615	Caetano Algarve I	C53F	1988	Prentice & McQuillan, Swanley, 1994
FP5992	Dennis Javelin 12SDA1907	Duple 320	C53F	1989	Bland, Cottesmoor, 1997
J3JCN	Mazda E2200	Howletts	M14	1991	Neild, Thrapston, 1993
M346TDO	Mercedes-Benz 711D	Autobus Classique	C25F	1994	

Previous Registrations:-

52GYY	NGS963V	FP5992	F21SBC	GIL4276	A60SEV

Livery:- Orange, red, white or silver.

Latterly with The Delaine where YPD128Y underwent much refurbishment the coach is now operated by Keystone. Originally, this Leyland Tiger operated on Green Line duties with London Country.
David Heath

L B TRAVEL

R S Lawman & R W Bull, Old Royal Blue Depot, Isham Road, Pytchley, Kettering, Northamptonshire, NN14 1EW

8	LJI8158	DAF MB230DKVL615	Van Hool Alizée H	C53FT	1985	Midland Fox, 1992
12	FIL9378	Bova FLD12.250	Bova Futura	C53FT	1986	Midland Fox, 1992
14	LBZ2937	Bedford YMT	Duple Dominant II	C53FT	1981	Wootton, Northampton, 1993
17	LBZ2936	DAF MB200DKFL600	Van Hool Alizée H	C55F	1984	Wilson, Carnwath, 1994
19	917ETV	Leyland Royal Tiger RTC	Leyland Doyen	C51FT	1986	Midland Fox, 1994
20	WUT866	DAF SB2305DHS585	Van Hool Alizée H	C53F	1989	Eastern Scottish, 1996
21	AEF368A	DAF SB2300DHTD585	Plaxton Paramount 3200 III	C53F	1987	Wootton, Northampton, 1996
22	660CUH	Scania K113CRB	Van Hool Alizée SH	C49FT	1990	Appleby, Conisholme, 1997
23	195CJU	Scania K113CRB	Van Hool Alizée SH	C49FT	1990	Appleby, Conisholme, 1997
24	SIB8349	DAF SB2300DHS585	Van Hool Alizée H	C51FT	1988	Swann, Blackpool, 1998

Previous Registrations:-

195CJU	G266WVL, BJV787, G904YBE	LBZ2936	A976ESF, GIL3271, A803WSU
660CUH	G333XFE, ASV895, G347AVL	LBZ2937	OED164W
917ETV	C69BFX	LJI8158	C310MRP
AEF368A	D286XCX	SIB8349	E332EVH
FIL9378	C725UMX	WUT866	F609HGO

Named Vehicles:- AEF368A *Highland Tourer*, 917ETV *Riviera Tourer*, FIL9378 *Benelux Tourer*, LBZ2936 *Rhineland Tourer*, LBZ2937 *Pennine Tourer*, LJI8158 *European Tourer*, WUT866 *Alpine Tourer*

Livery:- Cream, orange and two tone green.

LBZ2936 in the L B Travel fleet is a DAF MB2000 with Van Hool Alizée H bodywork. It is one of four of the combination with the operator which undertakes coaching and contract work in the Kettering area. *Colin Lloyd*

LANGSTON & TASKER
BRACKLEY BUZZER

J Langston & M A Fenner, 23 Queen Catherine Road, Steeple Claydon, Buckinghamshire, MK18 2PZ

LVS439P	Bedford YRT	Duple Dominant II	C53F	1976	Prairie, West Drayton, 1979
PJF909R	Bedford YLQ	Plaxton Supreme III	C45F	1976	Harris, Seven Kings, 1983
PKG651R	Bedford YMT	Plaxton Supreme III	C53F	1977	Waddon, Caerphilly, 1983
XUY159R	Ford R1114	Duple Dominant II	C53F	1977	Sunbeam, Hevingham, 1982
BWA21B	Bedford YLQ	Plaxton Supreme IV	C45F	1979	Green, Kirkintilloch, 1989
JMJ112V	Ford R1114	Duple Dominant II	C53F	1979	Butler, Kingswood, 1988
OAP17W	Dennis Dominator DDA134	East Lancashire	H43/31F	1981	Brighton Blue Bus, 1996
VJT612X	Ford R1114	Plaxton Supreme V	C53F	1982	Excelsior, Bournemouth, 1984
VJT618X	Ford R1114	Plaxton Supreme V	C53F	1982	Kinch, Mountsorrell, 1984
A730BSE	Bedford YNT	Plaxton Paramount 3200	C53F	1983	Mayne, Buckie, 1987
A396GVN	Fiat 60.10	Caetano Beja	C18F	1984	Oldfield, Wombwell, 1994
E930YAM	Mercedes-Benz 507D	Reeve Burgess	C16F	1988	Badgerline, 1995
E162TVR	Leyland Tiger TRCTL11/3RZ	Duple 320	C57F	1988	Bullock, Cheadle, 1994
E590PFR	Dennis Javelin 12SDA1907	Duple 320	C57F	1988	Tyrer, Trawden, 1998
F601DWB	Mercedes-Benz 609D	Whittaker	C20F	1988	Barry, Weymouth, 1996
F788GNA	Leyland Tiger TRCTL11/3ARZ	Duple 320	C53F	1989	Shearings, 1984
L223BUT	Dennis Javelin 12SDA2131	Plaxton Premiere 320	C53F	1994	Tate's, Markyate, 1998

Previous Registration:-

BWA21B	ZJ704B, WTC916T	E590PFR	E444OCW, 7529UK

Livery:- Grey, red and yellow.

Depot:- Buckingham Road, Steeple Claydon.

LAYSTON COACHES

M L George, Layston Garage, Hare Street, Buntingford, Hertfordshire, SG9 0EA

NCY626	AEC Reliance MU3RV	Weymann Fanfare	C37F	1956	Hulme Hall, Cheadle Hulme, 1981
TMJ643R	Bristol LHS6L	Plaxton Supreme III	C35F	1977	Thomas Bros, Llangadog, 1998
D83PPP	Ford Transit 150D	Ford	M8	1987	private owner, 1991
N207EAV	Peugeot Boxer	Devon Conversions	M12	1996	
P432JDT	Dennis Javelin 12SDA2136	Plaxton Premiére 320	C57F	1996	Costin, Stanbridge, 1998

Previous Registrations:-

NCY626	From new

Livery:- White, blue and red

LEN WRIGHT BAND SERVICES

Len Wright Band Services Ltd, 9 Elton Way, Watford, WD2 8HH

A16LWB	Volvo B10M-61	Van Hool Astral	CH6/6DT	1984	Cantabrica, Watford, 1991
E689NNH	Scania K112CRS	Jonckheere Jubilee P599	C10FT	1988	Cantabrica, Watford, 1991
E690NNH	Scania K112CRS	Jonckheere Jubilee P599	C10FT	1988	Cantabrica, Watford, 1991
A17LWB	Volvo B10M-53	Van Hool Astral 3	CH8/7FT	1988	Cantabrica, Watford, 1991
A18LWB	Volvo B10M-50	Van Hool Astral 3	CH8/7FT	1989	Cantabrica, Watford, 1991
A19LWB	Volvo B10M-50	Van Hool Astral 3	CH8/7FT	1989	Cantabrica, Watford, 1991
K2LWB	Scania K113CRB	Plaxton Excalibur	C10FT	1993	
L3LWB	Volvo B12	Plaxton Prestige 370	C10FT	1994	
M6LWB	Volvo B12(T)	Jonckheere Monaco	CH8/7CT	1995	RDJ International, Torquay1997
N4LWB	Scania K113TRB	Irizar Century 12.37	C10FT	1996	
N5LWB	Scania K113TRB	Irizar Century 12.37	C10FT	1996	
R7LWB	Bova FHD12.340	Bova Futura	C13FT	1998	

Previous Registrations:-

A16LWB	A59OTA, WSV505	A18LWB	G95VMM		M6LWB	M10TCC
A17LWB	F68SMC	A19LWB	G96VMM			

Livery:- Three-tone grey, or burgundy and silver

Note:- L3LWB is left hand drive. All vehicles are used exclusively for show business touring, frequently abroad. The low seating capacities reflect that they are each fitted with an equivalent number of bunks.

Named vehicles:- A17LWB *Gold II*, A18LWB *Gold III*, A19LWB *Gold IV*

Large quality coaches with just enough seats for each party are used by many music groups and their entourage to travel between venues. These contain large amounts of storage and extensive music/video systems and are commonly known as band buses. Painted in an all-over grey scheme, G96VMM has been modified to just eight on the upper deck and seven on the lower. Since being photographed the vehicle has received Select index mark A19LWB. *Colin Lloyd*

LONDON LUTON AIRPORT

London Luton Airport Ltd, Percival House, 96 Percival Way, Luton, LU2 9LY

	G938LFV	Renault PR100	Northern Counties	DP27D	1989	
	G939LFV	Renault PR100	Northern Counties	DP26D	1989	
	G940LFV	Renault PR100	Northern Counties	DP27D	1990	
	M846RCP	DAF SB220LT550	Northern Counties Paladin	B49F	1995	Speedlink, 1997
	M850RCP	DAF SB220LT550	Northern Counties Paladin	B49F	1995	Speedlink, 1997
2	A84MUR	Bedford VAS 5	Reeve Burgess	DP24C	1983	
3	A85MUR	Bedford VAS 5	Reeve Burgess	DP24C	1983	
761	E376XVS	Renault-Dodge G10	Reeve Burgess	B24F	1988	
809	UBH394W	Mercedes-Benz 0305G	Lex	AB35D	1981	
810	UBH395W	Mercedes-Benz 0305G	Lex	AB35D	1981	
811	UBH396W	Mercedes-Benz 0305G	Lex	AB35D	1981	
976	UWG820Y	Bedford VAS 5	Reeve Burgess	DP24C	1983	
AP1	P129RWR	DAF DE02GSSB220	Ikarus Citibus	B..D	1997	
AP2	G363ATM	Leyland Swift ST2R44C97A4	Reeve Burgess Harrier	C25F	1990	
AP3	N986FWT	DAF DE02GSSB220	Northern Counties Paladin	B32D	1996	Northern Counties demonstrator, 1997
AP4	N67FWU	DAF DE02LTSB220	Ikarus Citibus	DP33D	1996	
AP5	M832RCP	DAF SB220LT550	Ikarus Citibus	B49F	1995	Delta, Kirkby-in-Ashfield, 1996
AP6	M836RCP	DAF SB220LT550	Ikarus Citibus	B49F	1995	Delta, Kirkby-in-Ashfield, 1996
AP7	M834RCP	DAF SB220LT550	Ikarus Citibus	B49F	1995	Delta, Kirkby-in-Ashfield, 1996
AP8	P128RWR	DAF DE02LTSB220	Ikarus Citibus	B..D	1997	
AP9	P127RWR	DAF DE02LTSB220	Ikarus Citibus	B..D	1997	
	P130RWR	DAF DE02GSSB220	Optare Delta	B44D	1997	
	P131RWR	DAF DE02GSSB220	Optare Delta	B44D	1997	
	R74GNW	DAF DE02GSSB220	Ikarus Citibus	B..D	1998	

Livery:- Light grey and blue; white (Thompson Holidays) AP3, AP9; yellow & white (Crown Service) AP5; orange and white (Easyjet) AP8; white, blue and red (Airtours) AP1.

London Luton Airport operate services within the airport and to the town's rail station. Several of the fleet have been painted into liveries of the various airlines that operate out of Luton. Pictured here in Monarch Airlines scheme is Ikarus Citibus-bodied DAF M832RCP. *Richard Godfrey*

MAGPIE TRAVEL

M P Ash, Magpies, London Road, Wooburn Moor, High Wycombe,
Buckinghamshire, HP11

A142FLE	Ford Transit	Dormobile	B11FL	1984	Leeway, Hounslow, 1995
A611HNF	Ford Transit	Mellor	B8FL	1984	HB Transport, Faversham, 1993
A606OWW	Bedford CF	Dormobile	M6L	1984	private owner, 1995
D955ARE	Mercedes-Benz L608D	PMT Hanbridge	C21F	1986	Dereham Coachways, 1990
E342DRO	Iveco Daily 49.10	Dormobile Routemaker	B25F	1988	The Shires, 1997
E487FNP	Ford Transit VE6	Ford	M.L	1987	Brandish, Nuneaton, 1995
G478EOK	Leyland-DAF 400	Leyland-DAF	M6L	1990	Chiltern Dial-a-Ride, 1995
H561FLE	Mercedes-Benz 609D	North West Coach Sales	C16F	1990	Capital, West Drayton, 1995
H119YGG	Mercedes-Benz 709D	Dormobile Routemaker	B29F	1991	Timeline, 1996
K5JFS	Mercedes-Benz 814D	Autobus Classique	C29F	1993	Watermill, Fraserburgh, 1998
L334HFU	Mercedes-Benz 814D	Autobus Classique	C29F	1993	Lakeland, Kendal, 1998
L345HFU	Mercedes-Benz 814D	Autobus Classique	C33F	1993	Aztec, Bristol, 1998

Previous Registration:-

K5JFS   K721GBE

Livery:- White and black; green and white (Green Line) K5JFS, L334/45HFU

Depots:- Binders Industrial Estate, Cryers Hill, High Wycombe and Lisset Road, Maidenhead, Berkshire.

**Three Mercedes-Benz minibuses with Autobus Classique bodywork operate with Magpie Travel.
Pictured here working service 290 into London is K5JFS which was new to Fishwick of Leyland.**
Colin Lloyd

MARLOW COACHES

A Evans, 42 Slade Road, Stokenchurch, Buckinghamshire, HP14 3PX

JAZ9862	Leyland Leopard PSU5C/4R	Duple Dominant II	C57F	1979	Nip-On, St Helens, 1995
BBB539V	Bedford YMT	Plaxton Supreme IV	C53F	1980	Briscoe, Witley, 1993
NUF632	Leyland Tiger TRCTL11/3R	Plaxton Paramount 3500 II	C46FT	1986	Dunn-Line, Nottingham, 1997
E635NHP	Ford Transit VE6	Ford	M8	1988	private owner, 1993
F169UDP	Ford Transit VE6	Ford	M11	1989	private owner, 1991
G405DPD	Iveco Daily 49.10	Carlyle Dailybus	B25F	1989	AMS, Maidenhead, 1997
G972CPD	Ford Transit VE6	Carlyle Dailybus	M	1990	private owner, 1997
J948UBL	Leyland-DAF 400	Leyland-DAF	M16	1992	private owner, 1994

Previous Registration:-

JAZ9862	EBM436T	NUF632	C423WFH

Livery:- White, burgundy, lilac and pink.

Depot:- Booker Airfield, Booker, High Wycombe.

The last new styles of coachwork to emerge from Duple's Blackpool factory were the 320 and 340 designs in 1983, which replaced the short-lived Laser and Caribbean types. Following cessation of production in 1989, a handful of 320's were built by Plaxton as the 321, after which the design passed into history. Many Duple products continue to survive, for example this 320 based upon a Volvo B10M chassis operated by **Marlow Coaches**. *Colin Lloyd*

MARSHALL'S

F W Marshall, Firbank Way, Leighton Buzzard, Bedfordshire, LU7 8YP

1404FM	Volvo B10M-61	Jonckheere Bermuda	C53F	1981	Trathens, Roborough, 1983
GSU384	Volvo B58-61	Jonckheere Bermuda	C53F	1981	Transauto, Chesham, 1993
FSU379	Neoplan N122/3	Neoplan Skyliner	CH57/18CT	1982	Ronsway, 1997
WJI5277	Scania K112CRS	Jonckheere Jubilee P599	C49FT	1983	Scania demonstrator, 1984
MIL2408	Volvo B10M-61	Van Hool Alizée H	C49FT	1984	Bromwich, Southam, 1996
SJI8102	Volvo B10M-61	Jonckheere Jubilee P50	C53F	1985	Stonehouse Coaches, 1992
SJI8103	Volvo B10M-61	Jonckheere Jubilee P50	C53F	1985	Skill's, Nottingham, 1992
MIJ3409	Volvo B10M-53	Jonckheere Jubilee P95	C54/13DT	1985	Happy Al's, Birkenhead, 1993
SJI8106	Volvo B10M-61	Plaxton Paramount 3500 III	C53F	1988	Transauto, Chesham, 1993
MIL2406	Neoplan N122/3	Neoplan Skyliner	CH53/18CT	1988	Trathens, Plymouth, 1996
MBZ1759	Neoplan N122/3	Neoplan Skyliner	CH57/18CT	1989	Park's, Hamilton, 1997
SJI8100	Volvo B10M-60	Jonckheere Deauville P599	C34FT	1990	
L110RWB	Volvo B10M-60	Plaxton Excalibur	C49FT	1994	
M250TAK	Scania K113CRB	Irizar Century 12.35	C49FT	1994	
M148KJF	MAN 11.190	Caetano Algarve II	C35F	1995	
M254TAK	Scania K93CRB	Berkhof Excellence 1000L	C55F	1995	
M255TAK	Scania K93CRB	Berkhof Excellence 1000L	C55F	1995	
R4FWM	Iveco EuroRider 391.12.29	Beulas Intalina E29	C53F	1998	
R5FWM	Iveco EuroRider 391.12.29	Beulas Intalina E29	C53F	1998	
R6FWM	Iveco EuroRider 391.12.35	Beulas Stergo E35	C49FT	1998	
R7FWM	Iveco EuroRider 391.12.35	Beulas Stergo E35	C49FT	1998	
R8FWM	Iveco EuroRider 391.12.35	Beulas Stergo E35	C49FT	1998	
R9FWM	Iveco EuroRider 391.12.35	Beulas Stergo E35	C49FT	1998	
R10FWM	Iveco EuroRider 391.12.29	Beulas Intalina E29	C53F	1998	
R11FWM	Iveco EuroRider 391.12.29	Beulas Intalina E29	C53F	1998	
R12FWM	Dennis Javelin	UVG S320	C67F	1998	

Previous Registrations:-

1404FM	XNV150W	SJI8100	G166RBD
FSU379	GVL939Y	SJI8102	B450KAL, UBM880, B794EGG
GSU384	XNV138W	SJI8103	B43KAL
MBZ1759	F626CWJ	SJI8106	E754YKU
MIJ3409	B705EOF	SM9562	A112SNH
MIL2406	F515ETA	WJI5277	A112SNH, SM9562
MIL2408	A794TGG, 8918EL, A814ANH		

Livery:- Blue, red, orange and yellow.

The Plaxton Paramount was also built as a double-deck coach. Two base variants were offered, the 4000RS with a rear sunken saloon suitable for mid-engined underframes, and the conventional 4000 for rear-engined machines. Marshall's MIL1158 is one of the latter form with Scania running units.
Tony Wilson

M K METRO

MK Metro Ltd, Snowdon Drive, Winterhill, Milton Keynes, MK6 1AD

01-27 Mercedes-Benz L608D Robin Hood B20F 1986 Milton Keynes, 1997

01	D101VRP	06	D106VRP	14	D114VRP	23	D123VRP	27	D127VRP
02	D102VRP	08	D108VRP	22	D122VRP	25	D125VRP		

29	D129VRP	Mercedes-Benz L608D	Dormobile Routemaker (1990)	B25F	1986	Milton Keynes, 1997

32-45 Mercedes-Benz L608D Robin Hood B20F 1986 Milton Keynes, 1997

32	D132VRP	35	D135VRP	38	D138VRP	40	D140VRP	41	D141VRP
34	D134VRP							

57-65 Renault S75 Plaxton Beaver B28F 1991-92 Stagecoach Transit, 1997-98

57	J225JJR	61	K342PJR	63	J233JJR	64	K341PJR	65	J553NGS
58	J226JJR	62	J232JJR						

66-73 Mercedes-Benz 709D Robin Hood B25F 1988 Milton Keynes, 1997

66	E66MVV	67	E67MVV	68	E68MVV	72	E72MVV	73	E73MVV

No.	Reg	Chassis	Body	Seating	Year	History
74	F359GKN	Mercedes-Benz 709D	Dormobile Routemaker	B29F	1989	Milton Keynes, 1997
75	J920UNA	Mercedes-Benz 709D	Plaxton Beaver	B23F	1992	South Lancs, St.Helens, 1997
76	F920YWY	Mercedes-Benz 811D	Optare StarRider	B26F	1988	Bridge, Paisley, 1997
77	D177VRP	Mercedes-Benz L608D	Dormobile Routemaker (1990)	B25F	1986	Milton Keynes, 1997
78	G118KUB	Mercedes-Benz 811D	Optare StarRider	B26F	1989	MTL London, 1997
79	H426XGX	Mercedes-Benz 811D	Alexander AM	B28F	1991	London General, 1997
80	F906YWY	Mercedes-Benz 811D	Optare StarRider	B26F	1988	Bridge, Paisley, 1997
81	F156FWY	Mercedes-Benz 811D	Optare StarRider	B26F	1989	Stagecoach East London, 1998
82	F175FWY	Mercedes-Benz 811D	Optare StarRider	B26F	1989	Stagecoach East London, 1998
83	F913YWY	Mercedes-Benz 811D	Optare StarRider	B26F	1988	Stagecoach East London, 1998
84	M884DDS	Mercedes-Benz 709D	TBP	B29F	1994	Thompson, South Bank, 1997
85	M885DDS	Mercedes-Benz 709D	TBP	B29F	1994	Thompson, South Bank, 1997
86	G207YDL	Mercedes-Benz 811D	Phoenix	B31F	1990	Wilfreda-Beehive, Adwick-le-Street, 1997
87	G212YDL	Mercedes-Benz 811D	Phoenix	B31F	1990	Wilfreda-Beehive, Adwick-le-Street, 1997
88	G122PGT	Mercedes-Benz 811D	Alexander AM	B28F	1990	London Central,1998
89	H425XGK	Mercedes-Benz 811D	Alexander AM	B28F	1991	London Central,1998
90	H429XGK	Mercedes-Benz 811D	Alexander AM	B28F	1991	London Central,1998
91	H430XGK	Mercedes-Benz 811D	Alexander AM	B28F	1991	London Central,1998
92	H432XGK	Mercedes-Benz 811D	Alexander AM	B28F	1991	London Central,1998
93	H428XGK	Mercedes-Benz 811D	Alexander AM	B28F	1991	London Central,1998

94-100 Mercedes-Benz 709D Dormobile Routemaker B29F 1989/90 Milton Keynes, 1997

94	G94ERP	97	G97ERP	98	G98NBD	99	G99NBD	100	G100NBD
96	G96ERP							

No.	Reg	Chassis	Body	Seating	Year	History
101	J201JRP	Mercedes-Benz 709D	Plaxton Beaver	B27F	1991	Milton Keynes, 1997
102	J202JRP	Mercedes-Benz 709D	Plaxton Beaver	B27F	1991	Milton Keynes, 1997
103	J203JRP	Mercedes-Benz 709D	Plaxton Beaver	B27F	1991	Milton Keynes, 1997
104	J204JRP	Mercedes-Benz 709D	Plaxton Beaver	B27F	1992	Milton Keynes, 1997
106	L206MAV	Mercedes-Benz 709D	Marshall C19	B27F	1993	Booth & Wright, Wingham, 1997

107-113 Mercedes-Benz Vario 0814 Plaxton Beaver 2 B27F 1997

107	R107DNV	109	R109DNV	110	R110DNV	112	R112DNV	113	R113DNV
108	R108DNV							

Opposite:-

There have been many changes in Milton Keynes since the last edition, most noticeably the Citybus and Buckinghamshire Roadcar names have been replaced with yellow and blue livery with M K Metro fleetnames. All Bristol VRs and Leyland Nationals have been sold and great inroads have been made into the Mercedes-Benz L608D stock. From South Lancs Transport came 75, J920UNA to assist in L608D replacement.

114	R114DNV	Iveco TurboDaily 59.12	Marshall C31	B27F	1997		
115	R115DNV	Iveco TurboDaily 59.12	Marshall C31	B27F	1997		
116-121		Mercedes-Benz Vario 0814	Plaxton Beaver 2	B27F	1998		
116	R116DNV	118	R118DNV	119	R119DNV	120	R120NVV	121	R121NVV
117	R117DNV						
122-133		Optare Solo	Optare	B27F	1998	On order	
122	S122	125	S125	128	S128	130	S130	132	S132
123	S123	126	S126	129	S129	131	S131	133	S133
124	S124	127	S127				
268	NJA568W	Leyland B45/TL11/1R	Northern Counties	H43/30F	1980	Black Prince, Morley, 1997
CT393	F393DHL	Mercedes-Benz 709D	Reeve Burgess Beaver	B18FL	1988	London General, 1997
401	M801OJW	Dennis Dart 9.8SDL3040	Plaxton Pointer	B40F	1995	Buslink, Willenhall, 1997
CT419	K419FAV	Mercedes-Benz 709D	Marshall C19	DP16FL	1993	Milton Keynes, 1997
CT426	K426FAV	Mercedes-Benz 709D	Marshall C19	DP16FL	1993	Milton Keynes, 1997
CT428	K428FAV	Mercedes-Benz 709D	Marshall C19	DP16FL	1993	Milton Keynes, 1997

Opposite, top:- **Pictured with Premier livery just prior to its sale to Sovereign, Volvo B6 number 428, L428XVV illustrates the livery of this short-lived operation.** *Tony Wilson*
Opposite, bottom:- **The 1997 intake of minibuses for MK Metro comprised early editions of the Mercedes-Benz Vario 0814 model, the replacement of the 814D.** *Keith Vincent*

432	N132XND	Dennis Dart 9.8SDL3054	Plaxton Pointer	B40F	1995	Stuart, Dukinfield, 1997
433	N133XND	Dennis Dart 9.8SDL3054	Plaxton Pointer	B40F	1995	Stuart, Dukinfield, 1997
434	N134XND	Dennis Dart 9.8SDL3054	Plaxton Pointer	B40F	1995	Stuart, Dukinfield, 1997
CT447	C447NNV	Renault-Dodge S56	Harrops	B11FL	1986	Milton Keynes, 1997
CT448	C448NNV	Renault-Dodge S56	Harrops	B12FL	1986	Milton Keynes, 1997
448	J648XHL	Dennis Dart 9.8SDL3004	Plaxton Pointer	B43F	1991	Buslink, Willenhall, 1997
458	H858NOC	Dennis Dart 9.8SDL3004	Caryle Dartline	DP32D	1991	D & J, Silvertown, 1997
462	LPY462W	Leyland Leopard PSU3E/4R	Duple Dominant	B55F	1981	South Lancs, St Helens, 1997

Livery:-Yellow and blue.

Allocations:-

Milton Keynes (Snowdon Drive)

Mercedes-Benz	01	02	06	08	14	22	23	25
	27	29	32	34	35	38	40	41
	66	67	68	72	73	74	75	76
	77	78	79	80	81	82	83	84
	85	86	87	88	89	90	91	92
	93	94	96	97	98	99	100	101
	102	103	104	106	CT393	CT419	CT426	CT428
Iveco	114	115						
Renault-Dodge S56	CT447	CT448						
Reanult S75	57	58	61	62	63	64	65	
Mercedes-Benz Vari0	107	108	109	112	113	116	117	118
	119	120	121					
Dart	401	432	433	434	448	458		
Leyland Leopard	462							
Leyland B45	268							

PMT produced several interesting body designs, the Knype was no exception. Illustrated here by 446, H946LRE in M K Metro livery. Only two Leyland Swifts have joined the fleet, this example spending around a year serving the company before being sold as we went to press; the other example has yet to enter passenger service, having been used from new as a development vehicle by Leyland.
David Heath

MARTIN

G H Martin, 6 Hazel Road, Kettering, Northamptonshire, NN15 7AL

B787OUT	Bedford YNT	Plaxton Paramount 3200 II	C51F	1985	
C908FMP	Mercedes-Benz L608D	Reeve Burgess	C21F	1986	Tuer, Morland, 1993
D346KVA	Freight-Rover Sherpa	Dormobile	B16F	1986	Cambus, 1987
F333RJF	Leyland Swift LBM6T/2RS	Reeve Burgess Harrier	C37F	1989	
G845VAY	Dennis Javelin 11SDA1906	Plaxton Paramount 3200 III	C53F	1989	
G102SVM	Mazda E2200	Made-to-Measure	M14	1990	Simmonds, Letchworth, 1994
G744UFW	Leyland-DAF 400	Howells	M16	1990	Howells, Deri, 1991
G411YAY	Dennis Javelin 12SDA1907	Plaxton Paramount 3200 III	C53F	1990	
H238ANE	Leyland-DAF 400	Deansgate	M16	1990	
H922BPN	Mercedes-Benz 709D	Made-To-Measure	C24F	1991	Brighton Blue Bus, 1993
H613FFP	Leyland-DAF 400	Leyland-DAF	M15	1991	
J734KBC	Dennis Javelin 12SDA1919	Plaxton Paramount 3200 III	C53F	1992	
K395PJU	Dennis Javelin 12SDA2117	Plaxton Premiére 320	C53F	1992	
L357YNR	Dennis Javelin 12SDA2131	Plaxton Premiére 320	C57F	1993	
L491JFU	Mercedes-Benz 711D	Autobus Classique 2	C25F	1994	
M715HBC	Dennis Javelin 12SDA2136	Marcopolo Explorer	C53F	1995	
N94BHL	Mercedes-Benz 814D	Plaxton Beaver	C33F	1996	
N783SJU	Dennis Javelin 12SDA2136	Caetano Algarve II	C18F	1996	
P772BJF	Dennis Javelin	Caetano Algarve II	C57F	1997	
P173NAK	Mercedes-Benz 814D	Plaxton Beaver	C33F	1997	
P365RGV	LDV Convoy	LDV	M16	1997	
R951RCH	Volvo B10M-62	Plaxton Premiére 320	C57F	1997	
R418YWJ	Dennis Javelin	Plaxton Premiére 320	C57F	1998	

Previous Registration:-

H922BPN   H552EVM

Livery:- White, green and orange.

Depot:- Robinson Way, Kettering.

The majority of vehicles for Martins of Kettering are supplied new. One of the more recent arrivals to wear the attractive white, green and red fleet livery is R418YWJ a Plaxton Premiére 320 bodied Dennis Javelin. Eight Javelins are operated, with a variety of coachwork.
David Heath

MOTTS TRAVEL

Motts Coaches (Aylesbury) Ltd, Station Road, Stoke Mandeville, Buckinghamshire, HP22 5UL

Reg	Chassis	Body		Seating	Year	Previous owner
KON323P	Leyland Fleetline FE30ALR	MCW		H43/33F	1976	West Midlands, 1989
641UTO	Volvo B58-56	East Lancashire EL2000 (1991)	DP49F		1976	Black Prince, Morley, 1997
SUR283R	Leyland Leopard PSU3C/4R	Plaxton Supreme III		C53F	1977	Clarke's of London, 1997
OJD463R	Leyland Fleetline FE30ALR	Park Royal		H44/24D	1977	London Buses, 1992
OWG368X	Leyland Leopard PSU3F/4R	Plaxton Bustler		DP53F	1982	South Yorkshire, 1991
CUB539Y	MCW Metrobus DR102/32	MCW		H46/30F	1983	London Buses, 1994
CUB540Y	MCW Metrobus DR102/32	MCW		H46/30F	1983	London Buses, 1994
6601MT	Volvo B10M-61	Jonckheere Jubilee P50		C49FT	1983	Tellings, Byfleet, 1987
5705MT	Volvo B10M-53	Van Hool Astral 3		CH55/12FT	1985	Harris, Armadale, 1988
B10TMT	Volvo B10M-53	Jonckheere Jubilee P95		CH54/13DT	1985	Flight's, Birmingham, 1989
KSK965	DAF SB2300DHTD585	Plaxton Paramount 3200 II		C53DTL	1985	
KSK966	DAF SB2300DHTD585	Plaxton Paramount 3200 II		C53F	1986	Smith, Alcester, 1987
B12TMT	Neoplan N122/3	Neoplan Skyliner		CH57/20CT	1987	Crosskeys, Newingreen, 1996
5812MT	Volvo B10M-61	Jonckheere Jubilee P50		C51FT	1987	
KSK967	DAF SB2300DHTD585	Plaxton Paramount 3200 III		C53F	1987	Smith, Alcester, 1988
5814MT	Volvo B10M-61	Jonckheere Jubilee P50		C53F	1987	Clarke's of London, 1996
9775MT	Volvo B10M-61	Jonckheere Jubilee P50		C53F	1987	Clarke's of London, 1996
6957MT	Volvo B10M-61	Jonckheere Jubilee P50		C51FT	1988	Morriston Coaches, 1991
4442MT	Neoplan N122/3	Neoplan Skyliner		CH51/18CT	1988	Express Travel, Perth, 1994
B10MMT	Volvo B10M-61	Jonckheere Deauville P599		C51FT	1988	Sunseeker Tours, Torquay, 1991
F600DWB	Mercedes-Benz 609D	Whittaker		C24F	1988	Telford, Highworth, 1993
F648PLW	Mercedes-Benz 609D	Reeve Burgess		C22F	1989	Advance Rentals, Hemel Hempstead, '91
6247MT	Volvo B10M-60	Jonckheere Deauville P599		C47FT	1989	
5723MT	Volvo B10M-60	Jonckheere Deauville P599		C47FT	1989	
H882AVK	Neoplan N122/3	Neoplan Skyliner		CH57/22CT	1990	Durham Travel Services, 1998
5874MT	Volvo B10M-60	Jonckheere Deauville P599		C51FT	1990	
1746MT	Volvo B10M-60	Jonckheere Deauville P599		C51FT	1991	
B6RMT	Mercedes-Benz 814D	Optare StarRider		C28F	1992	Ralph's, Langley, 1996
9920MT	Volvo B10M-60	Jonckheere Deauville P599		C53FT	1992	Henry Crawford, Neilston, 1995
K229WNF	MAN 11.190	Jonckheere Deauville P35		C34FT	1992	Jones, Newton Aycliffe, 1995
90WFC	Volvo B10M-60	Jonckheere Deauville P599		C53F	1993	Clarke's of London, 1995
L214GJO	Volvo B10M-60	Jonckheere Deauville P599		C51FT	1993	Stagecoach Oxford, 1998
L744YGE	Volvo B10M-62	Jonckheere Deauville 45		C49FT	1994	Park's, Hamilton, 1997
M573DSJ	Volvo B10M-62	Jonckheere Deauville 45		C53F	1995	Park's, Hamilton, 1997
M575RJM	Dennis Javelin	Plaxton Première 320		C53FL	1995	Owen, Camberley, 1998
R968RCH	Volvo B10M-62	Jonckheere Mistral 50		C51FT	1998	
R902EDO	Mercedes-Benz Vario O814	Autobus Classique Nouvelle 2		C29F	1998	
S	Mercedes-Benz Vario O814	Plaxton Cheetah		C29F	1998	

Previous Registrations:-

90WFC	K914RGE	9775MT	D109BNV
641UTO	LUB512P	B6RMT	K935GWR
1746MT	H65XBD	B10MMT	F952RNV
4442MT	E93VWA	B10TMT	C712GOP, 278CFC
5705MT	B421CGG	B12TMT	C792PEM, 139MDV
5723MT	F903YNV	H882AVK	H882AVK, H5DTS
5812MT	D100BNV	KSK965	4932PH, C460JCP
5814MT	D108BNV	KSK966	C782MVH
5874MT	G380RNH, 90WFC	KSK967	D289XCX
6247MT	F902YNV	M573DSJ	LSK874
6601MT	ONV649Y		
6957MT	E209GNV		
9920MT	K266OGA		

Livery:- Yellow and blue (buses); yellow and cream (contract vehicles); yellow, cream and brown (coaches).

Depots:- Station Road, Stoke Mandeville; Bicester Road Kingswood and Aylesbury Road, Dinton.

Opposite:- **An unusual vehicle is Plaxton Bustler-bodied OWG368X in that it has been fitted with high-back seating. It is seen with Yellow Bus names outside Reading rail station. The lower picture shows 9775MT, a Volvo B10M with Jonckheere Jubilee bodywork while operating in Central London.** Colin Lloyd

NEW GREENS

H B Brown, Delaport Lodge, Lamer Lane, Wheathampstead, Hertfordshire, AL4 8RQ
J C & B A Vockings, 39 Vincent Drive, St Albans, Hertfordshire, AL1 5SL

XHE753T	Ford R1114	Plaxton Supreme III	C53F	1978	Ausden Clark, Leicester, 1995
IIL2485	Volvo B58-61	Plaxton Supreme IV	C49DL	1980	AB Coaches, Totnes, 1997
WSU451	MCW Metroliner CR126/8	MCW	C51F	1984	Provence, St Albans, 1996
B928XPP	Ford Transit 190D	Dormobile	M10L	1985	Buckinghamshire CC, 1993
B520BBD	Ford Transit 190D	Dormobile	M16	1985	Folds, Kensworth, 1995
C268XSC	Bedford Venturer YNV	Plaxton Paramount 3200 II	C53F	1985	Brice, Four Marks, 1994
C500DMP	Mercedes-Benz L608D	Reeve Burgess	C21F	1985	Chambers, Stevenage, 1993
C119TLO	Renault-Dodge S56	Reeve Burgess	B24FL	1985	Comm-Resource, Hammersmith, 1995
E786KHW	Ford Transit VE6	Steedrive	M14	1987	Maycock, Kidlington, 1989
F225OLO	Renault-Dodge S56	Leicester Carriage Builders	B9FL	1988	London Borough of Hillingdon, 1995
F22VVV	Mercedes-Benz 507D	Reeve Burgess	M16	1988	Country Lion, Northampton, 1997
JIL6902	DAF SB2305DHD585	Plaxton Paramount 3200 III	C53F	1988	City Tour, Bath, 1998
F405CKU	Mercedes-Benz 609D	Whittaker Europa	B26F	1988	Burton, Stanton, 1996
G971KWJ	Mercedes-Benz 811D	Whittaker Europa	C23F	1989	Brents, Watford, 1993
K362RNR	Mazda E2200	Howletts	M11	1992	

Previous Registrations:-

C268XSC	B885RMS, B977NSF	JIL6902	F214RJX
IIL2485	GPA610V	WSU451	B851TKL

Livery:- Cream and two tone green (Brown) C268XSC, XHE753T, WSU451; (Vockings) remainder.

Depot:- High Street, Kimpton (Brown) and Ryders Avenue, Colney Heath (Vockings)

Vehicles in the fleet of New Greens Travel wear a two-tone green and cream livery, effectively shown in this view of RLY630W, a vehicle that marries the Volvo B58 chassis with the IV version of the Plaxton Supreme. It was photographed passing through Welwyn Garden City. *Colin Lloyd*

OFFICE TRAVEL

Office Travel Ltd, 1 High Street, Elstree, Hertfordshire, WD6 3BY

2570PF	AEC Reliance 6U3ZR	Plaxton Supreme IV (1980)	C55F	1972	Shearer, Mayford, 1998
SDA710S	Leyland Fleetline FE30AGR	MCW	H43/33F	1978	Leisurelink, Newhaven, 1997
SDA714S	Leyland Fleetline FE30AGR	MCW	H43/33F	1978	Leisurelink, Newhaven, 1997
TVP891S	Leyland Fleetline FE30AGR	MCW	H43/33F	1978	Leisurelink, Newhaven, 1997
AFH389T	Bedford YMT	Duple Dominant II	C53F	1978	Busylink, Hemel Hempstead, 1995
YPL72T	AEC Reliance 6U2R ˙	Duple Dominant II Express	C53F	1979	Beard, Cinderford, 1997
505KVO	Bova EL26/581	Bova Europa	C47FT	1983	Fallon, Dunbar, 1995
TJI7508	Bova FHD12.280	Bova Futura	C49FT	1983	Keenan, Bellurgan, 1997
LBZ8368	Neoplan N122/3	Neoplan Skyliner	CH53/20CT	1984	Corbel, Edgware, 1998
D836CNV	Iveco 315-8-17	Caetano Algarve	C28F	1987	Telsons, Kings Cross, 1997

Previous Registrations:-

505KVO	SSX63Y, 503FYC, NRV953Y	LBZ8368	A102MWT, LSV621, A864RUG, CBA1L
2570PF	FAR728L	TJI7508	A548CTV

Livery:- White and blue; most double deckers are green and cream.

Depot:- West Hendon and South Mimms Service Area, St Albans Road, Potters Bar.

Office Travel have a mixed fleet of coaches, together with a small batch of Leyland Fleetlines that originated in the West Midlands PTE fleet. This view shows A129XNH, the fleet's Jonckheere Jubilee P599 bodied Volvo B10M, in the white and blue livery. *Colin Lloyd*

PAUL DALE

P P Dale, 83 Meadfield, Edgware, Middlesex, HA8 8XL

CTM418T	AEC Reliance 6U3ZR	Plaxton Supreme III	C57F	1979	Cooper, Perivale, 1994
ALJ990A	Mercedes-Benz 0303/15RHP	Mercedes-Benz	C53F	1983	Baxter, Hatch End, 1990
SIB3708	Mercedes-Benz L608D	Whittaker	C23F	1984	Heaton, Mayford, 1997
PBZ1451	Leyland Tiger TRCTL11/3R	Plaxton Paramount 3500	C53F	1985	Fell, Newbury Park, 1996
VIB6181	Leyland Tiger TRCTL11/3RZ	Plaxton Paramount 3500 II	C49FT	1986	Neild, Thrapston, 1995

Previous Registrations:-

ALJ990A	PUL98Y	SIB3708	A210YWE
PBZ1451	C530EMD	VIB6181	C66BEL, 166YHK, C316MWJ

Livery:- White and green

Depot:- South Mimms Service Area, St Albans Road, Potters Bar

Named Vehicle:- CTM418T *Billy's Bus*

POYNTER'S

J & S J Poynter, 411 Harlestone Road, New Duston, Northamptonshire, NN5 6PB

14	H982UBD	Ford Transit VE6	Crystals	M15	1990	
17	J230HVK	Toyota Coaster HDB30R	Caetano Optimo II	C21F	1991	
18	H152ANV	Ford Transit VE6	Ford	M8	1991	private owner, 1991
22	HIL5683	Leyland Swift LBM6T/2RS	Elme Galaxy	C28F	1989	Chartercoach, Dovercourt, 1992
24	L115WBX	Renault Master T35D	Cymric	M16	1993	
26	M78JNV	Scania K113CRB	Van Hool Alizée HE	C51FT	1995	
27	N572RJU	Iveco EuroMidi CC95.E18	Indcar Eco-3	C31FT	1995	
	D477DSX	Van Hool T815	Van Hool Acron	C55F	1987	Wilson, Carnwath, 1993
	J390MRP	Ford Transit VE6	Ford	M14	1992	
	K991GBD	Ford Transit VE6	Ford	M14	1993	private owner, 1998

Previous Registration:-

HIL5683	F471AFV

Livery:- White, red and blue.

Depot:- Cambridge Street, Northampton.

Poynter's have a small varied and well-appointed modern fleet. Two vehicles in the current fleet are illustrated here. Number 17, J230HVK, is a Toyota Coaster with Caetano Optimo III coachwork, while 26, M78JNV, is the fleets Van Hool Alizée bodied Scania K113. The clear and prominent position of the fleet numbers on both vehicles is noteworthy. *Colin Lloyd*

PREMIER

Premier Coaches (Watford) Ltd; J E Hewitt; 105-107 Queens Avenue, Watford, WD1 7NU

ENT778	Leyland Tiger PS1	Burlingham	C33F	1948	Combs, Ixworth, 1973
LTA904	Bedford OB	Duple Vista	C27F	1949	Rover, Chesham, 1988
LGV994	Bedford SB3	Duple Vega	C41F	1958	Wents, Boxted, 1982
CBM13X	Leyland Tiger TRCTL11/3R	Plaxton Supreme VI	C46FT	1982	
B21XKX	Leyland Tiger TRCTL11/3R	Plaxton Paramount 3200	C57F	1985	
B22XKX	Leyland Tiger TRCTL11/3R	Plaxton Paramount 3200	C57F	1985	
C24GKX	Iveco 79.14	Caetano Viana	C19F	1986	
J269NNC	Scania K93CRB	Plaxton Première 320	C53F	1992	Johnson, Hodthorpe, 1997

Livery:- Cream and red

Named Vehicle:- CBM13X *Tiger Executive*

Premier is a small, well respected operator based in Watford, Hertfordshire. Of particular interest are the classic vehicles operating in the fleet, a Burlingham-bodied Leyland Tiger and a Duple bodied Bedford OB. A Duple Vega bodied Bedford SB3 will bolster the classic fleet upon completion of its thorough restoration. Leyland Tiger CBM13X, seen here, has the relatively rare shallow windowed option of the Plaxton Supreme body, and is currently the company's executive coach. *Geoff Rixon*

PRESTWOOD TRAVEL

PB & GL Baird, 152 Wrights Lane, Prestwood, Great Missenden, Buckinghamshire, HP16 0LG

WRO438S	AEC Reliance 6U3ZR	Plaxton Supreme III	C53F	1978	J&L, St Leonards, 1995
APM111T	AEC Reliance 6U2R	Plaxton Supreme IV Express	C53F	1979	London Country, 1985
APM117T	AEC Reliance 6U2R	Plaxton Supreme IV Express	C49F	1979	London Country, 1985
EPM140V	AEC Reliance 6U2R	Plaxton Supreme IV Express	C53F	1979	Altonian, Cheltenham, 1990
EPM144V	AEC Reliance 6U2R	Plaxton Supreme IV Express	C53F	1979	London Country, 1985
EPM146V	AEC Reliance 6U2R	Plaxton Supreme IV Express	C53F	1979	London Country, 1985
RJI4670	Bova EL26/581	Bova Europa	C52F	1981	Altonian, Alton, 1992
PPJ162W	Leyland Leopard PSU5D/5R	Wadham Stringer Vanguard	B54F	1981	MoD, 1995
8726FH	Bova EL26/581	Bova Europa	C53F	1982	McAndrew, Leamington, 1990
RJI4669	Bova EL26/581	Bova Europa	C53F	1983	Pan Atlas, Harlesden, 1987
CPE480Y	Leyland Leopard PSU5D/5L	Wadham Stringer Vanguard	B54F	1983	MoD, 1995
C814FMC	Leyland Tiger RTC	Leyland Doyen	C49F	1986	Beard, Cinderford, 1997
C82YKK	Auwaeter Neoplan N122/3	Neoplan Skyliner	CH53/20CT	1986	Ham, Flimwell, 1997
E48TYG	Leyland Royal Tiger RTC	Leyland Doyen	C53F	1988	Holmeswood Coaches, 1995

Previous Registrations:-

8726FH	CLX573Y	PPJ162W	50AC03
C82YKK	C726JTL, B44HAM	RJI4669	DOY134Y
CPE480Y	51AC05	RJI4670	VPG339X

Livery:- White, orange and black.

Depot:- Binders Industrial Estate, Cryers Hill, High Wycombe.

Prestwood Travel use a varied fleet ranging from minibuses to double deck coaches, catering for private hire, school contract, local bus and shoppers services, mainly around High Wycombe. The AEC Reliance usually frequent the school contract and local services, while newer coaches such as the Leyland Royal Tiger Doyens, are most likely to be found on private hire work, as shown by C814FMC in this view.
David Heath

PROVENCE PRIVATE HIRE

Provence Private Hire Ltd, Heath Farm Lane, Harpenden Road, St Albans, Hertfordshire, AL3 5AE

KFO572P	Bedford VAS 5	Plaxton Supreme III	C28FL	1975	Roy Brown, Builth Wells,1990
XTM482S	Bedford YMT	Plaxton Supreme III	C53F	1978	H & F Hire, St Albans, 1989
AWB818T	Bedford YMT	Duple Dominant II	C53F	1979	Arenson, St Albans, 1986
FRM688V	Volvo B58-61	Unicar	C57F	1980	Gordon, Kirkbride, 1984
MUE314V	Volvo B58-61	East Lancashire EL2000(1997)	DP57F	1980	
LTY556X	Bedford YNT	Plaxton Supreme VI	C53F	1982	Wild, Clowne, 1990
CPP45X	Volvo B10M-61	Duple Dominant III	C53F	1982	
153XYC	Neoplan N122/3	Neoplan Skyliner	CH53/20CT	1982	H & F Hire, St Albans, 1993
SUK431Y	Ford R1115	Duple Dominant IV	C53F	1982	Meadway, Birmingham, 1991
CVH733Y	Ford R1114	Duple Dominant IV	C35F	1983	H & F Hire, St Albans, 1992
485SWL	Neoplan N122/3	Neoplan Skyliner	CH53/20CT	1983	Reilly, Maghull, 1993
A203ODY	MCW Hi-liner HR131/1	MCW	C49FT	1983	East Kent, 1996
WSU448	MCW Metroliner CR126/8	MCW	C51F	1984	East Kent, 1994
XMW285	MCW Metroliner CR126/8	MCW	C51F	1984	East Kent, 1994
WSU450	MCW Metroliner CR126/8	MCW	C51F	1984	East Kent, 1996
WSU452	MCW Metroliner CR126/8	MCW	C51F	1984	East Kent, 1996
WSU453	MCW Metroliner CR126/8	MCW	C51F	1984	East Kent, 1994
B946CMT	MCW Hi-liner HR131/6	MCW	C49FT	1985	East Kent, 1996
C985YFA	DAF MB200DKFL600	Duple Caribbean 2	C53F	1985	Rainbow, Westbury, 1996
C131CFB	MCW Hi-liner HR131/7	MCW	C55F	1986	Wessex, 1993
C215KMA	MCW Metroliner DR130/27	MCW	CH57/22DT	1986	Rainbow, Westbury, 1996
C759CWX	MCW Metroliner DR130/26	MCW	CH57/22DT	1986	Amberline, 1990
C425WFH	Leyland Tiger TRCTL11/3RZ	Plaxton Paramount 3500 II	C49FT	1986	Diocese of St Albans, 1997
E426ATT	Fiat Ducato	Devon Conversions	M14	1988	London Unit, Swanley, 1992
E854UKR	MCW Hi-liner HR131/12	MCW	C51F	1988	East Kent, 1996
E855UKR	MCW Hi-liner HR131/12	MCW	C51F	1988	East Kent, 1996
F862TNH	Volvo B10M-61	Caetano Algarve	C53F	1988	
TJT788	Leyland Tiger TRCL10/3ARZM	Plaxton Paramount 3500 III	C49FT	1990	Court, Fillongley, 1997
XGV226	Leyland Tiger TRCL10/3ARZM	Plaxton Paramount 3500 III	C49FT	1990	Court, Fillongley, 1997

Previous Registrations:-

153XYC	ADV160Y	WSU448	A848OKK
485SWL	MVL607Y, 4585SC	WSU450	B850TKL
A203ODY	A543WOB, ABM300A, XDU599	WSU452	B852TKL
B946CMT	B246JVA, XYK976	WSU453	B853TKL
C985YFA	C760UVT, MIB582	XGV226	G116JBO
TJT788	G117JBO	XMW285	A849OKK

Livery:- Yellow and blue

Depots:- Heath Farm Lane, St Albans; Acrewood Way, St Albans and Maxted Road, Hemel Hempstead.

Provence Private Hire operate five Metroliner single deck coaches, six of the high floor Hi-liner single deckers, and two Metroliner double deckers. Provence must be the largest operator of the type - apart from London Pride's large fleet of open top double deckers. C131CFB depicts the lines of the Hi-liner, and C215KMA, shows the more familiar double deck version. *David Heath/Colin Lloyd*

RED KITE COMMERCIAL SERVICES

G Hyde, 25 High Street North, Stewkley, Buckinghamshire, LU7 0EZ

PBH539R	Bedford YMT	Plaxton Supreme III	C53F	1976	Brown, Builth Wells, 1996
XRN716R	Bedford YMT	Plaxton Supreme III	C53F	1977	Guscott, Halwill, 1996
TEX405R	Bristol VRT/SL3/6LXB	Eastern Coach Works	H43/31F	1977	Metro, 1997
TEX872R	Bristol VRT/SL3/6LXB	Eastern Coach Works	H43/31F	1977	Stagecoach Cambus, 1997
CBV19S	Bristol VRT/SL3/501	Eastern Coach Works	H43/31F	1977	Metro, 1998
WPW201S	Bristol VRT/SL3/6LXB	Eastern Coach Works	H43/31F	1977	Stagecoach Cambus (Viscount), 1997
XNV890S	Bristol VRT/SL3/6LXB	Eastern Coach Works	H43/31F	1978	Metro, 1997
YVV896S	Bristol VRT/SL3/6LXB	Eastern Coach Works	H43/31F	1978	Stagecoach Cambus, 1997
YNG208S	Bristol VRT/SL3/6LXB	Eastern Coach Works	H43/31F	1978	Stagecoach Cambus (Viscount), 1997
FRP905T	Bristol VRT/SL3/6LXB	Eastern Coach Works	H43/31F	1979	Stagecoach Cambus, 1997
FRP910T	Bristol VRT/SL3/6LXB	Eastern Coach Works	H43/31F	1979	Metro, 1997
FWR218T	Bristol VRT/SL3/6LXB	Eastern Coach Works	H43/31F	1979	Stagecoach Cambus, 1997
FWR219T	Bristol VRT/SL3/6LXB	Eastern Coach Works	H43/31F	1979	Metro, 1998
URP942W	Bristol VRT/SL3/6LXB	Eastern Coach Works	H43/31F	1981	Metro, 1998
JFL729W	Bedford YMT	Plaxton Supreme IV	C43F	1981	Shaw, Maxey, 1996

Depot:- Leys Yard, Tilsworth, Bedfordshire.

RED ROSE TRAVEL

Red Rose Travel Ltd, 110 Oxford Road, Aylesbury, Buckinghamshire, HP1 8PB

Q956UOE	Bedford YRT	Willowbrook Warrior (1987)	B53F	1976	Sussex Bus, Ford, 1992
A128FDC	Leyland National 2 NL116HLXB/1R		B49F	1983	Arriva Northumbria, 1998
B63APP	Ford Transit	Chassis Developments	C16F	1985	Crosskeys, Newingreen, 1994
D217SKD	Mercedes-Benz L608D	Alexander AM	B20F	1986	North Western, 1996
D209FFX	Ford Transit 190D	Carlyle	B16F	1986	Expresslines, Bedford, 1997
D124PTT	Ford Transit VE6	Mellor	B16F	1987	Stagecoach Oxford, 1998
D607NOE	MCW MetroRider MF150/3	MCW	B23F	1987	West Midlands Travel,1997
F49ENF	Leyland Tiger TRBL10/3ARZA	Alexander N	B53F	1987	Timeline, 1998
E737WOC	Leyland Tiger TRCTLII/3LZ	Plaxton Derwent 2	B54F	1987	MoD, 1998
F190YDA	MCW MetroRider MF158/11	MCW	B28F	1988	Westlink, 1997
F725MNB	Ford Transit VE6	Ford	M15	1989	Stagecoach Darlington, 1995
F160AWO	MCW MetroRider MF154/19	MCW	B31F	1989	Cardiff Bus, 1997
H389SYG	Mercedes-Benz 811D	Optare StarRider E	B26F	1990	Optare demonstrator, 1991
K540OGA	Mercedes-Benz 811D	Dormobile Routemaker	B29F	1992	
M62MOG	Iveco TurboDaily 59.12	Mellor	B27F	1994	
M848MOL	Iveco TurboDaily 59.12	Mellor	B27F	1994	
M260VEJ	Dennis Dart 9.8SDL3040	East Lancashire	B43F	1995	Davies Bros, Pencoder, 1998
N802GRV	Mercedes-Benz 709D	UVG CitiStar	B29F	1996	
N803GRV	Mercedes-Benz 709D	UVG CitiStar	B29F	1996	
N219HBK	Dennis Dart 9.8SDL3054	UVG UrbanStar	B40F	1996	
N784JBM	Mercedes-Benz 711D	UVG CitiStar	B29F	1996	
P507NWU	Optare MetroRider MR17	Optare	B25F	1996	Optare demonstrator, 1997
R796GSF	Mercedes-Benz Vario 0814	Plaxton Beaver 2	B29F	1997	

Previous Registration:-

Q956UOE	NFP735P	E737WOC	?

Livery:- Red, cream and black (Red Rose)

Red Rose of Aylesbury have recently expanded their fleet, territory and vehicle variety. Featuring a red, cream and black livery are K540OGA, a Mercedes-Benz 811D with Dormobile Routemaker bodywork, and N219HBK, the first Dennis Dart for Red Rose. This example carries the comparatively rare UVG Urban Star bodywork. *Tony Wilson*

REG'S OF HERTFORD

Reg's Coaches Ltd, Spencer Street, Mead Lane, Hertford, Hertfordshire, SG13 7AH

PBZ9155	Leyland Leopard PSU5C/4R	Duple Dominant II	C57F	1980	Robinson, Great Harwood, 1986
PBZ9154	Leyland Leopard PSU5C/4R	Duple Dominant II	C57F	1981	Robinson, Great Harwood, 1988
LBZ2943	Leyland Tiger TRCTL11/3RZ	Plaxton Paramount 3200 III	C53F	1987	Shearings, 1993
LBZ2944	Leyland Tiger TRCTL11/3RZ	Plaxton Paramount 3200 III	C53F	1987	Shearings, 1993
LBZ7235	Bedford Venturer YNV	Duple 320	C57F	1987	Cabson, Yaxley, 1996
LBZ2940	Hestair Duple SDA1512	Duple 425	C51FT	1988	Pat's, New Broughton, 1994
LBZ2942	Dennis Javelin 12SDA1908	Plaxton Paramount 3200 III	C57F	1988	Go Whittle, Kidderminster, 1989
LBZ2941	Dennis Javelin 12SDA1908	Plaxton Paramount 3200 III	C49FT	1988	Go Whittle, Kidderminster, 1989
LBZ7234	Leyland Tiger TRCTL11/3ARZ	Duple 320	C53F	1989	Bennetts Silverline, Chieveley, 1996
PBZ9152	Dennis Javelin 11SDA1906	Duple 320	C55F	1989	Layston, Hare Street, 1997
PBZ9153	Dennis Javelin 12SDA1907	Duple 320	C57F	1989	Coombs, Weston super Mare, 1996
G541JBV	Dennis Dart 9SDL3002	Duple Dartline	B39F	1989	Carlyle demonstrator, 1990
L402XLM	Mercedes-Benz 814D	Optare StarRider	C20F	1994	Wings, Uxbridge, 1998
N990FNK	Mercedes-Benz 709D	Marshall C19	B27F	1995	
N991FNK	Mercedes-Benz 709D	Marshall C19	B27F	1995	
N617UEW	Dennis Dart 9.8SDL3054	Marshall C37	B40F	1996	
WSY601	Dennis Javelin	Plaxton Première 320	C53F	1993	Read Wing, Camberwell, 1997
WSY602	Dennis Javelin	Plaxton Première 320	C53F	1993	Martin's, Kettering, 1997
WSY691	Dennis Javelin	Plaxton Première 320	C53F	1993	Phil Anslow, Pontypool, 1997

Previous Registrations:-

LBZ7234	F783GNA	LBZ2943	D593MVR	PBZ9155	LVS418V
LBZ7235	D35ONY	LBZ2944	D594MVR	WSY601	K260FUV
LBZ2940	E612AEY	PBZ9152	F241OFP	WSY602	K263FUV
LBZ2941	E544JWP	PBZ9153	F684CYC	WSY691	L355YNR
LBZ2942	E502JWP	PBZ9154	HHG193W		

Named Vehicles:- PBZ9154 *Reg's Pathfinder*, LBZ7234 *Reg's Viewfinder*, LBZ7235 *Reg's Nightingale*, LBZ2940 *Reg's Enterprise*, LBZ2941 *Reg's Moonraker*, LBZ2942 *Reg's Starliner*, LBZ2943 *Reg's Highwayman*, LBZ2944 *Reg's Highlander*, PBZ9155 *Reg's Panoramic Cruiser*, N990FNK *Reg's Mini Hopper*, N991FNK *Reg's Mini Hopper*, PBZ9152 *Reg's Viewseeker*, PBZ9153 *Reg's Viewmaster*.

Livery:- Metallic green, black and orange replacing green, black and red.

Initially a trio of 10.3 metre Leyland Nationals formed Reg's bus fleet, though these were replaced by early examples of the Dennis Dart with Duple Dartline bodies. Two of the Darts have since left the fleet, while a similar-styled 9.8 metre example bodied by Marshall, N617UEW, has entered service and is shown here.
Tony Wilson

REYNOLDS DIPLOMAT

R Reynolds & SK Goodhand, 22 Bushey Hall Road, Bushey, Hertfordshire, WD2 2ED

FLD927Y	Volvo B10M-61	Jonckheere Jubilee	C48DT	1983	Prairie, Uxbridge, 1998
FLD928Y	Volvo B10M-61	Jonckheere Jubilee	C48DT	1983	Prairie, Uxbridge, 1998
B839NKA	Leyland Tiger TRCTL11/3RH	Plaxton Paramount 3500 II	C49FT	1985	Blue Triangle, Bootle, 1993
C460CNG	Leyland Tiger TRCTL11/3RZ	Plaxton Paramount 3500 II	C49FT	1986	Rosemary, Terrington St Clements, 1993
NIW4405	Volvo B10M-61	Jonckheere Jubilee P50	C51FT	1986	Thamesdown (Kingston Coaches), 1997
MIL4003	Mercedes-Benz O303.14RHD	Mercedes-Benz	C49F	1987	Mitchell of Plean, 1998
A1NYJ	Volvo B10M-60	Duple 340	C53F	1989	Westbus, Hounslow, 1996
N5RDC	Volvo B10M-62	Jonckheere Deauville 45	C51FT	1995	
N6RDC	Scania K113CRB	Irizar Century 12.35	C49FT	1996	

Previous Registrations:-

A1NYJ	F994UME	FLD928Y	ONV643Y, 315ASV
B839NKA	B27OBF, 4327PL, B457SFA, 449CLT	MIL4003	D348CBC, LSU113
FLD927Y	ONV641Y, 848KMX	NIW4405	C413LRP

Livery:- Green, white and gold. National Youth Jazz Orchestra :- A1NYJ

Depot:- Bushey Hall Drive, Bushey.

Reynolds Diplomat have recently introduced the Irizar Century to their fleet. Initially launched onto the UK market in 1994, the Century range has so far expanded to three models. The first model available was the Century 12.35, a standard model with two axles; 12 metres long and 3.5 metres in height similar to N6RDC, seen at Hyde Park Corner. *Colin Lloyd*

RICHARD TAYLOR'S TRAVEL

R W J Taylor, St Ibbs Farmhouse, London Road, St Ippolytts,
Hitchin, Hertfordshire, SG4 7NL

WIB4784	Bedford YMT	Plaxton Supreme IV	C49F	1979	D&G, Stevenage, 1997
MIW3853	DAF MB200DKFL600	Duple Caribbean	C55F	1984	D&G, Stevenage, 1996
RAZ5954	Volvo B10M-61	Berkhof Emperor 395	CH--/--FT	1986	?, 1998
PJI3531	Leyland Royal Tiger RTC	Leyland Doyen	C49FT	1987	Millership, Telford, 1996

Previous Registrations:-

MIW3853	A806REW		RAZ5954	?
PJI3531	D162HML		WIB4784	XDY942T

Livery:- Blue and white or silver

For a brief period in the 1980's, coaches with ultra-high floors and double-deck vehicles with or without rear sunken saloons were fashionable. Various manufacturers produced models for this market. One of these was Berkhof with their Everest and Eclipse designs, and the Emperor with sunken rear saloon. Richard Taylor Travel have one of the Emperors, RAZ5954 shown here. *David Heath*

RICHMOND'S

H V Richmond Ltd, The Garage, Barley, Royston, Hertfordshire, SG8 8JA

Reg	Chassis	Body	Seats	Year	History
239LYC	Volvo B10M-61	Plaxton Supreme V	C57F	1981	Smiths, Buntingford, 1994
275FUM	Volvo B10M-61	Plaxton Supreme VI	C57F	1982	
668PTM	Volvo B10M-61	Plaxton Supreme VI	C57F	1983	Ralph's, Longford, 1985
559ABX	Volvo B10M-61	Plaxton Paramount 3200	C53F	1984	
729KTO	Volvo B10M-61	Plaxton Paramount 3200 II	C57F	1985	
851FYD	Volvo B9M	Plaxton Paramount 3200 II	C39F	1986	
403NMM	Volvo B9M	Plaxton Paramount 3200 II	C39F	1987	Courtlands, Horley, 1989
E408YLG	Mercedes-Benz 609D	PMT	DP24F	1987	Cooper, Ashton, 1989
438XYA	Volvo B10M-61	Van Hool Alizée	C53F	1988	Sworder, Walkern, 1990
648EAU	Volvo B10M-60	Van Hool Alizée H	C53FT	1989	Kenzies, Shepreth, 1995
753LNU	Volvo B10M-60	Van Hool Alizée H	C52FT	1989	Tellings Golden Miller, Byfleet, 1995
593FGF	Volvo B10M-60	Van Hool Alizée H	C55F	1990	
577HYX	Toyota Coaster HDB30R	Caetano Optimo II	C18F	1991	Capital, West Drayton, 1997
539WVJ	Volvo B10M-60	Van Hool Alizée H	C53F	1991	Shearings, 1998
316UVX	Volvo B10M-60	Van Hool Alizée H	C49FT	1992	Shearings, 1997
153WAR	Volvo B10M-60	Van Hool Alizée HE	C49FT	1993	
649ETF	Toyota Coaster HDB30R	Caetano Optimo II	C18F	1993	
M587BFL	Mercedes-Benz 709D	Marshall C19	B23F	1994	
M588BFL	Mercedes-Benz 709D	Marshall C19	B23F	1994	
N895VEG	Mercedes-Benz 811D	Marshall C16	B33F	1996	
YER469	Volvo B10M-62	Van Hool Alizée HE	C53F	1996	
426YRA	Dennis Javelin (10m)	Berkhof Axial	C41F	1997	
892LTV	Dennis Javelin (10M)	Berkhof Axial	C43F	1998	

Previous Registrations:-

153WAR	From new	539WVJ	H198DVM	729KTO	B29ABH
239LYC	XPP693X	559ABX	B618AMD	753LNU	F810TMD
275FUM	OMM675X	577HYX	J135LLK	851FYD	C219FMF
316UVX	J208NNC	593FGF	G85AUR	892LTV	R588RRX
403NMM	D867YPH	648EAU	F37DAV	HDT375	-
426YRA	From new	649ETF	From new	YER469	N994EYA
438XYA	F238HRO	668PTM	RMH868Y		

Livery:- Cream and caramel.

Depot:- The Garage and Church Street, Barley.

Recent years have seen most of the major suppliers to the UK coach market launch completely new ranges. The latest model range from Berkhof is the Axial, a clean and attractive design with an unusual hump at roof level at the front of the vehicle. This feature of the Axial is visible in this picture of Richmond's 426YRA, which has been built on the short 10-metre version of the Dennis Javelin.
P J Stockwell

ROBINSONS

BJ & BE Robinson, Central Garage, Stewkley, Buckinghamshire, LU7 0EW

FFT684W	Volvo B58-61	Plaxton Supreme IV	C57F	1981	Barfordian, Gt Barford, 1997
BRY102Y	Bova EL26/581	Bova Europa	C53F	1983	
ODO918Y	Kässbohrer Setra S215HD	Kässbohrer Tornado	C49FT	1983	Lally, Galway, 1997
3253VU	Kässbohrer Setra S228DT	Kässbohrer Imperial	CH54/20CT	1984	Turner, Bristol, 1996
4542VU	Kässbohrer Setra S215HR	Kässbohrer Rational	C53F	1987	SSS, Euston, 1997
2522VU	Bova FHD12.290	Bova Futura	C51FT	1989	Henry Cooper, Annitsford, 1995
5302VU	Bova FHD12.290	Bova Futura	C51FT	1989	
J3TCC	Kässbohrer Setra S215HD	Kässbohrer Tornado	C47FT	1992	Travellers, Hounslow, 1996
L299HKM	MAN 11.190	Berkhof Excellence 1000 Midi	C33FT	1983	The Kings Ferry, Gillingham, 1998
N580GBW	Dennis Javelin 12SDA2147	Caetano Algarve II	C53F	1995	

Previous Registrations:-

2522VU	F240TBC, JJI4889, F543OVK	5302VU	G795URY
3253VU	A470WRL, 8909DF, A541YGL, XFV257, A137GAO, ASH293, A137GAO	ODO918Y	RAX24Y, 671BOF, 83-G-58
4542VU	C104TFP		

Livery:- Silver and two-tone blue.

Bova Futura integral coaches have been available in the UK for fifteen years and still look quite striking. Recent additions to the model have included a 15 metre tri-axle version which currently does not comply with UK regulations. Robinsons of Stewkley in Buckinghamshire have two 1989 models with cherished registration marks. Pictured here is 2522VU, one of the more common DAF engined high floor FHD models. *Geoff Rixon*

RODGERS

J W Rodger, 102 Kettering Road, Weldon, Corby, Northamptonshire, NN17 3JG

CBV20S	Bristol VRT/SL3/501(6LXB)	Eastern Coach Works	H43/31F	1977	Stagecoach Midland Red, 1996
RTH927S	Bristol VRT/SL3/501	Eastern Coach Works	H43/31F	1978	Mac, Roydon, 1993
FTU377T	Bristol VRT/SL3/501	Eastern Coach Works	H43/31F	1978	Crosville Cwmru, 1995
JMB359T	Bristol VRT/SL3/501	Eastern Coach Works	H43/31F	1979	Cerbydau Carreglefn, 1992
WTH960T	Bristol VRT/SL3/501	Eastern Coach Works	H43/31F	1979	Mac, Roydon, 1993
MEF826W	Bristol VRT/SL3/6LXB	Eastern Coach Works	H43/31F	1980	Jones, Llanfaethlu, 1997
GSB146Y	Dennis Dominator DDA163	Alexander RL	H45/31F	1983	Stott, Oldham, 1998
GSB147Y	Dennis Dominator DDA163	Alexander RL	H45/31F	1983	Stott, Oldham, 1998
A335GFF	Volvo B10M-61	East Lancashire (1998)	H45/35F	1983	Smith, Darenth, 1997
A37DTV	Volvo B10M-61	Van Hool Alizée H	C53F	1984	Drislane, Corby, 1995
B379FHK	Leyland Tiger TRCTL11/3RZ	Van Hool Alizée H	C53FT	1984	Lodge, High Easter, 1996
C47WLL	Volvo B10M-61	Duple 320	C53F	1986	Moor-Dale, Newcastle, 1994
D377VRM	Bedford YNT	Duple 320	C53F	1987	Dawson & Cowley, Chesterfield, 1995
E541EAL	Dennis Javelin 11SDL1905	Plaxton Paramount 3200 III	C45F	1988	Leah, Huthwaite, 1997
E448WAH	Dennis Javelin 12SDA1907	Duple 320	C53F	1988	Sanders, Holt, 1995
F28FCC	Volvo B10M-60	Plaxton Paramount 3500 III	C53F	1989	Vale of Llangollen, Cefn Mawr, 1997

Previous Registration:-

A335GFF	A123KCC, XDJ7, A3ARV	F28FCC	F993KFM, 8701VT, F438LTU, 791VT
E448WAH	E769HJF, SGF965		

Livery:- Red and yellow.

ROVER LUXURY TRAVEL

J R Dell, Delmar, Lycrome Road, Lye Green, Chesham, Buckinghamshire, HP5 3LF

SFU718	Bedford YMT	Plaxton Supreme III	C53F	1976	Morley, West Row, 1985
MIL2397	Bova FLD12.250	Bova Futura	C53F	1984	North Somerset Coaches, 1996
HIL3470	Volvo B10M-61	Duple 320	C53F	1986	Marton, West drayton, 1991
JIL9034	Mercedes-Benz 307D	Economy	M12	1986	Coles, Eversley, 1995
JOI9820	Volvo B10M-61	Van Hool Alizée H	C53F	1987	Clarkson, Hemyock, 1994
E240NSE	Mercedes-Benz 609D	Yeates	C19F	1988	Mayne, Buckie, 1989
OJR338	Volvo B10M-61	Plaxton Paramount 3500 III	C53F	1988	Shearings, 1992
F61RKX	Dennis Javelin 11SDL1905	Duple 320	C55F	1989	Horsham Coaches, 1993
760BUS	Volvo B10M-60	Plaxton Paramount 3500 III	C53F	1989	Horseshoe, Tottenham, 1991
TJI8299	Volvo B10M-60	Jonckheere Deauville P599	C51FT	1990	Redwood, Hemyock, 1994
OPT829	Mercedes-Benz 811D	Optare StarRider	C29F	1990	Reid, Chesham, 1997
J727CWT	Volvo B10M-60	Plaxton Excalibur	C53F	1992	Wallace Arnold, 1998
372DEL	Volvo B10M-60	Plaxton Excalibur	C49FT	1992	Flights, Birmingham, 1998

Previous Registrations:-

372DEL	K285XOG, K12FTG		
760BUS	F886SMU, 662JJO	MIL2397	A953JJN, 2942FH, VHY437
F61RKX	F491WPR, SRD733	OJR338	E659UNE
HIL3470	C949TLF	OPT829	H390SYG
JIL9034	C532VPM	SFU718	LHW508P
JOI9820	D560MVR, PJI5526, D710NYG	TJI8299	G648ONH

Named Vehicles:- E240NSE *Nessie*; JIL9034 *Jill*; MIL2397 *Nilly*

Livery:- Blue, cream and yellow.

SEAMARKS

Seamarks Coach & Travel Ltd, Seamarks House, 387-397 Dunstable Road, Luton, Bedfordshire, LU5 8BY

200	MJI7855	Kässbohrer Setra S215HR	Kässbohrer Rational	C53F	1984	
201	MJI7856	Kässbohrer Setra S215HR	Kässbohrer Rational	C53F	1984	
202	MJI7857	Kässbohrer Setra S215HR	Kässbohrer Rational	C53F	1984	
205	9569KM	Volvo B10M-61	Plaxton Paramount 3500 II	C57F	1985	
206	MJI8660	Volvo B10M-61	Plaxton Paramount 3500 II	C57F	1985	
208	MJI8662	Volvo B10M-61	Plaxton Paramount 3500 II	C53F	1985	
209	MJI8663	Volvo B10M-61	Plaxton Paramount 3500 II	C53F	1985	
210	25CTM	Volvo C10M-70	Ramseier & Jenser	C49FT	1985	
211	MJI7854	Volvo B10M-61	Caetano Algarve	C53F	1985	
214	F791DWT	DAF SB220LC550	Optare Delta	B47F	1989	
215	F370BUA	DAF SB220LC550	Optare Delta	B51F	1988	Optare demonstrator, 1989
220	G278WKX	DAF SB220LC550	Optare Delta	B47F	1989	
223	6101MV	Volvo C10M-70	Ramseier & Jenser	C49FT	1986	Park's, Hamilton, 1991
224	9683ML	Volvo C10M-70	Ramseier & Jenser	C37FT	1986	Park's, Hamilton, 1991
225	J208RVS	Optare MetroRider	Optare	DP31F	1992	Park's, Hamilton, 1991
226	H846UUA	MAN 11.190	Optare Vecta	B41F	1992	Optare demonstrator, 1989
229	J367BNW	MAN 11.190	Optare Vecta	B41F	1992	Optare demonstrator, 1993
230	L834MWT	MAN 11.190	Optare Vecta	B40F	1993	Optare demonstrator, 1994
231	M702RVS	MAN 11.190	Optare Vecta	B40F	1994	
232	M231SGS	Mercedes-Benz 709D	Marshall C19	B25F	1995	
	N75JUR	Mercedes-Benz 811D	Plaxton Beaver	B31F	1996	
	N76KVS	Mercedes-Benz 811D	Plaxton Beaver	B31F	1996	
	N57MDW	Volvo B10M-62	Plaxton Première 320	C53F	1996	Bebb, Llantwit Fardre, 1998
	N58MDW	Volvo B10M-62	Plaxton Première 320	C53F	1996	Bebb, Llantwit Fardre, 1998
	N61MDW	Volvo B10M-62	Plaxton Première 320	C53F	1996	Bebb, Llantwit Fardre, 1998
	S582VOB	Volvo B10BLE	Wright Renown	B F	1998	
	S583VOB	Volvo B6BLE	Wright Crusader	B F	1998	
	S584VOB	Volvo B6BLE	Wright Crusader	B F	1998	

Previous Registrations:-

25CTM	From new	MJI7856	B266XNK
6101MV	C651KDS	MJI7857	B267XNK
9683ML	C345GSD	MJI8660	B542BMH
9569KM	B817MPP, 9683ML, B541BMH	MJI8661	
MJI7854	B455AUR	MJI8662	B544BMH
MJI7855	B265XNK	MJI8663	B545BMH

Livery:- White and green

A varied selection of modern buses are used by Seamarks, including newly introduced Volvo B6 and B10BLE saloons. A trio of Mercedes-Benz minibuses are used on the quieter routes, this is Plaxton Beaver bodied N75JUR. Opposite are Delta F791DWT and Vecta J367BNW.
David Heath/ Colin Lloyd

SHIRE COACHES

M W & L Maney, 31 Frogmore, Park Street, St Albans, Hertfordshire, AL2 2NH

D523DWP	Scania K112TRS	Plaxton Paramount 4000 II	CH55/20DT	1987	Astons, Kempsey, 1997
G169ODH	Dennis Javelin 12SDA1907	Plaxton Paramount 3200 III	C53F	1989	Elizabethan, Walsall, 1997
G466JNH	Scania K113CRB	Jonckheere Deauville P599	C51FT	1989	Reynolds Diplomat, Bushey, 1997
G52BLX	Mercedes-Benz 609D	Rainbow	C24F	1990	Rainbow, Stanmore, 1995
K540CWN	DAF SB3000DKVF601	Caetano Algarve II	C49FT	1993	Diamond Glantawe, Morriston, 1997
L577ULY	Ford Transit VE6	Ford	M8	1994	
N934HPX	Dennis Javelin	UVG Unistar	C57F	1996	
P479FAN	Dennis Javelin 12SDA2136	Berkhof Excellence 1000L	C53F	1996	
P526NOT	Dennis Javelin	UVG S320	C55F	1997	
R503SCH	Iveco EuroRider 391-12-35	Beulas Stergo E35	C51FT	1997	
R205VJF	Iveco EuroRider 391-12-29	Beulas Intalina E29	C51FT	1998	
S106KJF	Iveco EuroMidi CC95.E.18	Indcar ECO4	C35F	1998	

Previous Registrations:-

D523DWP   3698E

Livery:- Maroon and gold

An attractive maroon livery adorns the Shire Coaches fleet, as seen on G466JNH. This Scania K113 has Jonckheere Deauville coachwork, the 1989 successor to the extensive Jubilee range. The Deauville remained available until 1997 when it was superseded by the Mistral which was introduced in from 1995. *David Heath*

SHOREYS

E C J Shorey, 119 Clophill Road, Maulden, Bedfordshire, MK45 2AE

GHV999N	Daimler Fleetline CRL6	Park Royal	H44/27D	1974	Ensign, Purfleet, 1986
GHV51N	Daimler Fleetline CRL6	Park Royal	H44/32F	1975	Pathfinder, Chadwell Heath, 1987
OJD351R	Leyland Fleetline FE30ALR	Park Royal	H44/24D	1977	London General, 1995
OJD357R	Leyland Fleetline FE30ALR	Park Royal	H44/24D	1977	London General, 1995
THX283S	Leyland Fleetline FE30ALR	MCW	H44/24D	1977	London General, 1995
THX304S	Leyland Fleetline FE30ALR	MCW	H44/24D	1978	London General, 1995
THX580S	Leyland Fleetline FE30ALR	Park Royal	H44/27D	1978	London Buses, 1992
SDA651S	Leyland Fleetline FE30AGR	Park Royal	H43/33F	1978	Stagecoach United Counties, 1998
BNO670T	Leyland National 11351A/1R		B49F	1978	Thamesway, 1995
YVN522T	Leyland Fleetline FE30AGR	Northern Counties	H43/31F	1979	Stagecoach United Counties, 1998
GAJ127V	Leyland Fleetline FE30AGR	Northern Counties	H43/31F	1980	Stagecoach United Counties, 1997
PIA892	Volvo B10M-53	Berkhof Emperor 395	CH51/11FT	1984	The Kings Ferry, Gillingham, 1993
17EJU	Volvo B10M-61	Van Hool Astral	CH47/10DT	1984	

Previous Registration:-

17EJU	From new	PIA892	B570YJN

Named Vehicle:- 17EJU *Lady Donna.*

Livery:- White, red and blue

In contrast to the Berkhof Emperor in two-axle layout with Richard Taylor Travel, here is PIA892, a similar vehicle but a Volvo B10M chassis in tri-axle form. Both of Shoreys coaches are twin deck machines to this layout, the balance of the fleet are double-deck buses and a Leyland National.

SIMMONDS

Simmonds Coaches Ltd, 9 Broadwater Avenue, Letchworth, Hertfordshire, SG6 3HE

KJD89P	Leyland Fleetline FE30ALR	Park Royal	H44/24D	1976	London Transport, 1983
A819XMK	Volvo B10M-61	Plaxton Paramount 3500	C53F	1984	
C117EMG	Volvo B10M-61	Plaxton Paramount 3200 II	C57F	1986	
C326DND	Volvo B10M-61	Van Hool Alizée H	C53F	1986	Shearings, 1992
F305RMH	Volvo B10M-61	Plaxton Paramount 3500 III	C57F	1988	
J61NTM	Volvo B10M-60	Plaxton Paramount 3500 III	C53F	1991	
L355HFU	Mercedes-Benz 814D	Autobus Classique	C33F	1993	
L980CRY	Toyota Coaster HZB50R	Caetano Optimo III	C21F	1994	
M136SKY	Volvo B10M-62	Van Hool Alizée HE	C53F	1995	
N996BWJ	Volvo B10M-62	Van Hool Alizée HE	C53F	1996	
P198OLC	Mercedes-Benz 412D	Autobus Classique	C16F	1997	

Livery:- Tan, orange and brown.

Depot:- Norton Way North, Letchworth.

Plaxton Paramounts can be found throughout Britain, emphasising the popularity of the type. It was available in three basic height options, 3.2 metre, 3.5 metre, and 4 metre double-decker. All options underwent updating to mark II and mark III specification before production ceased in favour of the Premiére and Excalibur products. Simmonds have four Paramounts, the newest being this 3500 mark II on a Volvo B10M chassis, J61NTM.

SMITH-IVINS / CARTERS / MARTINS

Smith's Travel (High Wycombe) Ltd, Halifax Road, Cressex Industrial Estate,
High Wycombe, Buckinghamshire, HP12 3ST

TRR892R	Leyland Leopard PSU3E/4R	Plaxton Supreme III	C47F	1977	Martin & Rodriguez, Chaddesden, 1997
NLP172V	Leyland Leopard PSU5C/4R	Duple Dominant IV	C57F	1980	Magpie, High Wycombe, 1995
OBD67V	Ford R1114	Plaxton Supreme IV	C49F	1980	York's, Cogenhoe, 1995
OHP10W	Ford R1114	Plaxton Supreme IV	C53F	1980	Plastow, Wheatley, 1997
IIL6765	Ford R1114	Plaxton Supreme IV	C53F	1980	Hyltone, Widmer End, 1997
JBZ3251	Leyland Leopard PSU3F/4R	Willowbrook 003	C47F	1982	Magpie, High Wycombe, 1995
JBZ4492	DAF SB2305DHTD585	Plaxton Paramount 3200 III	C57F	1986	Magpie, High Wycombe, 1995
JIL6902	DAF SB2305DHTD585	Plaxton Paramount 3200 III	C53F	1988	Chambers, Stevenage, 1994
F281GBW	DAF SB2305DHTD585	Plaxton Paramount 3200 III	C53FT	1988	Pearce, Berinsfield, 1994
G579WUT	TAZ D3200	TAZ Dubrava	C53F	1990	Bondhawk, Maidenhead, 1995
MIL5499	Kässbohrer Setra S215HD	Kässbohrer Tornado	C49FT	1989	Dick, Slough, 1996

Previous Registrations:-

IIL6765	JPG715V	JBZ4492	D295XCX	MIL5499	F22YBO, EAZ8415
JBZ3251	RVN244X	JIL6902	F214RJX	TRR892R	SCH1R, YRC180

Livery:- Cream, red and gold.

Depots:- Binders Industrial Estate, Cryers Hill, High Wycombe and Lisset Road, Maidenhead, Berkshire.

The fleet of Smith-Ivins comprises mostly Ford and DAF coaches with Plaxton bodywork. A recent interesting vehicle in the fleet was J97NJT which was used until recently for the high-end of the operators work. The vehicle is a Scania with Plaxton Premiére bodywork. *Geoff Rixon*

SMITH'S of TRING

G A Smith's Coaches Ltd, The Garage, Wiggington, Tring, Hertfordshire, HP23 6EJ

C23ENK	Mercedes-Benz L207D	Coachcraft	M12	1985	
XIB1907	Volvo B10M-56	Plaxton Paramount 3200 II	C57F	1986	
XIB1909	Volvo B10M-61	Plaxton Paramount 3500 III	C53F	1987	
XIB1906	Volvo B10M-60	Plaxton Paramount 3500 III	C53F	1989	Wallace Arnold, 1992
XIB1908	Volvo B10M-60	Plaxton Paramount 3500 III	C53F	1989	
WIB7180	Volvo B10M-60	Plaxton Paramount 3500 III	C53F	1990	Wallace Arnold, 1995
TJI4501	Toyota Coaster HB31R	Caetano Optimo	C18F	1991	The Kings Ferry, Gillingham, 1995
KAZ4130	Volvo B10M-60	Plaxton Excalibur	C53F	1994	Wallace Arnold, 1996
TBZ1008	Volvo B10M-62	Plaxton Premiere 350	C53F	19`	?, 1998

Previous Registrations:-

KAZ4130	L934NWW	XIB1906	F439DUG	XIB1908	G146TUR
TJI4501	H182EJF	XIB1907	C23KBH	XIB1909	E826YTM
WIB7180	G514LWU				

Livery:- Cream and red.

A new livery style has been adopted by Smiths of Tring, one that uses more red than hitherto with the cream relief reduced. Pictured here is XIB1908, one of several Volvo B10Ms in the fleet that carry Plaxton Paramount 3500 bodywork. *Geoff Rixon*

The Chilterns and West Anglia Bus Handbook

SOULS

Soul Bros Ltd, 7 Yardley Road Industrial Estate, Olney, Buckinghamshire, MK46 5EA

PBD345R	Bedford YMT	Duple Dominant II	C53F	1976	Johnsons, Rushden, 1985
EVC210T	Bedford YMT	Duple Dominant II	C53F	1979	Johnsons, Rushden, 1985
FLS733V	DAF MB200DKTL600	Plaxton Supreme IV	C57F	1980	Johnsons, Rushden, 1985
RNV303V	Bedford YMT	Duple Dominant II	C53F	1980	
YRP161W	Bedford YMT	Duple Dominant IV	C53F	1981	
GVV322X	Bedford YNT	Duple Dominant IV	C53F	1981	
GVV251X	Bedford YMT	Duple Dominant IV	C53F	1981	Griffin & Richardson, Hartwell, 1982
A31GJT	Bedford YNT	Duple Laser	C53F	1983	Marchwood, Totton, 1987
A35GJT	Bedford YNT	Duple Laser	C53F	1983	Marchwood, Totton, 1987
LSV146	Volvo B10M-61	Duple Dominant IV	C53F	1983	Smiths Shearing, Wigan, 1988
954CUH	Volvo B10M-61	Duple Dominant IV	C53F	1983	Smiths Shearing, Wigan, 1988
873DTU	Volvo B10M-61	Duple Dominant IV	C53F	1983	Smiths Shearing, Wigan, 1988
577HDV	Volvo B10M-61	Duple Dominant IV	C53F	1983	Smiths Shearing, Wigan, 1988
130VBJ	Volvo B10M-61	Duple Dominant IV	C53F	1983	Smiths Shearing, Wigan, 1988
230WYA	Bedford YNT	Duple Laser	C53F	1984	
855GAC	Bedford YNT	Duple Laser 2	C53F	1984	
IAZ5657	Volvo B10M-61	Plaxton Paramount 3200 II	C53F	1985	Safeguard, Guildford, 1996
LIL9811	Volvo B10M-61	Plaxton Paramount 3200 II	C53F	1985	Safeguard, Guildford, 1996
UND126	Bedford YNT	Duple Laser 2	C53F	1985	
RBW396	Bedford Venturer YNV	Duple Laser 2	C53F	1986	
239BUP	Bedford Venturer YNV	Duple Laser 2	C53F	1986	

A large fleet consisting mainly of Bedford and Volvo coaches is operated by Souls of Olney. Some of the later examples may be seen working feeder coaches for one of the large touring companies. VIJ4021was picking up passengers on behalf of Wallace Arnold at Bedford bus station in this view, before departing for South Mimms services where the passengers would interchange onto their tour coach. *Keith Grimes*

VUD483	DAF SB2300DHTD585	Plaxton Paramount 3200 II	C53F	1986	Smith, Alcester, 1987
872PYA	DAF SB2300DHTD585	Plaxton Paramount 3200 II	C53F	1986	Smith, Alcester, 1987
C88NNV	Bedford Venturer YNV	Caetano Algarve	C53F	1986	Hamilton, Stoney Stratford, 1987
KYU77	Volvo B10M-61	Plaxton Paramount 3500 III	C48FT	1988	Wallace Arnold, 1991
50DBD	Volvo B10M-61	Plaxton Paramount 3500 III	C48FT	1988	Wallace Arnold, 1991
821FHU	Volvo B10M-61	Plaxton Paramount 3500 III	C50F	1988	Wallace Arnold, 1991
751EKX	Volvo B10M-61	Plaxton Paramount 3500 III	C50F	1988	Wallace Arnold, 1992
459KBM	Volvo B10M-61	Plaxton Paramount 3500 III	C50F	1988	Premier Travel, 1992
VIJ4021	Volvo B10M-61	Plaxton Paramount 3500 III	C53F	1988	Addy & Bradley, Barnsley, 1997
HIL2282	Volvo B10M-61	Plaxton Paramount 3500 III	C48FT	1988	Lowland, 1993
966MBM	Volvo B10M-61	Plaxton Paramount 3500 III	C53F	1988	Lowland, 1993
HIL2386	Volvo B10M-61	Plaxton Paramount 3500 III	C48FT	1988	Owens, Yateley, 1995
PIW4127	Volvo B10M-60	Plaxton Paramount 3500 III	C50F	1989	The Londoners, Nunhead, 1995
675PBM	Volvo B10M-60	Plaxton Paramount 3500 III	C53F	1989	Knowles, Paignton, 1996
FAZ4494	Volvo B10M-60	Plaxton Paramount 3500 III	C50F	1989	The Londoners, Nunhead, 1995
G681BFC	Toyota Coaster HB31R	Caetano Optimo	C21F	1990	Heyfordian, Upper Heyford, 1994
H675ATN	Toyota Coaster HB31R	Caetano Optimo	C21F	1991	Thompson, Great Ayton, 1994
RAZ3785	Dennis Javelin 12SDA1929	Plaxton Paramount 3200 III	C53F	1992	Western Buses, 1998
WJI6166	Dennis Javelin 12SDA2117	Plaxton Premiére 320	C53F	1993	Go_Felix, Stanley, 1998
ALZ2490	Volvo B10M-60	Plaxton Premiére 320	C53F	1993	Wallace Arnold, 1997
TAZ4995	Volvo B10M-60	Plaxton Excalibur	C50F	1994	Wallace Arnold, 1998

Previous Registrations:-

50DBD	E313UUB	GVV251X	BBD93X, 459KBM
130VBJ	ENF557Y	GVV322X	XNH121X, 614MBM, 966MBM,
239BUP	From new	HIL2282	E314UUB
230WYA	From new	HIL2386	E319UUB
459KBM	E304UUB	IAZ5657	B906SPR
577HDV	ENF558Y	KYU77	E312UUB
675PBM	F443DUG	LIL9811	B907SPR
751EKX	E303UUB	LSV146	ENF556Y
821FHU	E320UUB	PIW4127	F414DUG
855GAC	A79ABD	RAZ3785	J13WSB
872PYA	C772MVH	RBW396	From new
873DTU	ENF552Y	RNV303V	821FHU
954CUH	ENF551Y	TAZ4995	L936NWW
966MBM	E308UUB	VIJ4021	E310UUB
ALZ2490	K849HUM	VUD483	C783MVH
FAZ4494	F418DUG	UND126	From new
G681BFC	G151ELJ, 1435VZ	YRP161W	751EKX

Named Vehicles:- 130VBJ *Hardmead*; 230WYA *Gayhurst*; 873DTU *Newport*; GVV322X *Lavendon*; GVV251X *Chicheley*; LSV146 *Astwood* ; RBW396 *Clifton*

Livery:-Red, cream, pink and lilac.

Depots:- Olney and Quorn Road, Rushden.

Pictured in Parliament Square is PIW4127 of Souls. This example of a Plaxton-bodied Volvo shows the extent to which operators gain from school contract duties - the temporary school sign being displayed only in certain circumstances. *Colin Lloyd*

SOUTH MIMMS TRAVEL

South Mimms Travel Ltd, 21 Gowarfield, Brookside, South Mimms, Hertfordshire, EN6 3NT

PUA408W	MCW Metrobus DR101/7	MCW	H46/31F	1982	Blue Triangel, Rainham, 1998
PBZ1450	DAF MB200DKFL600	Plaxton Paramount 3200	C51F	1983	Paul Dale, Edgware, 1997
MIL6993	Leyland Tiger TRCTL11/3RZ	Duple 320	C50FT	1987	London Cityrama, Battersea, 1994
MIL6994	Leyland Tiger TRCTL11/3RZ	Plaxton Paramount III	C53F	1987	Thamesway, 1996
MIL7852	Bedford Venturer YNV	Plaxton Paramount 3200 III	C55F	1987	FE Thorpe, North Kensington, 1995
MIL7853	Hestair Duple SDA1512	Duple 425	C51FT	1988	Owen, Oswestry, 1994
F607RPG	Dennis Dominator DDA1026	East Lancashire	H45/31F	1989	Arriva Croydon & N Surrey, 1998
F609RPG	Dennis Dominator DDA1026	East Lancashire	H45/31F	1989	Arriva Croydon & N Surrey, 1998
HBZ4674	Dennis Javelin 12SDA1907	Duple 320	C53F	1989	Lucketts, Fareham, 1997
G428YAY	Dennis Javelin 12SDA1907	Duple 320	C53FT	1990	Metrobus, Orpington, 1997
G303RJA	Dennis Javelin 12SDA1907	Plaxton Paramount 3200 III	C53F	1990	Gordon's, Rotherham, 1998
GSU305	Dennis Javelin 12SDA2102	Plaxton Première 320	C53F	199?	Stagecoach Western Buses. 1997

Named Vehicles:- MIL7852 *Big Ed*, MIL7853 *Curly*

Previous Registrations:-

GSU305	J15WSE		
HBZ4674	F698PAY	MIL7852	E403LPR
MIL6993	D132HML	MIL7853	E750JAY
MIL6994	D592MVR	PBZ1450	ANA454Y

Livery:- Red, black and gold.

Depot:- Harper Lane, Radlett

GSU305 is a Javelin with Plaxton Premiére 320 coachwork, now serving with the South Mimms travel fleet, it was seen parked on the Embankment, a location guaranteed to produce a line of coaches employed on day trips to the capital. *Colin Lloyd*

SOVEREIGN

Sovereign Bus & Coach Co Ltd, Babbage Road, Stevenage, SG1 2EQ
London SovereignLtd, Station Road, Borehamwood, Hertfordshire, WD6 1HB
Cambridge Coach Services Ltd, Kings Hedges Road, Impington, Cambridge, CB4 4PQ
Sovereign Buses (Harrow) Ltd, Babbage Road, Stevenage, SG1 2EQ

29	H139GGS	Leyland Olympian ON2R50C13Z4 Northern Counties Palatine		H47/30F	1991	
30	H140GGS	Leyland Olympian ON2R50C13Z4 Northern Counties Palatine		H47/30F	1991	
32	BPF132Y	Leyland Olympian ONTL11/1R	Roe	H43/29F	1983	London Country NE, 1989
33	BPF133Y	Leyland Olympian ONTL11/1R	Roe	H43/29F	1983	London Country NE, 1989
34	BPF134Y	Leyland Olympian ONTL11/1R	Roe	H43/29F	1983	Keighley & District, 1997
37	BPF137Y	Leyland Olympian ONTL11/1R	Roe	H43/29F	1983	London Country NE, 1989
38	A138DPE	Leyland Olympian ONTL11/1R	Roe	H43/29F	1983	London Country NE, 1989
39w	A139DPE	Leyland Olympian ONTL11/1R	Roe	H43/29F	1983	Keighley & District, 1993
40	A140DPE	Leyland Olympian ONTL11/1R	Roe	H43/29F	1983	Keighley & District, 1994

41-52

Leyland Olympian ON2R50C13Z4 Northern Counties Palatine   H47/30F   1991

41	H141GGS	44	H144GGS	47	H147GGS	49	H149GGS	51	H151GGS
42	H142GGS	45	H145GGS	48	H148GGS	50	H150GGS	52	H152GGS
43	H143GGS	46	H146GGS						

61	K711ASC	Leyland Olympian ON2R50G13Z4 Alexander RL		H47/32F	1992	MK Metro, 1998
62	K712ASC	Leyland Olympian ON2R50G13Z4 Alexander RL		H47/32F	1992	MK Metro, 1998
66	B266LPH	Leyland Olympian ONTL11/1R	Eastern Coach Works	H43/29F	1985	Keighley & District, 1997
68w	B268LPH	Leyland Olympian ONTL11/1R	Eastern Coach Works	H43/29F	1985	Keighley & District, 1997
69	B269LPH	Leyland Olympian ONTL11/1R	Eastern Coach Works	H43/29F	1985	Keighley & District, 1997
70	H650VVV	Leyland Olympian ON2R56G13Z4 Alexander RL		H51/34F	1990	MK Metro, 1998
71	H651VVV	Leyland Olympian ON2R56G13Z4 Alexander RL		H51/34F	1990	MK Metro, 1998
72	H652VVV	Leyland Olympian ON2R56G13Z4 Alexander RL		H51/34F	1990	MK Metro, 1998
73	H653VVV	Leyland Olympian ON2R56G13Z4 Alexander RL		H51/34F	1990	MK Metro, 1998

76-82

Leyland Olympian ONLXB/1R   Eastern Coach Works   H45/32F   1982-83   Keighley & District, 1998

76	DWW926Y	78	DWW928Y	80	DWW930Y	81	DWW931Y	82	DWW932Y
77	DWW927Y	79	DWW929Y					

91	R91GTM	Volvo Olympian	Northern Counties Palatine II	DPH39/29F	1998
92	R92GTM	Volvo Olympian	Northern Counties Palatine II	DPH39/29F	1998

101-105

Volvo B10B-58   Wright Endurance   DP49F   1995

101	M101UKX	102	M102UKX	103	M103UKX	104	M104UKX	105	M105UKX

106	N106GVS	Volvo B10B-58	Wright Endurance	B51F	1996	
107	N107GVS	Volvo B10B-58	Wright Endurance	B51F	1996	
108	N108GVS	Volvo B10B-58	Wright Endurance	B51F	1996	
109	N109GVS	Volvo B10B-58	Wright Endurance	B51F	1996	
110	M310KHP	Volvo B10B-58	Wright Endurance	B51F	1994	Volvo demonstrator, 1996
112	P112RGS	Volvo B10B-58	Wright Endurance	DP49F	1997	

120-127

Volvo B10BLE   Wright Endurance   DP47F   1998

120	R120HNK	122	R122HNK	124	R124HNK	126	R126HNK	127	R127HNK
121	R121HNK	123	R123HNK	125	R125HNK				

Opposite, top:- **Pictured on London Buses' service 13 is RML2627, NML627E, which Sovereign operate from their depot at Borehamwood.** *Tony Wilson*
Opposite, bottom:- **While many of the coach fleet work from Cambridge, Stevenage depot provide vehicle for the Jetlink service between Luton, Heathrow and Gatwick airports.** *Tony Wilson*

In 1998 the Huntingdon services acquired from Stagecoach along with the MK Metro operation were sold by Metro to Sovereign who established Huntingdon and District. One of the vehicles that came with the business was K712ASC, now numbered 62 in the Sovereign system. The vehicle is seen in Cambridge in its new colours. *Keith Grimes*

201-207

		Leyland Lynx LX2R11C15Z4S		Leyland Lynx		B49F	1989		
201	G201URO	**203**	G203URO	**205**	G205URO	**206**	G206URO	**207**	G207URO
202	G202URO	**204**	G204URO						

213	F203MBT	Leyland Lynx LX112TL11ZR1R	Leyland Lynx	B51F	1989	Keighley & District, 1993
214	F204MBT	Leyland Lynx LX112TL11ZR1R	Leyland Lynx	B51F	1989	Keighley & District, 1993
215	F205MBT	Leyland Lynx LX112TL11ZR1R	Leyland Lynx	B47F	1989	Keighley & District, 1992
216	F206MBT	Leyland Lynx LX112TL11ZR1R	Leyland Lynx	B51F	1989	Keighley & District, 1993
217	F207MBT	Leyland Lynx LX112TL11ZR1R	Leyland Lynx	B49F	1989	Keighley & District, 1993
218	F208MBT	Leyland Lynx LX112TL11ZR1R	Leyland Lynx	B51F	1989	Harrogate & District, 1993
240	E840EUT	Leyland Lynx LX112TL11ZR1R	Leyland Lynx	B51F	1987	County, 1990
258	F358JVS	Leyland Lynx LX112TL11ZR1R	Leyland Lynx	B49F	1988	Jubilee, Stevenage, 1989
259	F359JVS	Leyland Lynx LX112TL11ZR1R	Leyland Lynx	B49F	1988	County, 1990
271	E371YRO	Leyland Lynx LX112TL11ZR1R	Leyland Lynx	B51F	1987	County, 1990
284	G384MWU	Leyland Lynx LX112L10ZR1R	Leyland Lynx	DP47F	1990	Harrogate & District, 1995
296	G296KWY	Leyland Lynx LX112L10ZR1R	Leyland Lynx	B49F	1989	Harrogate & District, 1997
297	G297KWY	Leyland Lynx LX112L10ZR1R	Leyland Lynx	B49F	1989	Harrogate & District, 1997

301-308

		Volvo B10M-62		Plaxton Premiére 350		C52F	1994		
301	M301BAV	**303**	M303BAV	**305**	M305BAV	**307**	M307BAV	**308**	M308BAV
302	M302BAV	**304**	M304BAV	**306**	M306BAV				

309	N309VAV	Volvo B10M-62	Plaxton Premiére 350	C52F	1996
310	N310VAV	Volvo B10M-62	Plaxton Premiére 350	C52F	1996
311	N311VAV	Volvo B10M-62	Plaxton Premiére 350	C52F	1996
312	N312VAV	Volvo B10M-62	Plaxton Premiére 350	C52F	1996
313	P313CVE	Volvo B10M-62	Plaxton Premiére 350	C49FT	1996
314	P314CVE	Volvo B10M-62	Plaxton Premiére 350	C49FT	1996
315	P315DVE	Volvo B10M-62	Plaxton Premiére 350	C49FT	1996
316	P316RGS	Volvo B10M-62	Plaxton Premiére 320	C53F	1996
317	P317RGS	Volvo B10M-62	Plaxton Premiére 320	C53F	1996
318	P318RGS	Volvo B10M-62	Plaxton Premiére 320	C53F	1996

Blazefield Holdings have several subsidiaries in the area of this book, all sharing a common fleet-numbering system introduced by Sovereign. Cambridge Coach Services operate a large network of express services throughout, and radiating from East Anglia, including several important trunk routes serving Airports. Pictured entering Colchester bus station is 305, M305BAV whilst engaged on a service to London Heathrow. *Colin Lloyd*

319	G519LWU	Volvo B10M-61	Plaxton Paramount 3500 III	C50F	1990	Wallace Arnold, 1994
321	F421DUG	Volvo B10M-60	Plaxton Paramount 3500 III	C50F	1989	Wallace Arnold, 1992
325w	F425DUG	Volvo B10M-60	Plaxton Paramount 3500 III	C50F	1989	Wallace Arnold, 1992
327	H627UWR	Volvo B10M-60	Plaxton Paramount 3500 III	C50F	1991	Wallace Arnold, 1993
328	H628UWR	Volvo B10M-60	Plaxton Paramount 3500 III	C50F	1991	Wallace Arnold, 1993
329	H629UWR	Volvo B10M-60	Plaxton Paramount 3500 III	C50F	1991	Wallace Arnold, 1994
331	G431MWU	Leyland Tiger TRCL10/3ARZA	Plaxton Paramount 3200 III	C55F	1990	Keighley & District, 1998
347	H647UWR	Volvo B10M-60	Plaxton Paramount 3200 III	C50F	1991	Wallace Arnold, 1994
349	J749CWT	Volvo B10M-60	Plaxton Premiére 350	C50F	1991	Wallace Arnold, 1996
350	D350KVE	Volvo B10M-61	Van Hool Alizée H	C53FL	1987	Premier Travel, 1990
362	G92RGG	Volvo B10M-60	Plaxton Paramount 3500 III	C49FT	1990	Keighley & District, 1995
364	B264KPF	Leyland Tiger TRCTL11/2RH	Plaxton Paramount 3200 II E	C49F	1985	Ex Keighley & District, 1995
395	G95RGG	Volvo B10M-60	Plaxton Paramount 3500 III	C53F	1990	Park's, Hamilton, 1993
396	G96RGG	Volvo B10M-60	Plaxton Paramount 3500 III	C53F	1990	Park's, Hamilton, 1991
397	G97RGG	Volvo B10M-60	Plaxton Paramount 3500 III	C53F	1990	Park's, Hamilton, 1991
398	G98RGG	Volvo B10M-60	Plaxton Paramount 3500 III	C53F	1990	Park's, Hamilton, 1991

403-424   Mercedes-Benz 811D   Reeve Burgess Beaver   B31F   1990-91

403	H403FGS	410	H410FGS	415	H415FGS	419	H419FGS	423	H423FGS
404	H404FGS	411	H411FGS	417	H417FGS	421	H421FGS	424	H424FGS
409	H409FGS	413	H413FGS	418	H418FGS	422	H422FGS		

433-454   Mercedes-Benz 811D   Plaxton Beaver   B31F   1993-94

433	K3SBC	443	L3SBC	446	L946HTM	449	L949MBH	452	L952MBH
434	K4SBC	444	L944HTM	447	L947HTM	450	L950MBH	453	L953MBH
435	K5SBC	445	L945HTM	448	L948HTM	451	L951MBH	454	L954MBH
442	L2SBC								

455-461			Mercedes-Benz 811D		Plaxton Beaver		B31F	1995		
455	M455UUR	457	M457UUR	459	M459UUR	460	M460UUR	461	M461UUR
456	M456UUR	458	M458UUR						

501	P501VRO	Dennis Dart SLF		Plaxton Pointer		N39F	1997
601	P601RGS	Volvo B6LE		Wright Crusader		N38F	1997

602-608			Volvo B6LE		Wright Crusader		N38F	1998		
602	R602WMJ	604	R604WMJ	606	R606WMJ	607	R607WMJ	608	R608CNM
603	R603WMJ								

626-630			Volvo B6-9.9m		Alexander Dash		DP40F	1994	MK Metro, 1998	
626	L426XVV	627	L427XVV	628	L428XVV	629	M429BNV	630	M430BNV

706	OHV706Y	Leyland Titan TNLXB2RR	Leyland		H44/28F	1983	BTS, Borehamwood, 1994
720	NUW620Y	Leyland Titan TNLXB2RR	Leyland		H44/28F	1982	BTS, Borehamwood, 1994
757	WYV57T	Leyland Titan TNLXB2RRsp	Park Royal		H44/28F	1979	BTS, Borehamwood, 1994

901-909			Mercedes-Benz 709D		Reeve Burgess Beaver		B23F	1989		
901	G901UPP	903	G903UPP	905	G905UPP	907	G907UPP	909	G909UPP
902	G902UPP	904	G904UPP	906	G906UPP	908	G908UPP		

920-931			Mercedes-Benz 711D		Reeve Burgess Beaver		B23F	1990		
920	H920FGS	922	H922FGS	925	H925FGS	927	H927FGS	930	H930FGS
921	H921FGS	923	H923FGS	926	H926FGS	929	H929FGS	931	H931FGS

990	K390SLB	Mercedes-Benz 709D	Plaxton Beaver	B23F	1993
991	K391SLB	Mercedes-Benz 709D	Plaxton Beaver	B23F	1993
992	K392SLB	Mercedes-Benz 709D	Plaxton Beaver	B23F	1993
993	K393SLB	Mercedes-Benz 709D	Plaxton Beaver	B23F	1993

RML2265-2756			AEC Routemaster R2RH/1		Park Royal		H40/32R	1965-68	On loan from LT Buses	
2265	CUV265C	2487	JJD487D	2569	JJD569D	2663	SMK663F	2694	SMK694F
2322	CUV322C	2527	JJD527D	2582	JJD582D	2668	SMK668F	2719	SMK719F
2341	CUV341C	2538	JJD538D	2598	JJD598D	2674	SMK674F	2756	SMK756F
2404	JJD404D	2563	JJD563D	2627	NML627E	2686	SMK686F		

Ancilliary Vehicle:-

821	FUG321T	Leyland National 10351B/1R			B44F	1979	Ex Keighley & District, 1994

Named Vehicles:- 313 *Trinity Hall*; 314 *Christs*; 315 *Ian Roberts*

Liveries:- Blue and cream with black (Sovereign); grey and blue(Cambridge Coach Services); blue, cream, red and black (Huntingdon & District); red and yellow (London Sovereign); blue and cream (Sovereign Harrow); - red, cream and black (Welwyn - Hatfield Line)

Allocations

Borehamwood (Station Road) - London Sovereign

Routemaster	2265	2322	2341	2404	2487	2527	2538	2563
	2569	2582	2598	2627	2663	2668	2674	2686
	2694	2719	2756					
Leyland Titan	706	720	757					
Olympian	29	30	33	41	42	43	44	45
	46	47	48	49	50	51	52	

Opposite, top:- **The Mercedes-Benz minibus is by far the most common minibus type now supplied to the British market. Sovereign example 449, L949MBH is fitted with a Reeve Burgess Beaver body and is seen heading for London Colney.** *Tony Wilson*
Opposite, bottom:- **The only double-deck bus model operating with Sovereign is the Olympian, though four makes of bodywork are fitted. Originally delivered to London Country, 32, BPF132Y, shown here at Stevenage bus station, is fitted with a high-bridge Roe body that features many common parts to the Eastern Coach Works product, the main difference being the lower front panel and windscreen.** *Tony Wilson*

Photographed in Ware is Sovereign 501, P501VRO, a Dennis Dart with Plaxton Pointer bodywork, and the sole example of the type in the fleet.
Tony Wilson

Cambridge (Kilmaine Close) - Cambridge Coach Services

Volvo Coach	301	302	303	304	305	306	307	308
	309	310	311	312	313	314	315	319
	321	329	347	350	362	395	396	397
	398							
Olympian	91	92						

Harrow (Pinner Road) - Sovereign (Harrow)

Mercedes-Benz	409	410	411	413	415	417	418	419
	421	422	423	424	435	455	456	457
	458	459	460	461	909	921	922	923
	925	926	927	929	930	931		

Huntingdon (Stukeley Road) - Huntingdon & District

Outstation - Bishops Stortford, Little Paxton, St Neots, March, Mildenhall and Sumersham.

Volvo B6	626	627	628	629	630			
Volvo B10BLE	120	121	122	123	124	125	126	127
Olympian	61	62	69	70	71	72	73	76
	77	78	79	80	81	82		

St Albans (Sandridge Road) - Sovereign

Mercedes-Benz	403	404	442	443	444	445	446	447
	448	449	450	451	903	907	920	990
	991	992	993					
Volvo B6LE	602	604						
Lynx	201	202	203	204	205	213	214	216
	217	218	271	284				
Olympians	37	38						

Stevenage (Babbage Road) - Sovereign

Tiger Coach	331	364						
Volvo Coach	316	317	318	325	327	328	349	
Lynx	206	207						
Dart	501							
Volvo B6	601	603						
Volvo B10B	101	102	103	104	105	106	107	108
	109	110	112					
Olympian	32	34	40	66				

Pictured with the Welwyn-Hatfield Line is Mercedes-Benz 811, K4SBC, one of five Beavers with Select index marks.
Phillip Stephenson

Welwyn Garden City (Burrowfield) - Sovereign - Welwyn & Hatfield Line

Mercedes-Benz	433	434	453	454	902	904	905	906
	908							
Volvo B6LE	606	607	608					
Tiger Coach	331	364						
Volvo Coach	316	317	318	325	327	328	349	
Lynx	215	240	258	259	296	297		

SOVEREIGN TAXIS

A North & S J Williams, 48 Park Avenue, Tottenhoe, Bedfordshire, LU6 1PF

A210PBM	Ford Transit	Chassis Developments	M12	1983	Mower, Cheam, 1993
A648VOJ	Mercedes-Benz L608D	Devon Conversions	C19F	1984	Yarranton, Eardiston, 1993
A473ODY	Bedford YNT	Plaxton Paramount 3200	C53F	1984	Rambler, St Leonards, 1997
C626MEG	Ford Transit	Dormobile	C16F	1985	Chariots, Stanford-le-Hope, 1994
D290BBC	Volkswagen LT50	G C Smith	C19F	1987	Statham, Ibstock, 1994
F73UJX	Volvo B10M-61	Ikarus Blue Danube 358	C49FT	1988	Aintree Coachline, Bootle, 1997
F895URP	Toyota Coaster BB31R	Caetano Optimo	C21F	1988	Den Caney, Birmingham, 1998
G709JET	Mercedes-Benz 609D	Whittaker	C24F	1989	Hing, Slough, 1996
K652TUE	Leyland-DAF 400	Walsall Motor Bodies (1995)	M16	1992	van conversion, 1995
K18OMC	Toyota Coaster HDB30R	Caetano Optimo II	C18F	1992	Hills of Hersham, 1998
M314EEA	LDV 400	Walsall Motor Bodies (1995)	M16	1994	van conversion, 1995
P656JDT	LDV 400	Crystals	M16	1996	

Previous Registration:-
A473ODY   A383BNP, ODY607

Depots:- Park Avenue, Tottenhoe and High Street, Houghton Regis

STAGECOACH UNITED COUNTIES

United Counties Omnibus Co Ltd, Rothersthorpe Avenue,
Northampton, NN4 9UT

81	WLT682	Leyland Tiger TRCTL11/3RZ	Plaxton Paramount 3500 II	C46FT	1986
82	WLT908	Leyland Tiger TRCTL11/3RZ	Plaxton Paramount 3500 II	C46FT	1986
85	647DYE	Leyland Tiger TRCTL11/3RZ	Plaxton Paramount 3500 II	C46FT	1986

92-96

Volvo B10M-60   Plaxton Première 350   C49FT   1992   Park's, 1993
94/5 ex Rainworth Travel, 1993

| 92 | J430HDS | 93 | J439HDS | 94 | J445HDS | 95 | J446HDS | 96 | J450HDS |

107	F107NRT	Volvo B10M-61	Plaxton Paramount 3500 III	C49FT	1988	Cambus (Premier), 1996
116w	VLT255	Leyland Tiger TRCTL11/3RZ	Duple Laser 2	C44FT	1985	Stagecoach Malawi, 1993
120	C120PNV	Leyland Tiger TRCTL11/3RZ	Plaxton Paramount 3200 IIE	C53F	1986	
121	C121PNV	Leyland Tiger TRCTL11/3RZ	Plaxton Paramount 3200 IIE	C53F	1986	
122	C122PNV	Leyland Tiger TRCTL11/3RZ	Plaxton Paramount 3200 IIE	C53F	1986	

130-135

Volvo B10M-61   Plaxton Paramount 3200 III   C53F   1988

| 130 | E130ORP | 132 | E132ORP | 133 | E133ORP | 134 | E134ORP | 135 | F135URP |
| 131 | E131ORP | | | | | | | | |

144-149

Volvo B10M-60   Plaxton Première 350   C50F   1992   Wallace Arnold, 1995

| 144 | J752CWT | 146 | K758FYG | 147 | K759FYG | 148 | K760FYG | 149 | K761FYG |
| 145 | J753CWT | | | | | | | | |

150-162

Volvo B10M-60   Plaxton Première Interurban   DP53F*   1993   *155-162 are DP51F

150	K150DNV	153	K153DNV	156	L156JNH	159	L159JNH	161	L161JNH
151	K151DNV	154	K154DNV	157	L157JNH	160	L160JNH	162	L162JNH
152	K152DNV	155	L155JNH	158	L158JNH				

171-186

Volvo B10M-62   Plaxton Première Interurban   DP51F   1996-97

171	P171KBD	175	P175DNH	178	R178DNH	181	R181DNH	184	R184DNH
172	P172KBD	176	P176DNH	179	R179DNH	182	R182DNH	185	R185DNH
173	P173KBD	177	R177DNH	180	R180DNH	183	R183DNH	186	R186DNH
174	P174DNH								

301-326

Mercedes-Benz 709D   Alexander Sprint   B23F   1996

301	N301XRP	307	N307XRP	312	N312XRP	317	N317XRP	322	N322XRP
302	N302XRP	308	N308XRP	313	N313XRP	318	N318XRP	323	N323XRP
303	N303XRP	309	N309XRP	314	N314XRP	319	N319XRP	324	N324XRP
304	N304XRP	310	N310XRP	315	N315XRP	320	N320XRP	325	N325XRP
305	N305XRP	311	N311XRP	316	N316XRP	321	N321XRP	326	N326XRP
306	N306XRP								

Opposite, top:- **The choice for a suitable midi-bus has seen both the Volvo B6 and Dennis Dart delivered to Stagecoach fleets with both normal and low-floor variants now in service. United Counties was the recipient of many early versions of the Volvo product, all of which carry Alexander dash bodywork. Pictured here is 410, L410JBD. Like most of the model, it is currently allocated to Bedford.** *Colin Lloyd*
Opposite, bottom:- **Stagecoach Express services now form an important network of services connecting principal towns. United Counties provide vehicles for the Oxford-Cambridge service, and 147, K759FYG is seen on that route last winter. Before the end of 1998 some nineteen Jonckheere-bodied Volvo coaches will be added to the national network, to be followed in the new year by further models on Volvo articulated B10M chassis.** *Colin Lloyd*

332-349 — Mercedes-Benz 709D — Alexander Sprint — B25F — 1994

332	M332DRP	337	M337DRP	341	M341DRP	344	M344DRP	347	M347DRP
334	M334DRP	338	M338DRP	342	M342DRP	345	M345DRP	348	M348DRP
335	M335DRP	339	M339DRP	343	M343DRP	346	M346DRP	349	M349DRP
336	M336DRP	340	M340DRP						

350-383 — Mercedes-Benz 709D — Alexander Sprint — B25F* — 1992-93 — *351-66 are B21F

350	K350ANV	357	K357ANV	364	L364JBD	371	L371JBD	378	L378JBD
351	K351ANV	358	K358ANV	365	L365JBD	372	L372JBD	379	L379JBD
352	K352ANV	359	K359ANV	366	L366JBD	373	L373JBD	380	L380JBD
353	K353ANV	360	L360JBD	367	L367JBD	374	L374JBD	381	L381NBD
354	K354ANV	361	L361JBD	368	L368JBD	375	L375JBD	382	L382NBD
355	K355ANV	362	L362JBD	369	L369JBD	376	L376JBD	383	L383NBD
356	K356ANV	363	L363JBD	370	L370JBD	377	L377JBD		

401-422 — Volvo B6-9.9M — Alexander Dash — B40F — 1993

401	L401JBD	406	L406JBD	411	L411JBD	415	L415JBD	419	L419JBD
402	L402JBD	407	L407JBD	412	L412JBD	416	L416JBD	420	L420JBD
403	L403JBD	408	L408JBD	413	L413JBD	417	L417JBD	421	L421JBD
404	L404JBD	409	L409JBD	414	L414JBD	418	L418JBD	422	L422MVV
405	L405JBD	410	L410JBD						

423	L423XVV	Volvo B6-9.9M	Alexander Dash	DP40F	1994
424	L424XVV	Volvo B6-9.9M	Alexander Dash	DP40F	1994
425	L425XVV	Volvo B6-9.9M	Alexander Dash	DP40F	1994
450	P450KRP	Dennis Dart	Alexander Dash	B40F	1996
451	P451KRP	Dennis Dart	Alexander Dash	B40F	1996
452	P452KRP	Dennis Dart	Alexander Dash	B40F	1996

453-461 — Dennis Dart SLF — Alexander ALX200 — N40F — 1998

453	S453CVV	455	S455CVV	457	S457CVV	459	S459CVV	461	S461CVV
454	S454CVV	456	S456CVV	458	S458CVV	460	S460CVV		

500	LFR862X	Leyland National 2 NL106AL11/1R		B44F	1981	Cumberland, 1993
501	LFR864X	Leyland National 2 NL106AL11/1R		B41F	1982	Cumberland, 1993

559-568 — Volvo Olympian — Alexander RL — H45/27F — 1997

559	R703DNH	561	R561DRP	563	R563DRP	565	R565DRP	567	R567DRP
560	R560DRP	562	R562DRP	564	R564DRP	566	R566DRP	568	R568DRP

600	F110NES	Leyland Olympian ON6LXCT/5RZ	Alexander RL	H66/44F	1989	East Midland, 1992

601-611 — Leyland Olympian ONLXB/1R — Eastern Coach Works — H45/32F* — 1981 — *601 is DPH45/27F / *602/5/6 are DPH41/27F

601	ARP601X	604	ARP604X	606	ARP606X	608	ARP608X	610	ARP610X
602	ARP602X	605	ARP605X	607	ARP607X	609	ARP609X	611	ARP611X

612	WLT528	Leyland Olympian ONLXB/1RV	Alexander RL	H43/34F	1987	Bluebird, 1991
613	D383XRS	Leyland Olympian ONLXB/1RV	Alexander RL	H43/34F	1987	Bluebird, 1991
614	WLT512	Leyland Olympian ONLXB/1RV	Alexander RL	H47/34F	1987	Bluebird, 1991
615	685DYE	Leyland Olympian ONLXB/1RV	Alexander RL	H47/34F	1987	Bluebird, 1991
616	GSO6V	Leyland Olympian ONLXB/1RV	Alexander RL	H47/34F	1987	Bluebird, 1991
617	GSO7V	Leyland Olympian ONLXB/1RV	Alexander RL	H47/34F	1987	Bluebird, 1991
618	GSO2V	Leyland Olympian ONLXB/1RV	Alexander RL	H47/34F	1986	Bluebird, 1994

620-649 — Leyland Olympian ONLXB/2RZ — Alexander RL — H51/36F* — 1988-89 — *635-644 are H51/34F / *645-9 are DPH51/31F

620	F620MSL	626	F626MSL	632	F632MSL	638	F638YRP	644	G644EVV
621	F621MSL	627	F627MSL	633	F633MSL	639	G639EVV	645	G645EVV
622	F622MSL	628	F628MSL	634	F634MSP	640	G640EVV	646	G646EVV
623	F623MSL	629	F629MSL	635	F635YRP	641	G641EVV	647	G647EVV
624	F624MSL	630	F630MSL	636	F636YRP	642	G642EVV	648	G648EVV
625	F625MSL	631	F631MSL	637	F637YRP	643	G643EVV	649	G649EVV

Shortly before the privatisation and sale of United Counties to Stagecoach, the express routes received Coachlinks branding, which continues to be used and developed. Most of The Coachlinks network has now been upgraded with Stagecoach's standard Plaxton Interurban bodied Volvo B10M's, with a corresponding decrease in the previous generation, such as Paramount Express bodied Leyland Tiger 120, C120PNV seen at Stevenage.

| 654 | H654VVV | Leyland Olympian ON2R56G13Z4 Alexander RL | | H51/34F | 1990 | |

655-670
Leyland Olympian ON2R50G13Z4 Northern Counties Palatine   H47/29F   1992

655	K655UNH	658	K658UNH	661	K661UNH	664	K664UNH	668	K668UNH
656	K656UNH	659	K659UNH	662	K662UNH	665	K665UNH	669	K669UNH
657	K657UNH	660	K660UNH	663	K663UNH	667	K667UNH	670	K670UNH

671-685
Volvo Olympian YN2RV18Z4   Northern Counties Palatine   H47/29F   1993

671	L671HNV	674	L674HNV	677	L677HNV	680	L680HNV	683	L683HNV
672	L672HNV	675	L675HNV	678	L678HNV	681	L681HNV	684	L684HNV
673	L673HNV	676	L676HNV	679	L679HNV	682	L682HNV	685	L685JBD

686-692
Volvo Olympian YN2RV18Z4   Alexander RL   H51/36F   1996

| 686 | P686JBD | 688 | P688JBD | 690 | P690JBD | 691 | P691JBD | 692 | P692JBD |
| 687 | P687JBD | 689 | P689JBD | | | | | | |

693-702
Volvo Olympian   Alexander RL   H45/27F   1997

| 693 | R693DNH | 695 | R695DNH | 697 | R697DNH | 699 | R699DNH | 702 | R702DNH |
| 694 | R694DNH | 696 | R696DNH | 698 | R698DNH | 701 | R701DNH | | |

703	P569EFL	Leyland Olympian YN2RV18V3	Northern Counties Palatine	H49/33F	1997	Stagecoach Cambus (Viscount) 1998
704	P570EFL	Leyland Olympian YN2RV18V3	Northern Counties Palatine	H49/33F	1997	Stagecoach Cambus (Viscount) 1998
705	P571EFL	Leyland Olympian YN2RV18V3	Northern Counties Palatine	H49/33F	1996	Stagecoach Cambus (Viscount) 1998
708	J808WFS	Leyland Olympian ON2R50C13Z4	Alexander RL	H47/32F	1992	Fife Scottish, 1994
709	K709ASC	Leyland Olympian ON2R50C13Z4	Alexander RL	H47/32F	1992	Fife Scottish, 1994
710	K710ASC	Leyland Olympian ON2R50C13Z4	Alexander RL	H47/32F	1992	Fife Scottish, 1994
713	K713ASC	Leyland Olympian ON2R50C13Z4	Alexander RL	H47/32F	1992	Fife Scottish, 1994
714	J620GCR	Leyland Olympian ON2R56G13Z4	Alexander RL	H51/34F	1991	Bluebird, 1994
715	J621GCR	Leyland Olympian ON2R56G13Z4	Alexander RL	H51/34F	1991	Bluebird, 1994
716	J622GCR	Leyland Olympian ON2R56G13Z4	Alexander RL	H51/34F	1991	Bluebird, 1994

Shortly after United Counties became a Stagecoach subsidiary, Transit Holdings sold a large quantity of then youthful Bristol VRT's made surplus in the Devon General fleet by a major influx of minibuses. United Counties became one of the recipient of them, many still serving the area, such as 740, FDV832V seen operating a Wellingborough town service. *Colin Lloyd*

721-740

| | | | | | | | | | Bristol VRT/SL3/6LXB | | Eastern Coach Works | | H43/31F | 1980-81 | Devon General, 1988-89 |

721	LFJ862W	726	LFJ855W	734	FDV812V	736	LFJ865W	739	LFJ869W
722	LFJ863W	727	LFJ879W	735	LFJ864W	738	FDV835V	740	FDV832V
724	LFJ852W								

744	LFJ878W	Bristol VRT/SL3/6LXC	Eastern Coach Works	H43/31F	1981	Devon General, 1989
752	FAO419V	Bristol VRT/SL3/6LXB	Eastern Coach Works	H43/31F	1980	Cumberland, 1992

800-814

| | Leyland Titan TNLXB2RR | | Leyland | | H44/27F | 1982-85 | East London, 1998 |

	NUW554Y		NUW568Y		NUW584Y	800	NUW595Y		NUW608Y
	NUW557Y		NUW576Y	801	NUW588Y		NUW602Y		NUW610Y
	NUW565Y		NUW579Y		NUW590Y		NUW605Y	814	B96WUV

862	RRP862R	Bristol VRT/SL3/6LXB	Eastern Coach Works	H43/31F	1976	
863	RRP863R	Bristol VRT/SL3/6LXB	Eastern Coach Works	H43/31F	1976	
901	BAU179T	Bristol VRT/SL3/6LXB	Eastern Coach Works	H43/31F	1978	East Midland, 1993

912-967

| | | | | Bristol VRT/SL3/6LXB | | Eastern Coach Works | | H43/31F | 1978-81 | 919/61 are DPH41/27F |

912	FRP912T	923	LBD923V	937	SNV937W	945	URP945W	962	VVV962W
914	HBD914T	930	SNV930W	939	URP939W	949	VVV949W	963	VVV963W
915	HBD915T	931	SNV931W	940	URP940W	950	VVV950W	965	VVV965W
916	HBD916T	935	SNV935W	941	URP941W	952	VVV952W	966	VVV966W
920	LBD920V	936	SNV936W	944	URP944W	961	VVV961W	967	VVV967W
921	LBD921V								

970	KRU843W	Bristol VRT/SL3/6LXB	Eastern Coach Works	H43/31F	1980	Hampshire Bus, 1988
971	KRU845W	Bristol VRT/SL3/6LXB	Eastern Coach Works	H43/31F	1980	Hampshire Bus, 1988
973	KRU847W	Bristol VRT/SL3/6LXB	Eastern Coach Works	H43/31F	1980	Hampshire Bus, 1988
974	KRU852W	Bristol VRT/SL3/6LXB	Eastern Coach Works	H43/31F	1980	Hampshire Bus, 1988

At first glance, 615, 685DYE, appears to be a standard Stagecoach Alexander RL bodied Leyland Olympian. However the cherished plate carried disguises that this vehicle was built for Scottish Bus Group subsidiary Bluebird Buses, thus pre-dating the expansion and standardisation. *Tony Wilson*

Special event vehicles

703u	HVS937	AEC Routemaster R2RH	Park Royal	H36/28R	1961	London Buses, 1988
708u	CUV192C	AEC Routemaster R2RH	Park Royal	H36/28R	1965	London Buses, 1988

Ancilliary vehicles

1005t	TCL142R	Bristol LH6L	Eastern Coach Works	B43F	1977	Stagecoach Busways, 1998
1006t	WEX929S	Bristol LH6L	Eastern Coach Works	B43F	1978	Stagecoach Busways, 1998
1007t	SVL834R	Bristol LH6L	Eastern Coach Works	B43F	1977	Stagecoach Busways, 1998

Previous Registrations:

647DYE	C85PRP	GSO7V	D377XRS	WLT528	D382XRS
685DYE	D379XRS	HVS937	WLT682	WLT682	C81PRP
GSO2V	C472SSO	VLT255	B357KNH, Malawi ?,	WLT908	C82PRP
GSO6V	D376XRS	WLT512	D384XRS		

Allocations:-

Bedford (St Johns)

Outstations - Biggleswade; Huntingdon and Northampton

Mercedes-Benz	302	304	317	318	319	320	321	322
	323	324	325	326	332	334	335	336
	337	338	350	369	370	371	372	373
Tiger	120	121	122					
Volvo B6	402	403	404	405	406	407	408	409
	410	411	412	413	414	415	416	417
	418	419	420	421	422			
National	500							

Volvo B10M coach	130	131	132	133	134	144	145	148
	149	150	151	152	153	154	171	172
	173							
Bristol VR	722	726	738	862				
	916	920	921	923	930	931	936	944
	950	962	967	974				
Olympian	559	560	561	562	563	564	565	566
	567	568	600	612	613	614	615	616
	617	618	621	622	623	624	629	630
	631	632	634	635	636	637	638	639
	640	641	642	644	655	661	662	663
	664	665	703	704	705	708	709	710
	713	714	715	716				

Corby (Station Road)

Outstation - Uppingham

Mercedes-Benz	351	352	353	354	355	356	357	358
	359	360	361	362	363	364	365	366
	367	368						
Tiger	81	82	85					
Bristol VR	721	739	912	914	915	941	945	949
	952	963	970	971	973			
Olympian	604	607	608	609	620			

Kettering (Northampton Road)

Outstations - Chown's Mill; Desborough; Thrapston and Wellingborough

Mercedes-Benz	306	307	308	309	310	311	312	313
	314	315	316	339	340	341	342	343
	344	345	346	347	348	349	383	
Volvo B10M coach	92	93	94	95	96		135	174
	175	176	177	178	179	180	181	182
	183	184	185	186				
Bristol VR	724	727	736	740	744	752	939	940
	961	965	966					
Olympian	625	626	627	628	633	643	645	646
	647	648	649	654	667	668	669	670

Northampton (Rothersthorpe Avenue)

Outstations - Buckingham; Chown's Mill; Daventry; Husbands Bosworth and Milton Keymes

Mercedes-Benz	301	303	305	374	375	376	377	378
	379	380	381	382				
Volvo B6	401	423	424	425				
Dennis Dart	450	451	452					
National	501							
Volvo B10M coach	107	146	147	155	156	157	158	159
	160	161	162					
Bristol VR	734	735	935	937	962			
Olympian	601	602	605	606	610	611	656	657
	658	659	660	671	672	673	674	675
	676	677	678	679	680	681	682	683
	684	685	686	687	688	689	690	691
	692	693	694	695	696	697	698	699
	701	702						

Unallocated or delicenced

Tiger	116	
Routemaster	703	708

STAR TRAVEL

S Hussain, 177 Cambridge Street, Aylesbury, Buckinghamshire, HP20 1BQ

C329OFL	Ford Transit 190D	Dormobile	B16F	1986	Pickford, Grittleton, 1993
D72KRL	Ford Transit VE6	Dormobile	B16F	1986	Filers, Ilfracombe, 1995
D600PKO	Ford Transit VE6	Ford	M8	1986	private owner, 1992
F816XUG	Ford Transit VE6	Dormobile	B16F	1988	Garfoot, Consett, 1996

Livery:- various

Star Travel is a small operator based in Aylesbury, whose fleet consists entirely of Ford Transits, mostly bodied by Dormobile. D72 KRL was one of the few VE6 Transits variants supplied to the National Bus Company, being new to Western National in 1986. It latterly operated for Filers of Ilfracombe, whose livery was still carried when photographed in service at Watford.
David Heath

Starline (overleaf) operate a variety of vehicles from mini-buses through to double-deck buses. Pictured here is Plaxton-bodied Volvo B10M EBZ6296 with boards for school service 831.
Colin Lloyd

STARLINE

E B Mullany, 117 Hempstead Road, Watford, Hertfordshire, WD1 8DG

D2143	OJD143R	Leyland Fleetline FE30AGR	Park Royal	H45/28D	1976	London Buses, 1990
T85	CUL85V	Leyland Titan TNLXB2RRSp	Park Royal	H44/26D	1980	Sullivan, Harrow, 1997
	YDN504	Mercedes-Benz L307D	Reeve Burgess	M12	1983	Simmonds, Letchworth, 1989
	EBZ6294	Volvo B10M-61	Duple Laser	C57F	1983	Link Line, Harlesden, 1987
	EBZ6296	Volvo B10M-61	Plaxton Paramount 3500	C57F	1983	Skills, Sheffield, 1989
	EBZ6295	Volvo B10M-61	Plaxton Paramount 3500	C57F	1983	Skills, Nottingham, 1989
T896	A896SYE	Leyland Titan TNLXB2RR	Leyland	H44/27D	1983	London United, 1996
T986	A986SYE	Leyland Titan TNLXB2RR	Leyland	H44/26D	1984	London Central, 1998
T987	A987SYE	Leyland Titan TNLXB2RR	Leyland	H44/27D	1984	London Central, 1998
	FDZ4730	Volvo B10M-61	Van Hool Alizée H	C53F	1984	Shearings, 1990
	FDZ5348	Volvo B10M-61	Van Hool Alizée H	C53F	1984	Shearings, 1991
	B21CYS	Mercedes-Benz L307D	Reeve Burgess	M12	1985	Barrett, Great Mongeham, 1992
	C938RPK	Mercedes-Benz L608D	Coachcraft	C21F	1986	
	C518DND	Volvo B10M-61	Plaxton Paramount 3200 II	C53F	1986	Metroline (Brents), 1997
	E219JJF	Volvo B10M-61	Van Hool Alizée H	C53F	1988	Clarkes of London, 1997
	E299GMY	Volvo B10M-61	Van Hool Alizée H	C49FT	1988	Clarkes of London, 1998
	F796FKU	Mercedes-Benz 811D	Whittaker Europa	C24F	1989	
	G870MAH	Volvo B10M-60	Plaxton Paramount 3500 III	C53F	1990	The Londoners, Nunhead, 1996
	H254LOX	Mercedes-Benz 709D	Blythswood (1994)	C24FL	1991	van, 1994
	K712GBE	Mercedes-Benz 407D	Autobus Classique	M16	1993	Metroline (Brents), 1997
	M669UCT	Mercedes-Benz 814D	Autobus Classique	C33F	1995	

Previous Registrations:-

E299GMY	GPL-066(B), XEL24, E455SEL, BIL1977		
EBZ6294	MSU598Y, EJV248, FLB453Y	FDZ4730	A179MNE
EBZ6295	YNN31Y	FDZ5348	A180MNE
EBZ6296	YNN30Y	YDN504	HBH420Y

Livery:- White

Depot:- Clarendon Garage, Cardiff Road, Watford,

Named Vehicle:- D2143 *Tornado*; T896 *Titan*; T986 *Telstar*; T897 *Early Bird*

Former London Buses Leyland Titans are proving to be popular second-hand purchases with operators of all sizes. Starline of Watford have four used mostly on schools services, as witnessed by A896SYE seen here prepared for route 835A. Interestingly, Starline have retained the London Buses fleet numbers this one being T896 and aptly named Titan.
Peter Graves

The Chilterns and West Anglia Bus Handbook

SWORDER'S

C W Sworder & Sons Ltd, Walkern Garage, Walkern, Stevenage, Hertfordshire, SG2 7PD

	Reg	Chassis	Body	Seating	Year	History
	SKN491R	Bedford YRT	Willowbrook 001	B53F	1977	Ipswich, 1989
	XTW856S	Bedford YMT	Duple Dominant	B55F	1978	Sampsons, Hoddesdon, 1993
	JIL9345	Volvo B58-56	Duple Dominant II Express	DP53F	1979	Weetabix, Burton Latimer, 1993
	JIL9346	Volvo B58-56	Duple Dominant II Express	DP53F	1979	Weetabix, Burton Latimer, 1993
u	18KB14	Bedford VAS5	Wadham Stringer Vanguard	B30F	1984	MoD, 1996
	B436RJU	Dodge G13	Reeve Burgess	B38F	1984	USAF, 1995
	B43BRO	Freight-Rover Sherpa	Freight-Rover	M8	1985	private owner, 1994
	B814BRO	Dodge G13	Reeve Burgess	B38F	1985	USAF, 1996
	B437RJU	Dodge G13	Reeve Burgess	B38F	1985	USAF, 1995
	C55MAR	Freight-Rover Sherpa	Freight-Rover	M8	1986	Layston, Hare Street, 1994
	C152SLN	Leyland Cub CU335	Wadham Stringer Vanguard	DP21FL	1985	LB Islington, 1994
	C336LBH	Renault-Dodge G13	Wadham Stringer Vanguard	B38F	1985	MoD, 1996
	D165OJN	Leyland Cub CU335	Wadham Stringer Vanguard	B20FL	1986	LB Redbridge, 1994
	D81UBM	Renault-Dodge G13	Wadham Stringer Vanguard	B38F	1986	MoD, 1996
	D331HMF	Bedford VAS5	Wadham Stringer Vanguard	B26FL	1987	LB Enfield, 1993
	D983OUH	Renault-Dodge G13	Wadham Stringer Vanguard	B38F	1987	MoD, 1994
	M969ONK	Ford Transit VE6	Ford	M14	1994	

Previous Registrations:-

B814BRO	85B...	C336LBH	31KC64	JIL9345	CAV620V
B436RJU	84B279	D983OUH	80KF27	JIL9346	CAV625V
B437RJU	85B...	D81UBM	80KF91		

Livery:- Tan, grey and orange

Named Vehicles:- JIL9345 *Vera*; RBD102M *Tom*.

Sworders of Walkern have a fleet dedicated to contract and school service work. Unusually there are no coaches in the current fleet, although initial impressions of JIL9345 and JIL9346 may suggest otherwise. Both vehicles are fitted with 53 bus seats in Duple Dominant II Express coach bodies. The vehicles were acquired from Weetabix of Burton Latimer, where they were used as staff transport for the cereal manufacturer. This view shows Vera, alias JIL9345 at Stevenage, having worked School service 889. *Richard Godfrey*

T & M TRAVEL / LANES COACHES

M E Kennedy & T A Ward, 100 Newton Road, Bletchley, Buckinghamshire, MK3 5BY

LIL2183	Bedford YNT	Duple Dominant II	C53F	1977	Alwynes, Elmswell, 1995
XBR657R	Ford R1114	Plaxton Supreme III	C53F	1977	Lucky Bus, Watford, 1994
NJI8869	Bedford YNT	Plaxton Supreme IV	C53F	1979	APT, Rayleigh, 1995
AJD20T	Bedford YMT	Plaxton Supreme IV	C53F	1979	Staples, Lincoln, 1998
CDT322T	Bedford YNT	Duple Dominant II	C53F	1979	Knotty Bus, Chesterton, 1996
RKE154W	Bedford YMT	Plaxton Supreme IV	C53F	1981	D J Transport, Bletchley, 1998
RIB8815	Bedford YNT	Duple Dominant II	C53F	1980	APT, Rayleigh, 1996

Previous Registrations:-

CDT322T	APH513T, CIB3683	NJI8869	BVE107V, MJI2374, LKE499V
LIL2183	OKY73R, 102SYB, DFC932R	RIB8815	DHT667W

Depot:- Bletchley Park, Wilton Avenue, Bletchley.

Tates operate an example of the 10 metre long Bedford YMQ. Pictured with a German school party, EIB502 features a Plaxton Supreme IV body with accommodation for 45. *Colin Lloyd*

The Chilterns and West Anglia Bus Handbook

TATES

S J & A M Tate, 44 High Street, Markyate, Hertfordshire, AL3 8PA

EIB502	Bedford YMQ	Plaxton Supreme IV	C45F	1980	Tates B & B, Markyate, 1983
FOD943Y	Dennis Dorchester SDA802	Wadham Stringer Vanguard	B59F	1983	Tillingbourne, Cranleigh, 1997
B327KPD	Bedford YMT	Plaxton Bustler	B53F	1984	Tillingbourne, Cranleigh, 1996
CAZ3687	Leyland Tiger TRCTL11/3RZ	Plaxton Paramount 3500 II	C53F	1985	Abbey Howe, Waddington, 1996
133MBJ	Bova FLD12.250	Bova Futura	C53F	1986	
VLV815	Van Hool T815H	Van Hool Alizée HE	C49FT	1993	Whyte & Urquhart, Newmachar, 1996
WIJ297	MAN 11.180	Caetano Algarve II	C35F	1994	Britannia, Telford, 1998
L223BUT	Dennis Javelin 12SDA2131	Plaxton Première 320	C53F	1994	
P955DNR	Dennis Javelin	Caetano Algarve II	C53F	1997	
R291NYG	Bova FLD12.300	Bova Futura	C49FT	1998	

Previous Registrations:-

133MBJ	C34VJF	VLV815	K545GSS
CAZ3687	B508UNB, RJI6239	WIJ297	L65YJF
EIB502	RKX26W		

Named Vehicle:- VLV815 *Tates European Goldliner*

Livery:- Cream, blue and orange. VLV815 is gold with orange and blue fleetnames.

Depot:- Water End Road, Potton End.

Tates run a solitary example of the lower Bova FLD variant. If this photograph of Tates 133MBJ and 2522VU with Robinsons are compared, it will be noticed that the black rubbing strip is lower down the bodyside.

TAYLOR'S RELIANCE COACHES

W C & R G Taylor, 77 High Street, Meppershall, Shefford, Bedfordshire, SG17 5LY

617MUR	Volvo B10M-61	Plaxton Paramount 3500	C53F	1983	Richardson, Mortlake, 1991
A33MTW	Leyland Tiger TRCTL11/2R	Plaxton Paramount 3200	C57F	1983	
2290PK	Volvo B10M-61	Plaxton Paramount 3500	C57F	1984	Epsom Coaches, 1993
1056AR	Volvo B10M-61	Plaxton Paramount 3500	C49FT	1984	Epsom Coaches, 1993
FIL8604	Leyland Tiger TRCTL11/3RZ	Plaxton Paramount 3500	C49F	1984	Dance & Evans, Catford, 1989
TSU477	Leyland Tiger TRCTL11/3RZ	Plaxton Paramount 3500 II	C51F	1985	Hills, Tredegar, 1992
93JNM	Leyland Tiger TRCTL11/3RZ	Plaxton Paramount 3200 II	C53F	1986	Frames Rickards, Brentford, 1990
SMJ521	Leyland Tiger TRCTL11/3RZ	Plaxton Paramount 3500 II	C49FT	1986	Robinson, Stewkley, 1996
578CYA	Volvo B10M-61	Plaxton Paramount 3500 III	C49FT	1988	Hoare, Chickerell, 1995
SVO89	Volvo B10M-60	Plaxton Paramount 3500 III	C49FT	1990	MTL, London, 1997

Previous Registrations:-

93JNM	C806FMC	FIL8604	C406DML, C409DML
2290PK	A503WGF	SMJ521	A131MBA, SMJ521
578CYA	E578NMK	SVO89	G44RGG
617MUR	PGH687Y	TSU477	B617CKG
1056AR	A401WGH		

Livery:- Lilac, pink and maroon

Taylor's Reliance coaches are adorned in an unusual, yet pleasing livery of lilac, pink and maroon. The fleet is almost entirely of Plaxton Paramount-bodied Leyland Tiger and Volvo B10M coaches, though several have been modernised by the substitution of later grille and dash panels. Volvo B10M 2290PK has mark III panels grafted onto its original 3500 bodywork. *David Heath*

The Chilterns and West Anglia Bus Handbook

THOMPSON TRAVEL

EA Thompson, 69 Lemonfield Drive, Garston, Hertfordshire, WD2 7TR

YAA130V	Ford R1114	Plaxton Supreme IV	C53F	1980	Edwards, Edmonton, 1985
PNB782W	Ford R1114	Plaxton Supreme IV	C53F	1981	Hammond, Lakenheath, 1988
VJT622X	Ford R1114	Plaxton Supreme V	C53F	1982	Titchen, Benfleet, 1990
FNA908Y	DAF MB200DKFL600	Plaxton Paramount 3200	C57F	1983	Healing, Oldham, 1997
B222NUT	DAF SB2300DHS585	Plaxton Paramount 3200 II	C53F	1985	Mills, Gornal Wood, 1997
F979LTM	Ford Transit	Crystals	M16	1989	
H367WPN	Renault Master T35	Oatia	M14	1991	Frank Thorpe, N Kensington, 1998
J350MBX	Renault Master T35	Cymric	M16	1991	Croxford, Farnham, 1993

Livery:- Cream with red and tan relief.

Depot:-Sutton Sidings Coach Park, Sutton Road, St Albans.

TIMEBUS

D Pring, 7 Boleyn Drive, St Albans, Hertfordshire, AL1 2BP

RLH23	MXX223	AEC Regent III 9613E	Weymann	L27/26R	1952	preservation, 1988
RF491	MXX468	AEC Regal IV 9821LT	Metro Cammell	B39F	1953	preservation, 1995
RM1871	ALD871B	AEC Routemaster R2RH	Park Royal	H36/24R	1964	Watford & District, 1997
RMA37	KGJ612D	AEC Routemaster R2RH/2	Park Royal	H32/24F	1966	Shaftesbury & District, 1996

Livery:- London Transport red.

Depot:- South Mimms Service Area, St Albans Road, Potters Bar, and c/o Classic Coaches, Fifield, Windsor.

Timebus operate a small, but very interesting fleet of heritage vehicles, all of which have at some time served with London Transport. The oldest is also the rarest, and one of the relatively few double-deck buses purchased by London to lowbridge layout for routes with restricted clearance. Always favourite buses with London enthusiasts, Timebus' RLH23, MXX223 was nostalgically employed on route 230 on the occasion of a Leyton garage open day. It is seen here in red livery, though this vehicle operated in green when new. *Colin Lloyd*

TRAVEL LINE

Travel Line Coaches Ltd, 29 The Fairway, Abbots Langley, Watford, Hertfordshire, WD5 0JX

TJI6756	Ford R1114	Duple Dominant II	C53F	1979	Universitybus, Hatfield, 1994
TJI6575	Ford R1114	Duple Dominant IV	C53F	1981	Harrod, Wormegay, 1995
PAZ3276	Volvo B10M-61	Duple Goldliner	C48FT	1982	P&H Travel, Dagenham, 1998
DSK562	Mercedes-Benz L307D	Reeve Burgess	M12	1984	Felix, Long Melford, 1990
LSK642	Volvo B10M-61	Jonckheere Jubilee P599	C49FT	1985	Case, Watford, 1992
FSU386	Scania K112CRS	Jonckheere Jubilee P599	C49FT	1985	Voel, Dyserth, 1993

Previous Registrations:-

| DSK562 | A72NPP | LSK642 | B24XVS, PSU608 | TJI6575 | RDH586W |
| FSU386 | B704EOF, 8214VC, B528FFM | PAZ3276 | LSF575X | TJI6756 | JFD285V |

Livery:- various

Depot:- Watford Metropolitan Station Approach, Watford and London Road, Bourne End

The newest coaches in the Travel Line fleet are Jonkheere Jubillee P599 coaches with the optional low driving position. FSU386 was photographed at Maidstone services on the M20 during the brief 1998 summer.

The Chilterns and West Anglia Bus Handbook

TURNER'S MINIBUSES

D W Turner, Turnwood, 105 Asheridge Road, Chesham, Buckinghamshire, HP5 2PZ

585EBP	Ford Transit 190D	Mellor	B16F	1983	Wings, Hayes, 1989
B57AOP	Ford Transit 190D	Carlyle	B16F	1985	Perry, Bromyard, 1991
B964BPP	Ford Transit 190D	Ford	M8	1985	MoD, 1992
C288CKN	Ford Transit 190D	Coachcraft	M16	1986	Gilbert, Chesham, 1995
C726JJD	Ford Transit 190D	Carlyle	B16F	1986	Stevensons, 1997
D121PTT	Ford Transit VE6	Mellor	B16F	1987	Thames Transit, 1997
D343SKX	Ford Transit 190D	Chassis Developments	C16F	1987	Charnley, Coleshill, 1991
F603PWS	Iveco Daily 49.10	Dormobile Routemaker	B20F	1989	City Line, 1996
F91JGE	Ford Transit VE6	Steedrive	B20F	1989	Waddell, Duns, 1996
F198ARP	Ford Transit VE6	Ford	M	1989	private owner, 1997
H789DBW	Ford Transit VE6	Ford	M	1991	private owner, 1997

Previous Registrations:-

585EBP	A598HNF	B964BPP	?

Pictured while operating a rail replacement service is Timebus' forward entrance Routemaster KGJ612D which, when new, was operated by London Transport for BEA, connecting the central London terminal to Heathrow Airport. For this operation a luggage trailer was towed. The vehicle carries fleet number RMA37 and red livery. *David Heath*

UNIVERSITYBUS

University Bus Ltd, College Lane, Hatfield, Hertfordshire, AL10 9AB

Reg	Chassis	Body	Seating	Year	Notes
THX261S	Leyland National 10351A/2R	EL Greenway (1993)	B41F	1978	London Buses,1992
EUI4415	Volvo B10M-61	Berkhof Everest 370	C48FT	1983	Time Travel, Thornton Heath, 1995
B761OPJ	Mercedes-Benz L608D	Reeve Burgess	C21F	1984	Chivers, Elstead, 1995
F930TBP	Mercedes-Benz 609D	?	C24F	1989	van, 1995
G472PGE	Leyland Lynx LX112L10ZR1R	Leyland Lynx	B51F	1989	Stonehouse Coaches, 1993
H748CBP	Mercedes-Benz 811D	Phoenix	B33F	1990	Hertfordshire CC,1992
H840NOC	Dennis Dart 9.8SDL3004	Carlyle Dartline	B40F	1991	Hertfordshire CC,1992
H849NOC	Dennis Dart 9.8SDL3004	Carlyle Dartline	B43F	1991	Hertfordshire CC,1992
K754UJO	Dennis Javelin 12SDA2118	Plaxton Premiere 320	C53F	1992	Lewis, Llanrhystyd, 1998
L94GVL	Dennis Javelin	Plaxton Premiere 320	C53F	1993	Metropolitan Police,1998
M47HUT	Bluebird CSRE 2700	Bluebird Q-Bus	B51F	1994	
M48HUT	Bluebird CSRE 2700	Bluebird Q-Bus	B51F	1994	
M49HUT	Bluebird CSRE 2700	Bluebird Q-Bus	B51F	1994	
M51HUT	Bluebird CSRE 2700	Bluebird Q-Bus	B51F	1994	
M419UWY	LDV 400	LDV	M16	1994	
M527UGS	Mercedes-Benz OH1416	Wright Urbanranger	B47F	1995	
M255UKX	Mercedes-Benz OH1416	Wright Urbanranger	B47F	1995	
M146VVS	Dennis Dart 9.8SDL3054	Wright Handy-bus	B42F	1995	
M148VVS	Dennis Dart 9.8SDL3054	Wright Handy-bus	B42F	1995	
N421ENM	Dennis Dart 9.8SDL3054	Marshall C37	B40F	1995	
N422ENM	Dennis Dart 9.8SDL3054	Marshall C37	B40F	1995	
N423ENM	Dennis Dart 9.8SDL3054	Marshall C37	B40F	1995	
N424ENM	Dennis Dart 9.8SDL3054	Marshall C37	B40F	1995	
P980PTM	Marshall Minibus	Marshall	B29F	1996	
P664PNM	Dennis Dart SLF	Wright Crusader	N41F	1996	
P665PNM	Dennis Dart SLF	Wright Crusader	N41F	1996	
P667PNM	Dennis Dart SLF	Wright Crusader	N41F	1996	
P668PNM	Dennis Dart SLF	Wright Crusader	N41F	1996	
P647SBH	Dennis Dart SLF	Wright Crusader	N38F	1997	
R648VMJ	Dennis Dart SLF	Wright Floline	N41F	1998	
R649VBM	Dennis Dart SLF	Wright Crusader	N41F	1997	
R650VBM	Dennis Dart SLF	Wright Crusader	N41F	1997	
R651VBM	Dennis Dart SLF	Wright Crusader	N41F	1997	
R652VBM	Dennis Dart SLF	Wright Crusader	N41F	1997	
R653VBM	Dennis Dart SLF	Wright Crusader	N41F	1997	
R654VBM	Dennis Dart SLF	Wright Crusader	N41F	1997	
R532YRP	Dennis Dart SLF	Wright Crusader	N41F	1997	
YDZ2082	Dennis Dart SLF	Wright Crusader	N41F	1998	Wright demonstrator, 1998
R71BUR	Optare MetroRider	Optare	B29F	1998	
R72JTM	Optare MetroRider	Optare	B29F	1998	

Previous Registrations:-

B761OPJ   B967MLF, KXI599   EUI4415   BDV862Y

Livery:-   White, grey and purple

Depot:-   Bishops Square Business Park, Hatfield.

Opposite:- **From humble beginnings transferring students between the various Campuses of Hertfordshire University, Universitybus have expanded into a well respected company with a route network and modern fleet that many companies would be proud of. Significant quantities of new Dennis Dart low floor buses have entered service rubbing shoulders with earlier standard Darts. Interesting vehicles feature strongly in the fleet, with rare Mercedes-Benz OH1416 and a Bluebird Q-Bus saloons on fleet strength. Of this latter model, M48HUT is seen heading for Hitchin while the lower picture shows Marshall Minibus P980PTM.** *Tony Wilson*

THE VILLAGE BUS

R F Litchfield, 14 Old Wheatsheaf Yard, Woburn, Bedfordshire, MK17 9PZ

KTY873X	Ford R1014	Duple Dominant II	C35F	1981	Wallace, Bardon Mill, 1984
UIA8946	Mercedes-Benz O303/15	Mercedes-Benz	C53F	1983	MHS Travell, Stourport, 1998
C138KVV	Ford Transit 190D	Carlyle	DP20F	1986	Gibbs, Milton Keynes, 1992
D218NUR	Ford Transit 190D	Chassis Developments	C16F	1986	Sapwell, Ashton, 1991
F702GWJ	Renault-Dodge S56	Reeve Burgess	B25F	1989	Wrights, Wrexham, 1993
F630DEG	Ford Transit	Dormobile	B20F	1989	Myall, Bassingbourne, 1995
H310BGD	Ford Transit	Made-to-Measure	C20F	1991	Broomfield, Hawick, 1996

Previous registrations:-

UIA8946   PUL97Y, ALJ857A

Welham Travel operate in the Hatfield area using a white and green livery. Most of their regular work is school contract services. Three Plaxton Supreme IVs are in use but on differing chassis. One is a heavyweight Volvo B58-61chassis, while the other pair are lightweight units on Ford R1114 and one of the last Bristol LHS underframes built, below is VBT201V on a Ford chassis and *(opposite)* SJI5617 on Volvo.

WELHAM TRAVEL

Nash Brothers Ltd, 26 Dellsome Lane, North Mymms, Hatfield, Hertfordshire, AL9 7NF
G E Hoskins, 9 Sibthorpe Road, Welham Green, Hatfield, Hertfordshire, AL9 7PA

NWU852M	Bedford YRQ	Plaxton Panorama Elite III	C45F	1973	Nash Brothers, North Mymms, 1994
VBT201V	Ford R1114	Plaxton Supreme IV	C53F	1979	Brown, St Albans, 1995
NMJ268V	Bedford YMT	Duple Dominant II	C53F	1980	Brown, Wheathampstead, 1993
SJI5617	Volvo B58-61	Plaxton Supreme IV	C57F	1980	Dawney, Halfway, 1995
DNK583Y	Bristol LHS6L	Plaxton Supreme V	C33F	1983	Hoskins, Welham Green, 1995
RXI9280	DAF SB2300DHS585	Berkhof Esprite 350	C49FT	1983	P J Reynolds, Bushey, 1995
IIL2255	Ford R1115	Plaxton Paramount 3200 II	C53F	1985	Rainbow, Westbury, 1997

Previous Registrations:-

IIL2255	B590CYS	RXI9280	A648NOO	SJI5617	MGD942V

Livery:- White and green. Nash Brothers - DNK583Y, IIL2255. Hoskins - remainder.

Depot:-Dellsome Lane, North Mymms

WEST LONDON TRAVEL

West London Travel Ltd, 24 Court Lawns, Tylers Green, Buckinghamshire, HP10 8DH

DHT528W	Bedford VAS5	Duple Dominant	C29F	1981	Hudson, Downley, 1994
IUI2768	Bedford YNT	Plaxton Paramount 3200	C53F	1984	York Pullman, 1997
A639AWA	Bedford YNT	Plaxton Paramount 3200	C53F	1984	York Pullman, Elvington, 1995
A927XNL	Ford Transit 190	Dormobile	B16F	1984	Pope, Reading, 1994
C913WVT	Ford Transit 190	Ford	M15	1986	private owner, 1994
D453CKV	Freight-Rover Sherpa	Rootes	B16F	1986	WMRCC, Shrewley, 1994
F613CKR	Ford Transit VE6	Ford	M14	1989	private owner, 1993
F598PLY	Ford Transit VE6	Ford	M11	1989	private owner, 1994
G233NWF	Ford Transit VE6	Advanced Vehicles Bodies	M11	1990	CPS Parking, Heathrow, 1994
G523BRK	Ford Transit VE6	Ford	M8	1990	private owner, 1992
G244ERE	Ford Transit VE6	Ford	M11	1990	private owner, 1992
J203BAH	Ford Transit VE6	Ford	M8	1992	private owner, 1995
M397NVR	Ford Transit VE6	Deansgate	M14	1995	
M398NVR	Ford Transit VE6	Deansgate	M14	1995	
P52KCA	Mercedes-Benz 814D	Buscraft	C24F	1996	

Previous Registration:-
IUI2768   A839AWA

Named Vehicles:- M397NVR *Charlotte*; M398NVR *Dave*

Livery:- Silver and black (Ambassador-Line) P52KCA.

Depot:- Binders Industrial Estate, Cryers Hill, High Wycombe.

Photographed carrying a black and silver livery and adorned with Ambassador Line Executive fleet names is P52KCA. This unusual vehicle is a Buscraft bodied Mercedes-Benz 814D, although the origins of the Mercedes-Benz chassis have been hidden, with few clues to the identity of the manufacturer. *David Heath*

WESTWAYS

M J & J J West, Unit 3 Chiltern Works, Lincoln Road, High Wycombe, HP12 3RQ

WXI4359	Bedford YMT	Plaxton Supreme III	C53F	1978	Wing, Sleaford, 1992
DMJ401X	Leyland Tiger TRCTL11/3R	Plaxton Supreme V	C57F	1982	Taylor's Reliance, Meppershall, 1995
853SEH	DAF MB200DKFL600	Plaxton Paramount 3500	C53F	1983	Smith-Ivins, High Wycombe, 1997
KIW3768	Leyland Tiger TRCTL11/3R	Plaxton Paramount 3200	C57F	1983	Rover, Chesham, 1992
F953ENH	Dennis Javelin 12SDA1907	Plaxton Paramount 3200 III	C53F	1989	Wainfleet, Nuneaton, 1996
F847OEB	Dennis Javelin 12SDA1907	Caetano Algarve	C51FT	1991	Grey, Ely, 1998
J532SRX	Mercedes-Benz 811D	Autobus Classique	C29F	1991	

Previous Registrations:-

853SEH	From new	KIW3768	BFP261Y
DMJ401X	VGV50X, 578CYA	WXI4359	CRW511T, SCT330, JFW853T
F953ENH	F867RFP, MIW5790	F847OEB	F169XLJ, ESU350

Livery:- White, burgundy and grey.

Depots:- Lincoln Road, High Wycombe and New Road, Sands, High Wycombe.

Westways have two Leyland Tiger coaches, KIW3768 has Plaxton Paramount 3200 coachwork in its original form. It was seen arriving at this years Hampton Court flower show looking very smart and denying its fifteen years age. *Geoff Rixon*

YORKS

York Brothers (Northampton) Ltd, Short Lane, Cogenhoe, Northamptonshire, NN7 1LT

16	M116MBD	LDV 400	Deansgate	M16	1995	
17	P117ORP	LDV Convoy	Coachliners	M16	1997	
50	RBD287Y	Ford R1115	Plaxton Supreme VI Express	C53F	1982	Ralph, Longford, 1983
51	XYN591	Volvo B10M-61	Van Hool Alizée H	C53F	1987	
52	ESK896	Volvo B10M-61	Van Hool Alizée H	C53F	1987	Shearings, 1992
53	ESK897	Volvo B10M-61	Van Hool Alizée H	C53F	1988	Park's, Hamilton, 1994
54	XVY392	Volvo B10M-61	Plaxton Paramount 3200 II	C53F	1985	Stainton, Kendal, 1995
55	XEA745	Volvo B10M-61	Plaxton Paramount 3200 II	C53F	1988	Wray, Harrogate, 1995
62	KHB34W	Ford R1114	Plaxton Supreme IV Express	C53F	1981	Ferrers, South Woodham Ferrers, 1989
70	UFC221	Volvo B10M-61	Plaxton Paramount 3500 III	C53F	1988	
71	R636VNN	MAN	Noge Catalan	C49F	1998	
80	EOW288	Kässbohrer Setra S215HD	Kässbohrer Tornado	C49FT	1983	
81	OOW233	Kässbohrer Setra S215HD	Kässbohrer Tornado	C49FT	1983	
82	XPO987	Kässbohrer Setra S215HR	Kässbohrer Rational	C53F	1985	
83	927NOF	Kässbohrer Setra S215HR	Kässbohrer Rational	C53F	1985	
84	946BKH	Kässbohrer Setra S215HR	Kässbohrer Rational	C53F	1985	
85	XHO856	Kässbohrer Setra S215HR	Kässbohrer Rational	C53F	1988	
86	FSV305	Kässbohrer Setra S215HR	Kässbohrer Rational	C53F	1988	
87	XLC516	Kässbohrer Setra S215HD	Kässbohrer Tornado	C49F	1985	
88	VHM847	Kässbohrer Setra S215HD	Kässbohrer Tornado	C49FT	1989	Ball, Felixstowe, 1991
89	387TYD	Volvo B10M-61	Van Hool Alizée H	C39DT	1988	Travellers, Hounslow, 1994
90	HSK511	Volvo B10M-61	Van Hool Alizée H	C49FT	1990	Shearings, 1996
91	335RHX	Kässbohrer Setra S215HD	Kässbohrer Tornado	C49F	1982	
92	846FHA	Kässbohrer Setra S215HD	Kässbohrer Tornado	C49FT	1993	Spirit Of London, Hounslow, 1996
95	SYK901	Kässbohrer Setra S215HR	Kässbohrer Rational	C49FT	1986	Skelton, Chilton Polden, 1992
96	KPR698	Kässbohrer Setra S215HR	Kässbohrer Rational	C53F	1986	
97	405MDV	Kässbohrer Setra S215HR	Kässbohrer Rational	C53F	1986	
98	TVY659	Kässbohrer Setra S215HR	Kässbohrer Rational	C53F	1986	

Heritage vehicles:

	FJ6154	Maudsley Marathon ML3B	Northern Counties	B33D	1929	Arden, Haldon, 1965
	AYH93	Maudsley Marathon ML3B	chassis only	N/A	1934	Heslop, Hexham, 1976

Previous Registrations:-

335RHX	ENH91X	OOW233	MRP81Y
387TYD	E263OMT	RBD287Y	FNM710Y, SYK901
405MDV	C97RVV	SYK901	C28JBO
846FHA	K121OCT	TVY659	C98RVV
927NOF	B83GBD	UFC221	E70LVV
946BKH	B84GBD	VHM847	F992MTW
EOW288	MRP80Y	XEA745	E607VNW, A20MCW
ESK896	D610MVR	XHO856	E85LVV
ESK897	E655UNE, LSK839, E619CDS	XLC516	B87GBD
FSV305	E86LVV	XPO987	B82GBD
HSK511	G880VNA, WSV528, G791YND	XVY392	B711PEC, LIB3766, B196MAO
KPR698	C96RVV	XYN591	D51DNH

Named Vehicles:- 335RHX *HMS Nelson*; 387TYD *HMS Dreadnought*; 405MDV *HMS Battleaxe*; 846FHA *HMS Iron Duke*; 946BKH *HMS Braven*; 927NOF *HMS Boxer*; EOW288 *HMS Endurance*; ESK896 *HMS Conqueror*; ESK897 *HMS Sovereign*; FSV305 *HMS Trafalgar*; HSK511 *HMS Somerset*; KHB34W *HMS Swallow*; KPR698 *HMS Campbeltown*; M116MBD *HMS Spey*; OOW233 *HMS Edinburgh*; P117ORP *HMS Cromer*; RBD287Y *HMS Manchester*; SYK901 *HMS Courageous*; TVY659 *HMS Beaver*; UFC221 *HMS Torbay*; VHM847 *HMS Ark Royal*; XEA745 *HMS Cornwall*; XHO856 *HMS Trenchant*; XLC516 *HMS Brilliant*; XPO987 *HMS Brave*; XVY392 *HMS Cumberland*; XYN591 *HMS Turbulent;* R636VNN *HMS Vengence.*

Livery:- Silver, blue and red.

---

*Opposite:-***Yorks operate a number of the top-class Kässbohrer Setra range and illustrated here are the two principal models seen in Britain. The upper picture shows 81, OOW233, which is a Tornado model, while the lower picture shows 86, FSV305, which is a Rational. Production of both of these models has now been replaced by the 300 series, though only a 250 special has been produced in right-hand drive form so far.** *Colin Lloyd*

Z & S TRAVEL

S Zaman, 38-40 Fleet Street, Aylesbury, Buckinghamshire, HP20 2PA

TCG333M	Bedford YRT	Duple Dominant	C53F	1974	Aylesbury Scouts, 1987
HPK502N	Leyland National 11351/1R		B49F	1975	London & Country, 1997
KPA364P	Leyland National 11351/1R		B49F	1975	London & Country, 1997
DJO32R	Bedford YMT		C53F	1977	Hartwool, Bicester, 1996
211WVT	AEC Reliance 6U2R	Plaxton Supreme III	C49F	1979	Lincoln, 1987
DGS626X	Volvo B10M-61	Plaxton Supreme IV Express	C49FT	1982	Club Cantabrica, St Albans, 1990
A502LUD	Renault-Dodge S56	Jonckheere Bermuda	B25F	1983	MoD, 1997
A891LWL	Renault-Dodge S56	Rootes	B25F	1983	MoD, 1997
A132XNH	Scania K112CRS	Rootes	C49FT	1984	Club Cantabrica, St Albans, 1992
B234PKV	Ford Transit 190D	Jonckheere Jubilee P599	C16F	1984	Allen, Coventry, 1990
C736XRU	Ford Transit 190D	Mellor	M12	1985	Souls, Olney, 1989
C125AHP	Toyota Coaster BB30R	Chassis Developments	C19F	1986	Allison, Haddenham, 1989
D718PGS	Freight-Rover Sherpa	Caetano Optimo	M6	1986	private owner, 1993
E374AMJ	Ford Transit	Freight-Rover	C16F	1987	Cedric, Wivenhoe, 1993
TIB8570	Scania K112CRS	Chassis Developments	C57F	1987	Scancoaches, North Acton, 1996
E261OMT	Volvo B10M-61	Jonckheere Jubilee P50	C49FT	1988	Travellers, Hounslow, 1994
		Van Hool Alizée DH			

Previous Registrations:-

211WVT	EPM147V	DJO32R	SBA200R, EOI4376
DGS626X	BNK853X, 450CCH	TIB8570	D325VVV

Livery:- Yellow, blue and white or silver, blue and orange.

Depts:- Fleet Street, Aylesbury and c/o Arriva The Shires, Brunel Park, Aylesbury.

Z&S Travel operated E261OMT during the summer of 1998, when it was pictured while on hire to Jeff Amos Coaches. The vehicle is a Volvo B10M with the DH variant of the Van Hool Alizée body. *Colin Lloyd*

Index to vehicles

Reg	Operator	Reg	Operator	Reg	Operator	Reg	Operator
17EJU	Shoreys	927NOF	Yorks	A138DPE	Sovereign	ARP618X	Arriva The Shires
18KB14	Sworder's	938HNM	Jeffs	A139DPE	Sovereign	ARP619X	Arriva The Shires
25CTM	Seamarks	946BKH	Yorks	A140DPE	Sovereign	ARP620X	Arriva The Shires
38CRC	Chambers	954CUH	Souls	A140TNV	Geoff Amos	AUD465R	Jeffs
50DBD	Souls	966MBM	Souls	A141DPE	Arriva The Shires	AWB818T	P P H
52GYY	Keystone	993HNW	Drury	A142FLE	Magpie Travel	AYH93	Yorks
90WFC	Motts	1056AR	Taylor's Reliance	A143DPE	Arriva The Shires	B6RMT	Motts
93JNM	Taylor's Reliance	1404FM	Marshall's	A143EPA	Arriva The Shires	B10MMT	Motts
112AXN	Jeffs	1746MT	Motts	A149FPG	Arriva The Shires	B10TMT	Motts
130VBJ	Souls	1774RU	Barfordian	A151FPG	Arriva The Shires	B12TMT	Motts
133MBJ	Tates	2522VU	Robinsons	A152EPA	Arriva The Shires	B21CYS	Starline
147VKN	Jeffs	2570PF	Office Travel	A152FPG	Arriva The Shires	B21XKX	Premier
153WAR	Richmond's	2583KP	Buffalo Travel	A153EPA	Arriva The Shires	B22XKX	Premier
153XYC	P P H	2997HL	Buffalo Travel	A153FPG	Arriva The Shires	B43BRO	Sworder's
195CJU	L B Travel	3085KX	Alec Head	A154FPG	Arriva The Shires	B45TVR	Harris
195JOH	Jeffs	3253VU	Robinsons	A155FPG	Arriva The Shires	B57AOP	Turner's
211WVT	Z & S Coaches	3493CD	Jeffs	A157EPA	Arriva The Shires	B63APP	Red Rose Travel
224ASV	Barfordian	4388WX	Alec Head	A203ODY	P P H	B64APP	Herberts Travel
2290PK	Taylor's Reliance	4442MT	Motts	A210PBM	Sovereign Taxis	B96WUV	United Counties
230WYA	Souls	4542VU	Robinsons	A320HFP	J&L Travel	B222NUT	Thompson Travel
239BUP	Souls	5228NW	Classic Coaches	A335GFF	Rodgers	B234PKV	Z & S Coaches
239LYC	Richmond's	5280NW	Classic Coaches	A355YOX	Chambers	B248RHP	Chambers
261HTF	Central Cars	5302VU	Robinsons	A396GVN	Langston & Tasker	B262LPH	Arriva The Shires
264KTA	Classic Coaches	5615RO	Jeffs	A473ODY	Sovereign Taxis	B264KPF	Sovereign
275FUM	Richmond's	5705MT	Motts	A481WCA	Abbey Coaches	B266LPH	Sovereign
279JJO	Jeffs	5723MT	Motts	A502LUD	Z & S Coaches	B268LPH	Sovereign
316UVX	Richmond's	5812MT	Motts	A520NCL	Enfieldian	B269LPH	Sovereign
335RHX	Yorks	5814MT	Motts	A606OWW	Magpie Travel	B270LPH	Arriva The Shires
372DEL	Rover Luxury Travel	5874MT	Motts	A611HNF	Magpie Travel	B271LPH	Arriva The Shires
387TYD	Yorks	6101MV	Seamarks	A639AWA	West London Travel	B272LPH	Arriva The Shires
403NMM	Richmond's	6247MT	Motts	A648VOJ	Sovereign Taxis	B273LPH	Arriva The Shires
405MDV	Yorks	6447PO	Alec Head	A659MWR	Hyltone	B274VRO	Chambers
426YRA	Richmond's	6601MT	Motts	A660KUM	First Northampton	B327KPD	Tates
438XYA	Richmond's	6957MT	Motts	A691ERB	Acclaim Travel	B368KNH	Geoff Amos
459KBM	Souls	7178NP	Souls	A698EAU	Arriva The Shires	B379FHK	Rodgers
485SWL	P P H	7195BY	Alec Head	A699EAU	Arriva The Shires	B436RJU	Sworder's
487VYA	Jeffs	7804PP	Cantabrica	A730BSE	Langston & Tasker	B437RJU	Sworder's
489SYB	Barfordian	8098NK	Alec Head	A819XMK	Simmonds	B520BBD	New Greens
505KVO	Office Travel	8726PH	Prestwood Travel	A839TOO	Herberts Travel	B638XJX	Central Cars
512AUO	Cedar Coaches	9349KP	Buffalo Travel	A847MAC	Keystone	B761OPJ	Universitybus
539WVJ	Richmond's	9569KM	Seamarks	A891LWL	Z & S Coaches	B787OUT	Martin
554JPP	Herberts Travel	9683ML	Seamarks	A896SYE	Starline	B814BRO	Sworder's
559ABX	Richmond's	9775MT	Motts	A927XNL	West London Travel	B839NKA	Reynolds Diplomat
570EFJ	Classic Coaches	9920MT	Motts	A933YOX	Jeffs	B928XPP	New Greens
572CNW	Classic Coaches	A1NYJ	Reynolds Diplomat	A969SKK	Herberts Travel	B946CMT	P P H
574CNW	Classic Coaches	A8CLN	Country Lion	A986SYE	Starline	B964BPP	Turner's
577HDV	Souls	A8EAD	Alec Head	A987SYE	Starline	BAU179T	United Counties
577HYX	Richmond's	A8KRT	Buffalo Travel	ABD74X	First Northampton	BAZ6869	Arriva The Shires
578CYA	Taylor's Reliance	A9CLN	Country Lion	ABD75X	First Northampton	BBB539V	Marlow Coaches
585EBP	Turner's	A10CLC	Country Lion	ABD76X	First Northampton	BBW141V	Keystone
591HNM	Herberts Travel	A11EAD	Alec Head	ABD253B	Classic Coaches	BKE847T	Arriva The Shires
593FGF	Richmond's	A12CLN	Country Lion	ADC277A	Jeffs	BLJ714Y	Greenway Travel
617MUR	Taylor's Reliance	A14CLC	Country Lion	ADZ4731	Arriva The Shires	BNO670T	Shoreys
641UTO	Motts	A15CLC	Country Lion	AEF368A	L B Travel	BNO686T	Jeffs
647PJO	Jeffs	A15CLN	Country Lion	AFH389T	Office Travel	BPF132Y	Sovereign
648EAU	Richmond's	A15NFC	Country Lion	AJD20T	T & M Travel	BPF133Y	Sovereign
649ETF	Richmond's	A16CLC	Country Lion	ALD871B	Timebus	BPF134Y	Sovereign
660CUH	L B Travel	A16LWB	Len Wright	ALJ990A	Paul Dale	BPF135Y	Arriva The Shires
668PTM	Richmond's	A17CLN	Country Lion	ALZ2490	Souls	BPF136Y	Arriva The Shires
675PBM	Souls	A17LWB	Len Wright	AML641H	Bryans of Enfield	BPF137Y	Sovereign
685DYE	United Counties	A18CLN	Country Lion	ANW710C	Classic Coaches	BRW738Y	Harris
713WAF	Cedar Coaches	A18LWB	Len Wright	APM111T	Prestwood Travel	BRY102Y	Robinsons
729KTO	Richmond's	A19CLN	Country Lion	APM117T	Prestwood Travel	BTV659T	Cedar Coaches
751EKX	Souls	A19LWB	Len Wright	ARP601X	United Counties	BTV661T	Cedar Coaches
753LNU	Richmond's	A20CLC	Country Lion	ARP602X	United Counties	BTX152T	Arriva The Shires
760BUS	Rover Luxury Travel	A31GJT	Souls	ARP604X	United Counties	BUT18Y	First Northampton
781CRC	Chambers	A33MTW	Taylor's Reliance	ARP605X	United Counties	BVV545T	Arriva The Shires
802AOJ	Jeffs	A33PFE	Abbey Coaches	ARP606X	United Counties	BWA21B	Langston & Tasker
821FHU	Souls	A35GJT	Souls	ARP607X	United Counties	BWU691H	Classic Coaches
846FHA	Yorks	A37DTV	Rodgers	ARP608X	United Counties	C23ENK	Smith's of Tring
851FYD	Richmond's	A58YMH	Hyltone	ARP609X	United Counties	C24GKX	Premier
853SEH	Westways	A61NPP	Herberts Travel	ARP610X	United Counties	C42MAK	Enfieldian
855GAC	Souls	A84MUR	Luton Airport	ARP611X	United Counties	C47WLL	Rodgers
872KMY	Jeffs	A85MUR	Luton Airport	ARP612X	Arriva The Shires	C55MAR	Sworder's
872PYA	Souls	A94GLD	Buckby's-Coopers	ARP613X	Arriva The Shires	C78MAK	Harris
873DTU	Souls	A104GBC	Greenway Travel	ARP614X	Arriva The Shires	C82YKK	Prestwood Travel
892LTV	Richmond's	A111OAV	Alec Head	ARP615X	Arriva The Shires	C88NNV	Souls
910OCV	Exodus	A113EPA	Arriva The Shires	ARP616X	Arriva The Shires	C95NNV	Harris
917ETV	L B Travel	A132XNH	Z & S Coaches	ARP617X	Arriva The Shires	C101OTW	Bryans of Enfield

Reg	Operator	Reg	Operator	Reg	Operator	Reg	Operator
C106KVS	Chambers	D101XNV	First Northampton	E374AMJ	Z & S Coaches	F135URP	United Counties
C108SDX	First Northampton	D102XNV	First Northampton	E376XVS	Luton Airport	F151KGS	Arriva The Shires
C109SDX	First Northampton	D121PTT	Turner's	E408YLG	Richmond's	F152KGS	Arriva The Shires
C114MAK	Country Lion	D124PTT	Red Rose Travel	E413YLG	Anita's	F153KGS	Arriva The Shires
C117EMG	Simmonds	D138HML	Chambers	E420EBH	Arriva The Shires	F160AWO	Red Rose Travel
C119TLO	New Greens	D149HML	ABC Travel	E426ATT	P P H	F164SMT	Cedar Coaches
C120PNV	United Counties	D165OJN	Sworder's	E448WAH	Rodgers	F169UDP	Marlow Coaches
C121MAK	Country Lion	D208SKD	Arriva The Shires	E486CNM	Arriva The Shires	F190YDA	Red Rose Travel
C121PNV	United Counties	D209FFX	Red Rose Travel	E487FNP	Magpie Travel	F198ARP	Turner's
C122MAK	Country Lion	D210SKD	Arriva The Shires	E541EAL	Rodgers	F203MBT	Sovereign
C122PNV	United Counties	D217SKD	Red Rose Travel	E590PFR	Langston & Tasker	F204MBT	Sovereign
C125AHP	Z & S Coaches	D218NUR	Village Bus	E601LBF	Herberts Travel	F205MBT	Sovereign
C131CFB	P P H	D220PVS	Herberts Travel	E635NHP	Marlow Coaches	F206MBT	Sovereign
C138KVV	Village Bus	D290BBC	Sovereign Taxis	E658UNE	Anita's	F207MBT	Sovereign
C140KVV	Expresslines	D331HMF	Sworder's	E677GRF	ABC Travel	F208MBT	Sovereign
C147SPB	Arriva The Shires	D343SKX	Turner's	E681MWP	AR Travel	F222BFL	Alec Head
C148SPB	Cedar Coaches	D346KVA	Martin	E689NNH	Len Wright	F225OLO	New Greens
C149SPB	Arriva The Shires	D350KVE	Sovereign	E690NNH	Len Wright	F266CEY	Arriva The Shires
C152SLN	Sworder's	D351JUM	Expresslines	E741DJO	Jeffs	F273CEY	Arriva The Shires
C215KMA	P P H	D377VRM	Rodgers	E777MCE	Alec Head	F279GNB	Herberts Travel
C268XSC	New Greens	D381JUM	Berko Bus	E786KHW	New Greens	F281GBW	Smith-Ivins
C288CKN	Turner's	D383XRS	United Counties	E854UKR	P P H	F305RMH	Simmonds
C317URF	Berko Bus	D393SGS	Keystone	E855UKR	P P H	F314RMH	Arriva The Shires
C318URF	Harris	D453CKV	West London Travel	E881YKY	Arriva The Shires	F331NLN	Central Cars
C326DND	Simmonds	D461PON	Classic Coaches	E882YKY	Arriva The Shires	F333RJF	Martin
C329OFL	Star Travel	D462PON	Classic Coaches	E903EAY	J&L Travel	F358JVS	Sovereign
C336LBH	Sworder's	D477DSX	Poynter's	E913PNV	Geoff Amos	F359JVS	Sovereign
C425WFH	P P H	D516WNV	Acclaim Travel	E930YAM	Langston & Tasker	F370BUA	Seamarks
C460CNG	Reynolds Diplomat	D523DWP	Shire Coaches	E940RWR	ABC Travel	F400PUR	Arriva The Shires
C500DMP	New Greens	D600PKO	Star Travel	E965PME	Arriva The Shires	F401PUR	Arriva The Shires
C513DND	Enfieldian	D603ACW	Arriva The Shires	E966PME	Arriva The Shires	F402PUR	Arriva The Shires
C518DND	Starline	D607NOE	Red Rose Travel	E969PME	Arriva The Shires	F403PUR	Arriva The Shires
C626MEG	Sovereign Taxis	D654BPL	Anglia	E970NMK	Arriva The Shires	F404PUR	Arriva The Shires
C681KFW	Greenway Travel	D718PGS	Z & S Coaches	E970PME	Arriva The Shires	F405CKU	New Greens
C726JJD	Turner's	D778JUB	Hyltone	E976YKO	Herberts Travel	F421DUG	Sovereign
C736XRU	Z & S Coaches	D836CNV	Office Travel	E990DNK	Arriva The Shires	F425DUG	Sovereign
C756OVV	Buckby's-Coopers	D849CRY	A to B Team	E995DNK	Arriva The Shires	F480AKC	Jeffs
C759CWX	P P H	D864PYS	Beeslty Enterprises	EBD188X	Buckby's-Coopers	F506OYW	Arriva The Shires
C814FMC	Prestwood Travel	D955ARE	Magpie Travel	EBZ6294	Starline	F540OEB	Cliffs Coaches
C820FMC	Chambers	D957ENH	Geoff Amos	EBZ6295	Starline	F567HPP	Jeffs
C875JCP	Acclaim Travel	D983OUH	Sworder's	EBZ6296	Starline	F598CET	Arriva The Shires
C908FMP	Martin	DBJ969Y	Barfordian	EDV505D	Classic Coaches	F598PLY	West London Travel
C913WVT	West London Travel	DGS626X	Z & S Coaches	EDV546D	Classic Coaches	F600DWB	Motts
C938RPK	Starline	DHT528W	West London Travel	EHL336	Classic Coaches	F601DWB	Langston & Tasker
C985YFA	P P H	DJO32R	Z & S Coaches	EIB502	Tates	F603PWS	Turner's
CAZ3687	Tates	DKG270V	Classic Coaches	ENT778	Premier	F613CKR	West London Travel
CAZ6852	Arriva The Shires	DMJ401X	Westways	EOW288	Yorks	F61RKX	Rover Luxury Travel
CBD897T	Arriva The Shires	DNK583Y	Welham Travel	EPH224V	Kellys Coaches	F620MSL	United Counties
CBD899T	Arriva The Shires	DSK562	Travel Line	EPM140V	Prestwood Travel	F621MSL	United Counties
CBD900T	Arriva The Shires	DSU296	Bryans of Enfield	EPM144V	Prestwood Travel	F622MSL	United Counties
CBD904T	Arriva The Shires	DWF195V	Classic Coaches	EPM146V	Prestwood Travel	F623MSL	United Counties
CBM13X	Premier	DWW926Y	Sovereign	ERP19T	Jeffs	F624MSL	United Counties
CBV19S	Red Kite	DWW927Y	Sovereign	ESK896	Yorks	F625MSL	United Counties
CBV20S	Rodgers	DWW928Y	Sovereign	ESK897	Yorks	F626MSL	United Counties
CDT322T	T & M Travel	DWW929Y	Sovereign	ESU635	Jeffs	F627MSL	United Counties
CFX305T	Acclaim Travel	DWW930Y	Sovereign	ESU939	J&L Travel	F628MSL	United Counties
CJO466R	Jeffs	DWW931Y	Sovereign	EUI4415	Universitybus	F628OHD	Acclaim Travel
CNH48T	First Northampton	DWW932Y	Sovereign	EVC210T	Souls	F629FNA	Herberts Travel
CNH49T	First Northampton	E48TYG	Prestwood Travel	EWR651Y	First Northampton	F629MSL	United Counties
CNH50T	First Northampton	E81HPG	Jeffs	EWR652Y	First Northampton	F630DEG	Village Bus
CNH52T	First Northampton	E94OUH	Barfordian	EWR653Y	First Northampton	F630MSL	United Counties
CNH53T	First Northampton	E111NNV	First Northampton	F22VVV	New Greens	F631MSL	United Counties
CNH54T	First Northampton	E130ORP	United Counties	F28FCC	Rodgers	F632MSL	United Counties
CNH56T	Country Lion	E131ORP	United Counties	F37ENF	First Northampton	F633LMJ	Arriva The Shires
CNH57T	First Northampton	E132ORP	United Counties	F41YNH	Country Lion	F633MSL	United Counties
CNH58T	First Northampton	E133ORP	United Counties	F47CVV	Jeffs	F634LMJ	Arriva The Shires
CPE480Y	Prestwood Travel	E134MHN	Herberts Travel	F48CVV	Jeffs	F634MSP	United Counties
CPO351W	Geoff Amos	E134ORP	United Counties	F50ENF	First Northampton	F635LMJ	Arriva The Shires
CPP45X	P P H	E148RNY	Balmoral Autos	F83XBD	First Northampton	F635YRP	United Counties
CRP120T	Classic Coaches	E162TVR	Langston & Tasker	F84XBD	First Northampton	F636LMJ	Arriva The Shires
CTM418T	Paul Dale	E176KNH	Keystone	F85XBD	First Northampton	F636YRP	United Counties
CUB539Y	Motts	E219JJF	Starline	F86DVV	First Northampton	F637LMJ	Arriva The Shires
CUB540Y	Motts	E235ADO	ABC Travel	F87GAO	J&L Travel	F637YRP	United Counties
CUL85V	Starline	E240EUT	Sovereign	F88DVV	First Northampton	F638LMJ	Arriva The Shires
CUV192C	United Counties	E240NSE	Rover Luxury Travel	F91JGE	Turner's	F638YRP	United Counties
CUV198C	Classic Coaches	E261OMT	Z & S Coaches	F107NRT	United Counties	F639LMJ	Arriva The Shires
CUV265C	Sovereign	E299GMY	Starline	F110NES	United Counties	F640LMJ	Arriva The Shires
CUV322C	Sovereign	E323OMG	Arriva The Shires	F115OVL	Balmoral Autos	F641LMJ	Arriva The Shires
CUV341C	Sovereign	E331HNV	Keystone	F121TRU	Arriva The Shires	F642LMJ	Arriva The Shires
CVH733Y	P P H	E335DRO	Arriva The Shires	F122TRU	Arriva The Shires	F643LMJ	Arriva The Shires
D23RPP	Arriva The Shires	E341DRO	Arriva The Shires	F123TRU	Arriva The Shires	F644LMJ	Arriva The Shires
D72KRL	Star Travel	E342DRO	Magpie Travel	F124TRU	Arriva The Shires	F648PLW	Motts
D81UBM	Sworder's	E351UOH	Beeslty Enterprises	F125TRU	Arriva The Shires	F689RKX	Arriva The Shires
D83PPP	Layston Coaches	E371YRO	Sovereign	F128TRU	Arriva The Shires	F696GMA	Arriva The Shires

Reg	Operator	Reg	Operator	Reg	Operator	Reg	Operator
F702GWJ	Village Bus	G113ENV	First Northampton	G657UPP	Arriva The Shires	H6CRC	Chambers
F723PFP	First Northampton	G114ENV	First Northampton	G681BFC	Souls	H27LHP	ABC Travel
F724SML	Expresslines	G129YEV	Arriva The Shires	G702LKW	Alec Head	H35DGD	Arriva The Shires
F725MNB	Red Rose Travel	G130YEV	Arriva The Shires	G709JET	Sovereign Taxis	H65XBD	Motts
F727EKR	Red Rose Travel	G131YWC	Arriva The Shires	G715PGA	Arriva The Shires	H119YGG	Magpie Travel
F737KGJ	Berko Bus	G132YWC	Arriva The Shires	G726CEM	Abbey Coaches	H125JTW	Expresslines
F73UJX	Sovereign Taxis	G140WPP	Central Cars	G736LEP	Cantabrica	H139GGS	Sovereign
F747XCS	Arriva The Shires	G145GOL	Arriva The Shires	G744UFW	Martin	H140GGS	Sovereign
F788GNA	Langston & Tasker	G146GOL	Arriva The Shires	G775WBE	Expresslines	H141GGS	Sovereign
F791DWT	Seamarks	G148GOL	Arriva The Shires	G820LAT	Expresslines	H142GGS	Sovereign
F791TBC	A to B Team	G156UYK	Buckby's-Coopers	G830RDS	Cedar Coaches	H143GGS	Sovereign
F796FKU	Starline	G167XJF	Hallmark	G838VAY	Chambers	H144GGS	Sovereign
F797MGB	Abbey Coaches	G169ODH	Shire Coaches	G843HRN	Cantabrica	H145GGS	Sovereign
F808LBM	Herberts Travel	G201URO	Sovereign	G845VAY	Martin	H146GGS	Sovereign
F816XUG	Star Travel	G202URO	Sovereign	G870MAH	Starline	H147GGS	Sovereign
F847OEB	Westways	G203URO	Sovereign	G896TGG	Arriva The Shires	H148GGS	Sovereign
F862TNH	P P H	G205URO	Sovereign	G901UPP	Sovereign	H149GGS	Sovereign
F895URP	Sovereign Taxis	G206URO	Sovereign	G902UPP	Sovereign	H150GGS	Sovereign
F930TBP	Universitybus	G207URO	Sovereign	G903UPP	Sovereign	H151GGS	Sovereign
F936MTM	Herberts Travel	G225GSG	Arriva The Shires	G904UPP	Sovereign	H152ANV	Poynter's
F953ENH	Westways	G233NWF	West London Travel	G905UPP	Sovereign	H152GGS	Sovereign
F969GKJ	Arriva The Shires	G244ERE	West London Travel	G906UPP	Sovereign	H183EJF	Jeffs
F979LTM	Thompson Travel	G276HDW	Arriva The Shires	G907UPP	Sovereign	H184EJF	Jeffs
F985GKJ	Arriva The Shires	G277HDW	Arriva The Shires	G907WAY	Jeffs	H187GKM	Expresslines
F996SVX	Anita's	G278WKX	Seamarks	G908UPP	Sovereign	H189GKM	Expresslines
F997MTM	Expresslines	G281UMJ	Arriva The Shires	G908WAY	Jeffs	H196GRO	Arriva The Shires
F999UME	Chambers	G282UMJ	Arriva The Shires	G909UPP	Sovereign	H197GRO	Arriva The Shires
FAO419V	United Counties	G283ANK	Expresslines	G909WAY	Jeffs	H198AOD	Arriva The Shires
FAZ4494	Souls	G283UMJ	Arriva The Shires	G910WAY	Jeffs	H198GRO	Arriva The Shires
FDF276T	Jeffs	G284UMJ	Arriva The Shires	G911WAY	Jeffs	H199AOD	Arriva The Shires
FDV812V	United Counties	G285UMJ	Arriva The Shires	G912WAY	Jeffs	H199GRO	Arriva The Shires
FDV832V	United Counties	G286UMJ	Arriva The Shires	G913WAY	Jeffs	H202GRO	Arriva The Shires
FDV835V	United Counties	G287UMJ	Arriva The Shires	G914WAY	Jeffs	H203GRO	Arriva The Shires
FDZ4730	Starline	G288UMJ	Arriva The Shires	G933JKY	Jeffs	H231KBH	Arriva The Shires
FDZ5348	Starline	G289UMJ	Arriva The Shires	G938LFV	Luton Airport	H238ANE	Martin
FEV178	Arriva The Shires	G290UMJ	Arriva The Shires	G939LFV	Luton Airport	H243MUK	Arriva The Shires
FFK312	First Northampton	G291UMJ	Arriva The Shires	G940EEH	Herberts Travel	H245MUK	Arriva The Shires
FFT684W	Robinsons	G292UMJ	Arriva The Shires	G940LFV	Luton Airport	H254LOX	Starline
FIL4892	Bryans of Enfield	G293UMJ	Arriva The Shires	G947VBC	Balmoral Autos	H289VRP	First Northampton
FIL4919	Arriva The Shires	G294UMJ	Arriva The Shires	G956VVR	Jeffs	H290VRP	First Northampton
FIL6282	Drury	G295UMJ	Arriva The Shires	G968WNR	ABC Travel	H291VRP	First Northampton
FIL7674	Hats & Herts Coaches	G296KWY	Sovereign	G971KWJ	New Greens	H292VRP	First Northampton
FIL8604	Taylor's Reliance	G297KWY	Sovereign	G972CPD	Marlow Coaches	H293VRP	First Northampton
FIL9378	L B Travel	G360FGP	Arriva The Shires	GAJ126V	Cedar Coaches	H294VRP	First Northampton
FJ6154	Yorks	G363ATM	Luton Airport	GAJ127V	Shoreys	H310BGD	Village Bus
FJR776L	Arriva The Shires	G384MWX	Sovereign	GBF79N	Abbey Coaches	H319OEV	Abbey Coaches
FKM866V	Arriva The Shires	G405DPD	Marlow Coaches	GDG442V	Jeffs	H367WPN	Thompson Travel
FKM874V	Arriva The Shires	G411PGG	Cedar Coaches	GDN704N	Acclaim Travel	H389SYG	Red Rose Travel
FLD927Y	Reynolds Diplomat	G411YAY	Martin	GFE836Y	Keystone	H403FGS	Sovereign
FLD928Y	Reynolds Diplomat	G421YAY	Chambers	GFR799W	Arriva The Shires	H404FGS	Sovereign
FLJ869V	Hyltone	G427PWW	First Northampton	GGM86W	Classic Coaches	H406FGS	Arriva The Shires
FLS733V	Souls	G428YAY	South Mimms Travel	GHB574V	Arriva The Shires	H407ERO	Arriva The Shires
FNA908Y	Thompson Travel	G441ETW	Expresslines	GHV51N	Shoreys	H407FGS	Arriva The Shires
FNM5Y	Greenway Travel	G466JNH	Shire Coaches	GHV70N	Bryans of Enfield	H408BVR	Arriva The Shires
FNM850Y	Chambers	G472PGE	Universitybus	GHV979N	Buffalo Travel	H408ERO	Arriva The Shires
FOD943Y	Tates	G478EOK	Magpie Travel	GHV999N	Shoreys	H408FGS	Arriva The Shires
FP5992	Keystone	G500MFV	ABC Travel	GIL4276	Keystone	H409BVR	Arriva The Shires
FRM688V	P P H	G519LWU	Sovereign	GIL5979	Enfieldian	H409CJF	Jeffs
FRP905T	Red Kite	G523BRK	West London Travel	GPD304N	Classic Coaches	H409ERO	Arriva The Shires
FRP910T	Red Kite	G541JBV	Reg's	GPJ640V	Hyltone	H409FGS	Sovereign
FRP912T	United Counties	G579WUT	Smith-Ivins	GSB146Y	Rodgers	H410ERO	Arriva The Shires
FSU379	Marshall's	G639EVV	United Counties	GSB147Y	Rodgers	H410FGS	Sovereign
FSU386	Travel Line	G640EVV	United Counties	GSL898N	Buffalo Travel	H411FGS	Sovereign
FSV305	Yorks	G641EVV	United Counties	GSL908N	Cedar Coaches	H413FGS	Sovereign
FSV720	Jeffs	G642EVV	United Counties	GSO2V	United Counties	H415FGS	Sovereign
FTO560V	Buckby's-Coopers	G643EVV	United Counties	GSO6V	United Counties	H417FGS	Sovereign
FTU377T	Rodgers	G644EVV	United Counties	GSO7V	United Counties	H418FGS	Sovereign
FUG321T	Sovereign	G645EVV	United Counties	GSU305	South Mimms Travel	H419FGS	Sovereign
FWR218T	Red Kite	G645UPP	Arriva The Shires	GSU384	Marshall's	H421FGS	Sovereign
FWR219T	Red Kite	G646EVV	United Counties	GUP647H	Classic Coaches	H422FGS	Sovereign
G37HDW	ABC Travel	G646UPP	Arriva The Shires	GUW441W	Arriva The Shires	H423FGS	Sovereign
G40OHS	Arriva The Shires	G647EVV	United Counties	GUW447W	Arriva The Shires	H424FGS	Sovereign
G42HKY	Cliffs Coaches	G647UPP	Arriva The Shires	GUW456W	Arriva The Shires	H448VNH	Anglia
G52BLX	Shire Coaches	G648EVV	United Counties	GUW457W	Arriva The Shires	H475KSG	Arriva The Shires
G58BEL	Arriva The Shires	G648UPP	Arriva The Shires	GUW461W	Arriva The Shires	H523SWE	Arriva The Shires
G92RGG	Sovereign	G649EVV	United Counties	GUW462W	Arriva The Shires	H561FLE	Magpie Travel
G95RGG	Sovereign	G649UPP	Arriva The Shires	GUW465W	Arriva The Shires	H613FFP	Martin
G96RGG	Sovereign	G650UPP	Arriva The Shires	GUW475W	Arriva The Shires	H614CGG	Arriva The Shires
G97RGG	Sovereign	G651UPP	Arriva The Shires	GUW494W	Arriva The Shires	H627UWR	Sovereign
G97VMM	Arriva The Shires	G652UPP	Arriva The Shires	GVV251X	Souls	H628UWR	Sovereign
G98RGG	Sovereign	G653UPP	Arriva The Shires	GVV322X	Souls	H629UWR	Sovereign
G102SVM	Martin	G654UPP	Arriva The Shires	GWT630	Classic Coaches	H641UWE	Arriva The Shires
G103YNK	Cedar Coaches	G655UPP	Arriva The Shires	H3CRC	Chambers	H642UWE	Arriva The Shires
G112ENV	First Northampton	G656UPP	Arriva The Shires	H5CRC	Chambers	H647UWR	Sovereign

Reg	Operator	Reg	Operator	Reg	Operator	Reg	Operator
H650VVV	Sovereign	J115MRP	First Northampton	K2CRC	Chambers	K665UNH	United Counties
H651VVV	Sovereign	J171GGG	Arriva The Shires	K2LWB	Len Wright	K667UNH	United Counties
H652VVV	Sovereign	J200CCH	Cantabrica	K3ERN	Anita's	K668UNH	United Counties
H653VVV	Sovereign	J200CCH	Cantabrica	K3SBC	Sovereign	K669UNH	United Counties
H654VVV	United Counties	J203BAH	West London Travel	K4SBC	Sovereign	K670UNH	United Counties
H668ATN	Red Rose Travel	J208RVS	Seamarks	K5JFS	Magpie Travel	K700CCH	Cantabrica
H675ATN	Souls	J210GNV	First Northampton	K5SBC	Sovereign	K709ASC	United Counties
H741LHN	A to B Team	J230HVK	Poynter's	K8BUS	Arriva The Shires	K710ASC	United Counties
H748CBP	Universitybus	J269NNC	Premier	K17FTG	Hallmark	K711ASC	Sovereign
H789DBW	Turner's	J295GNV	First Northampton	K18OMC	Sovereign Taxis	K712ASC	Sovereign
H809RWJ	Alec Head	J296GNV	First Northampton	K25WND	Arriva The Shires	K712GBE	Starline
H832JNK	Anita's	J297GNV	First Northampton	K26WND	Arriva The Shires	K713ASC	United Counties
H840NOC	Universitybus	J298GNV	First Northampton	K27WND	Arriva The Shires	K758FYG	United Counties
H846UUA	Seamarks	J299GNV	First Northampton	K28WND	Arriva The Shires	K759FYG	United Counties
H848AUS	Arriva The Shires	J350MBX	Thompson Travel	K29WND	Arriva The Shires	K760FYG	United Counties
H849NOC	Universitybus	J367BNW	Seamarks	K31WND	Arriva The Shires	K761FYG	United Counties
H882AVK	Motts	J390MRP	Poynter's	K32WND	Arriva The Shires	K777KGM	Buffalo Travel
H920FGS	Sovereign	J430HDS	United Counties	K97UFP	Jeffs	K800CCH	Cantabrica
H921FGS	Sovereign	J439HDS	United Counties	K98UFP	Jeffs	K900CCH	Cantabrica
H922BPN	Martin	J445HDS	United Counties	K121URP	First Northampton	K991GBD	Poynter's
H922FGS	Sovereign	J446HDS	United Counties	K123URP	First Northampton	K999CCH	Cantabrica
H922LOX	Arriva The Shires	J450HDS	United Counties	K124URP	First Northampton	KAZ4130	Smith's of Tring
H923FGS	Sovereign	J465UFS	Arriva The Shires	K125URP	First Northampton	KAZ6898	Buffalo Travel
H923LOX	Arriva The Shires	J470NJU	Jeffs	K126URP	First Northampton	KAZ6900	Funstons
H925FGS	Sovereign	J471NJU	Jeffs	K127GNH	First Northampton	KAZ6901	Funstons
H925LOX	Arriva The Shires	J472NJU	Jeffs	K128GNH	First Northampton	KAZ6902	Funstons
H926FGS	Sovereign	J473NJU	Jeffs	K129GNH	First Northampton	KAZ6903	Funstons
H926LOX	Arriva The Shires	J474NJU	Jeffs	K130GNH	First Northampton	KAZ6904	Funstons
H927FGS	Sovereign	J475NJU	Jeffs	K131GNH	First Northampton	KBM647Y	Acclaim Travel
H929FGS	Sovereign	J476NJU	Jeffs	K132GNH	First Northampton	KCG627L	Classic Coaches
H930FGS	Sovereign	J477NJU	Jeffs	K150DNV	United Counties	KFO572P	P P H
H931FGS	Sovereign	J520LRY	Jeffs	K151DNV	United Counties	KGJ612D	Timebus
H934JDP	Harris	J521LRY	Jeffs	K152DNV	United Counties	KHB34W	Yorks
H941WNH	Buckby's-Coopers	J532SRX	Westways	K153DNV	United Counties	KHD921K	Classic Coaches
H951LSF	Expresslines	J620GCR	United Counties	K154DNV	United Counties	KIW3768	Westways
H982UBD	Poynter's	J621GCR	United Counties	K184GDU	Arriva The Shires	KIW8800	Buffalo Travel
HAY201V	Harris	J622GCR	United Counties	K202FEH	Arriva The Shires	KJD89P	Simmonds
HBD914T	United Counties	J727CWT	Rover Luxury Travel	K203FEH	Arriva The Shires	KJD268P	Alec Head
HBD915T	United Counties	J734KBC	Martin	K221CBD	Barfordian	KON323P	Motts
HBD916T	United Counties	J749CWT	Sovereign	K226WNH	Hallmark	KPA364P	Z & S Coaches
HBZ4674	South Mimms Travel	J752CWT	United Counties	K227WNH	Hallmark	KPC405W	Classic Coaches
HC6422	Hallmark	J753CWT	United Counties	K230WNH	Alec Head	KPJ238W	Geoff Amos
HIL2282	Souls	J781KHD	Berkeleys	K231WNH	Alec Head	KPJ241W	Arriva The Shires
HIL2386	Souls	J808WFS	United Counties	K265FUV	Chambers	KPJ242W	Arriva The Shires
HIL2833	A to B Team	J828JFG	ABC Travel	K318FYG	Cantabrica	KPJ243W	Arriva The Shires
HIL3470	Rover Luxury Travel	J917HGD	Arriva The Shires	K350ANV	United Counties	KPJ244W	Geoff Amos
HIL5683	Poynter's	J948UBL	Marlow Coaches	K351ANV	United Counties	KPJ256W	Geoff Amos
HIL7595	Arriva The Shires	J964NLL	Arriva The Shires	K352ANV	United Counties	KPJ262W	Arriva The Shires
HIL7597	Arriva The Shires	JAZ9862	Marlow Coaches	K353ANV	United Counties	KPJ271W	Geoff Amos
HIL7749	Buckby's-Coopers	JBZ3251	Smith-Ivins	K354ANV	United Counties	KPM429P	Classic Coaches
HIL9273	Funstons	JBZ4492	Smith-Ivins	K355ANV	United Counties	KPR698	Yorks
HJB451W	Barfordian	JBZ8933	Balmoral Autos	K356ANV	United Counties	KRU843W	United Counties
HLP10C	Classic Coaches	JCY870	Classic Coaches	K357ANV	United Counties	KRU845W	United Counties
HNW366D	Classic Coaches	JFL729W	Red Kite	K358ANV	United Counties	KRU847W	United Counties
HOD55	Cedar Coaches	JHL983	Classic Coaches	K359ANV	United Counties	KRU852W	United Counties
HPB814V	Classic Coaches	JIL6902	New Greens	K362RNR	New Greens	KSK965	Motts
HPK502N	Z & S Coaches	JIL6902	Smith-Ivins	K390SLB	Sovereign	KSK966	Motts
HSK511	Yorks	JIL7424	Buffalo Travel	K391SLB	Sovereign	KSK967	Motts
HVS937	United Counties	JIL9034	Rover Luxury Travel	K392SLB	Sovereign	KTY873X	Village Bus
HXI252	Herberts Travel	JIL9345	Sworder's	K393SLB	Sovereign	KYU77	Souls
IAZ2314	Arriva The Shires	JIL9346	Sworder's	K395PJU	Martin	L1CRC	Chambers
IAZ3915	Barfordian	JJD404D	Sovereign	K447XPA	Arriva The Shires	L1ONB	Country Lion
IAZ3977	Arriva The Shires	JJD487D	Sovereign	K448XPA	Arriva The Shires	L1ONC	Country Lion
IAZ4037	Arriva The Shires	JJD527D	Sovereign	K525RJX	Hallmark	L1OND	Country Lion
IAZ5657	Souls	JJD538D	Sovereign	K540CWN	Shire Coaches	L2SBC	Sovereign
IIL2255	Welham Travel	JJD563D	Sovereign	K540OGA	Red Rose Travel	L3LWB	Len Wright
IIL2485	New Greens	JJD569D	Sovereign	K543OGA	Sovereign	L3SBC	Sovereign
IIL4821	Arriva The Shires	JJD582D	Sovereign	K578YOJ	Arriva The Shires	L7CCH	Cantabrica
IIL4822	Arriva The Shires	JJD598D	Sovereign	K579YOJ	Arriva The Shires	L8CCH	Cantabrica
IIL4823	Arriva The Shires	JKW303W	Kellys Coaches	K580YOJ	Arriva The Shires	L9CCH	Cantabrica
IIL4824	Arriva The Shires	JMB359T	Rodgers	K600CCH	Cantabrica	L10CCH	Cantabrica
IIL6441	Classic Coaches	JMJ112V	Langston & Tasker	K647SBX	Cliffs Coaches	L10NBB	Country Lion
IIL6567	Hyltone	JNK238V	ABC Travel	K652TUE	Sovereign Taxis	L10NCC	Country Lion
IIL6765	Smith-Ivins	JOI9820	Rover Luxury Travel	K655UNH	United Counties	L10NKK	Country Lion
IUI2768	West London Travel	JPE233V	Arriva The Shires	K656UNH	United Counties	L15ALU	Herberts Travel
J3JCN	Keystone	JPE236V	Arriva The Shires	K657KNL	Arriva The Shires	L35CAY	Jeffs
J3TCC	Robinsons	JPE237V	Arriva The Shires	K657UNH	United Counties	L36CAY	Jeffs
J4CRC	Chambers	JRV416X	Classic Coaches	K658UNH	United Counties	L37CAY	Jeffs
J31UTG	Arriva The Shires	JUG356N	Classic Coaches	K659UNH	United Counties	L38CAY	Jeffs
J32UTG	Arriva The Shires	JUG357N	Classic Coaches	K660UNH	United Counties	L39CAY	Jeffs
J37VDW	Arriva The Shires	JVH378	Classic Coaches	K661UNH	United Counties	L43MEH	Arriva The Shires
J61NTM	Simmonds	JWF47W	Geoff Amos	K662UNH	United Counties	L94GVL	Universitybus
J65UNA	Arriva The Shires	JWV267W	Classic Coaches	K663UNH	United Counties	L100BUS	Arriva The Shires
J100CCH	Cantabrica	K1OLE	Exodus	K664UNH	United Counties	L110RWB	Marshall's

L115WBX	Poynter's	L421JBD	United Counties	LFR862X	United Counties	M336DRP	United Counties
L128GBA	Hallmark	L422MVV	United Counties	LFR864X	United Counties	M337DRP	United Counties
L129GBA	Hallmark	L423XVV	United Counties	LGV994	Premier	M338DRP	United Counties
L130GBA	Hallmark	L424XVV	United Counties	LHK644V	Hats & Herts	M339DRP	United Counties
L133HVS	Arriva The Shires	L425XVV	United Counties	LIL2183	T & M Travel	M340DRP	United Counties
L140BPH	Central Cars	L426XVV	Sovereign	LIL5379	Buffalo Travel	M341DRP	United Counties
L155JNH	United Counties	L427XVV	Sovereign	LIL7234	Alec Head	M342DRP	United Counties
L156JNH	United Counties	L428XVV	Sovereign	LIL9811	Souls	M343DRP	United Counties
L157JNH	United Counties	L491JFU	Martin	LJI8158	L B Travel	M344DRP	United Counties
L158JNH	United Counties	L500BUS	Arriva The Shires	LJX198	Classic Coaches	M345DRP	United Counties
L159JNH	United Counties	L530EHD	Hallmark	LSK527	First Northampton	M346DRP	United Counties
L160JNH	United Counties	L531EHD	Hallmark	LSK642	Travel Line	M346TDO	Keystone
L161JNH	United Counties	L555GSM	Buffalo Travel	LSV146	Souls	M347DRP	United Counties
L162JNH	United Counties	L577ULY	Shire Coaches	LTA904	Premier	M348DRP	United Counties
L200BUS	Arriva The Shires	L579MVV	Buckby's-Coopers	LTY556X	P P H	M349DRP	United Counties
L214GJO	Motts	L600BUS	Arriva The Shires	LVS439P	Langston & Tasker	M397NVR	West London Travel
L223BUT	Tates	L671HNV	United Counties	LXI2743	Buffalo Travel	M398NVR	West London Travel
L299HKM	Robinsons	L671PWT	Cantabrica	M1CRC	Chambers	M419UWY	Universitybus
L300BUS	Arriva The Shires	L672HNV	United Counties	M6CLS	Hallmark	M429BNV	Sovereign
L305HPP	Arriva The Shires	L673HNV	United Counties	M6ERN	Anita's	M430BNV	Sovereign
L306HPP	Arriva The Shires	L674HNV	United Counties	M6LWB	Len Wright	M455UUR	Sovereign
L307HPP	Arriva The Shires	L675HNV	United Counties	M7CCH	Cantabrica	M456UUR	Sovereign
L308HPP	Arriva The Shires	L676HNV	United Counties	M8CCH	Cantabrica	M457UUR	Sovereign
L309HPP	Arriva The Shires	L677HNV	United Counties	M9CCH	Cantabrica	M458UUR	Sovereign
L310HPP	Arriva The Shires	L678HNV	United Counties	M9CJN	Cliffs Coaches	M459UUR	Sovereign
L311HPP	Arriva The Shires	L679HNV	United Counties	M10CCH	Cantabrica	M460UUR	Sovereign
L312HPP	Arriva The Shires	L680HNV	United Counties	M15HMC	Hallmark	M461UUR	Sovereign
L313HPP	Arriva The Shires	L681HNV	United Counties	M16HMC	Hallmark	M495XWF	Cliffs Coaches
L314HPP	Arriva The Shires	L682HNV	United Counties	M38WUR	Arriva The Shires	M521FAC	Hallmark
L315HPP	Arriva The Shires	L683HNV	United Counties	M39WUR	Arriva The Shires	M527FAC	Hallmark
L316HPP	Arriva The Shires	L684HNV	United Counties	M41WUR	Arriva The Shires	M527UGS	Universitybus
L326AUT	Arriva The Shires	L685JBD	United Counties	M42WUR	Arriva The Shires	M573DSJ	Motts
L327AUT	Arriva The Shires	L700BUS	Arriva The Shires	M43WUR	Arriva The Shires	M575RJM	Motts
L328AUT	Arriva The Shires	L744YGE	Motts	M45WUR	Arriva The Shires	M581BVL	AR Travel
L334HFU	Magpie Travel	L777GSM	Buffalo Travel	M46WUR	Arriva The Shires	M582BVL	AR Travel
L345HFU	Magpie Travel	L800BUS	Arriva The Shires	M47HUT	Universitybus	M587BFL	Richmond's
L355HFU	Simmonds	L834MWT	Seamarks	M47WUR	Arriva The Shires	M588BFL	Richmond's
L357YNR	Martin	L863BEA	Arriva The Shires	M48HUT	Universitybus	M601RCP	Hallmark
L360JBD	United Counties	L864BEA	Arriva The Shires	M49HUT	Universitybus	M602RCP	Hallmark
L361JBD	United Counties	L922LJO	Arriva The Shires	M51HUT	Universitybus	M603RCP	Hallmark
L362JBD	United Counties	L923LJO	Arriva The Shires	M62MOG	Red Rose Travel	M604RCP	Hallmark
L363JBD	United Counties	L944HTM	Sovereign	M78JNV	Poynter's	M612RCP	Hallmark
L364JBD	United Counties	L945HTM	Sovereign	M95BPX	Cliffs Coaches	M633RCP	Berkeleys
L365JBD	United Counties	L945JFU	Barfordian	M101UKX	Sovereign	M669UCT	Starline
L366JBD	United Counties	L946HTM	Sovereign	M102UKX	Sovereign	M685UUR	Hallmark
L367JBD	United Counties	L946JFU	Barfordian	M103UKX	Sovereign	M687UUR	Hallmark
L368JBD	United Counties	L947HTM	Sovereign	M104UKX	Sovereign	M702RVS	Seamarks
L369JBD	United Counties	L948HTM	Sovereign	M105UKX	Sovereign	M710OMJ	Arriva The Shires
L370JBD	United Counties	L949MBH	Sovereign	M111EAD	Alec Head	M711OMJ	Arriva The Shires
L371JBD	United Counties	L950MBH	Sovereign	M116MBD	Yorks	M712OMJ	Arriva The Shires
L372JBD	United Counties	L951MBH	Sovereign	M136SKY	Simmonds	M713OMJ	Arriva The Shires
L373JBD	United Counties	L952MBH	Sovereign	M146VVS	Universitybus	M714OMJ	Arriva The Shires
L374JBD	United Counties	L953MBH	Sovereign	M148KJF	Marshall's	M715HBC	Martin
L375JBD	United Counties	L954MBH	Sovereign	M148VVS	Universitybus	M715OMJ	Arriva The Shires
L376JBD	United Counties	L980CRY	Simmonds	M150RBH	Arriva The Shires	M716OMJ	Arriva The Shires
L377JBD	United Counties	LAZ4364	Buffalo Travel	M151RBH	Arriva The Shires	M717OMJ	Arriva The Shires
L378JBD	United Counties	LAZ5827	Anglia	M152RBH	Arriva The Shires	M718OMJ	Arriva The Shires
L379JBD	United Counties	LBD837P	Arriva The Shires	M153RBH	Arriva The Shires	M719OMJ	Arriva The Shires
L380JBD	United Counties	LBD920V	United Counties	M154RBH	Arriva The Shires	M720OMJ	Arriva The Shires
L381NBD	United Counties	LBD921V	United Counties	M156RBH	Arriva The Shires	M721OMJ	Arriva The Shires
L382NBD	United Counties	LBD923V	United Counties	M157RBH	Arriva The Shires	M722OMJ	Arriva The Shires
L383NBD	United Counties	LBL990W	Abbey Coaches	M158RBH	Arriva The Shires	M723OMJ	Arriva The Shires
L400BUS	Arriva The Shires	LBZ2936	L B Travel	M159RBH	Arriva The Shires	M724OMJ	Arriva The Shires
L401JBD	United Counties	LBZ2937	L B Travel	M160RBH	Arriva The Shires	M725OMJ	Arriva The Shires
L402JBD	United Counties	LBZ2940	Reg's	M231SGS	Seamarks	M726OMJ	Arriva The Shires
L402XLM	Reg's	LBZ2941	Reg's	M239XLV	Arriva The Shires	M727OMJ	Arriva The Shires
L403JBD	United Counties	LBZ2942	Reg's	M240XLV	Arriva The Shires	M728OMJ	Arriva The Shires
L404JBD	United Counties	LBZ2943	Reg's	M250TAK	Marshall's	M729OMJ	Arriva The Shires
L405JBD	United Counties	LBZ2944	Reg's	M254TAK	Marshall's	M752UKX	Hallmark
L406JBD	United Counties	LBZ7234	Reg's	M255TAK	Marshall's	M754UKX	Hallmark
L407JBD	United Counties	LBZ7235	Reg's	M255UKX	Universitybus	M759UKX	Hallmark
L408JBD	United Counties	LBZ8368	Office Travel	M301BAV	Sovereign	M832RCP	Luton Airport
L409JBD	United Counties	LDV469F	Classic Coaches	M302BAV	Sovereign	M834RCP	Luton Airport
L410JBD	United Counties	LDV847F	Classic Coaches	M303BAV	Sovereign	M836RCP	Luton Airport
L411JBD	United Counties	LFJ852W	United Counties	M304BAV	Sovereign	M839RCP	Hallmark
L412JBD	United Counties	LFJ855W	United Counties	M305BAV	Sovereign	M841DDS	Arriva The Shires
L413JBD	United Counties	LFJ862W	United Counties	M306BAV	Sovereign	M842DDS	Arriva The Shires
L414JBD	United Counties	LFJ863W	United Counties	M307BAV	Sovereign	M843DDS	Arriva The Shires
L415JBD	United Counties	LFJ864W	United Counties	M308BAV	Sovereign	M844DDS	Arriva The Shires
L416JBD	United Counties	LFJ865W	United Counties	M310KHP	Sovereign	M845DDS	Arriva The Shires
L417JBD	United Counties	LFJ869W	United Counties	M314EEA	Sovereign Taxis	M846DDS	Arriva The Shires
L418JBD	United Counties	LFJ878W	United Counties	M332DRP	United Counties	M846RCP	Luton Airport
L419JBD	United Counties	LFJ879W	United Counties	M334DRP	United Counties	M846RCP	Luton Airport
L420JBD	United Counties	LFO800Y	Harris	M335DRP	United Counties	M847DDS	Arriva The Shires

Reg	Operator	Reg	Operator	Reg	Operator	Reg	Operator
M848MOL	Red Rose Travel	N67FWU	Luton Airport	N508FVS	Hallmark	NRP581V	Arriva The Shires
M849LFP	Jeffs	N75JUR	Seamarks	N509FVS	Hallmark	NSP323R	Classic Coaches
M850LFP	Jeffs	N76KVS	Seamarks	N539DNW	Buffalo Travel	NSP324R	Classic Coaches
M969ONK	Sworder's	N94BHL	Martin	N572RJU	Poynter's	NTL655	First Northampton
MBZ1759	Marshall's	N106GVS	Sovereign	N580GBW	Robinsons	NUF632	Marlow Coaches
MBZ6455	Arriva The Shires	N107GVS	Sovereign	N617UEW	Reg's	NUW554Y	United Counties
MDS228V	Jeffs	N108GVS	Sovereign	N660EWJ	Barfordian	NUW557Y	United Counties
MEF826W	Rodgers	N109GVS	Sovereign	N693EUR	Arriva The Shires	NUW565Y	United Counties
MGR671P	Classic Coaches	N124GNM	Arriva The Shires	N694EUR	Arriva The Shires	NUW568Y	United Counties
MHW285K	Classic Coaches	N186EMJ	Arriva The Shires	N695EUR	Arriva The Shires	NUW576Y	United Counties
MIJ3409	Marshall's	N187EMJ	Arriva The Shires	N696EUR	Arriva The Shires	NUW579Y	United Counties
MIL2350	Arriva The Shires	N188EMJ	Arriva The Shires	N697EUR	Arriva The Shires	NUW584Y	United Counties
MIL2397	Rover Luxury Travel	N189EMJ	Arriva The Shires	N698EUR	Arriva The Shires	NUW588Y	United Counties
MIL2406	Marshall's	N190EMJ	Arriva The Shires	N699EUR	Arriva The Shires	NUW590Y	United Counties
MIL2408	Marshall's	N191EMJ	Arriva The Shires	N701EUR	Arriva The Shires	NUW595Y	United Counties
MIL4003	Reynolds Diplomat	N192EMJ	Arriva The Shires	N702EUR	Arriva The Shires	NUW602Y	United Counties
MIL4418	Buffalo Travel	N193EMJ	Arriva The Shires	N703EUR	Arriva The Shires	NUW605Y	United Counties
MIL5499	Smith-Ivins	N194EMJ	Arriva The Shires	N704EUR	Arriva The Shires	NUW608Y	United Counties
MIL6993	South Mimms Travel	N195EMJ	Arriva The Shires	N705EUR	Arriva The Shires	NUW610Y	United Counties
MIL6994	South Mimms Travel	N196EMJ	Arriva The Shires	N706EUR	Arriva The Shires	NUW620Y	Sovereign
MIL7852	South Mimms Travel	N207EAV	Layston Coaches	N707EUR	Arriva The Shires	NVS707	Classic Coaches
MIL7853	South Mimms Travel	N219HBK	Red Rose Travel	N708EUR	Arriva The Shires	NWU852M	Welham Travel
MIL8741	Alec Head	N244NNR	Hallmark	N709EUR	Arriva The Shires	OAP17W	Langston & Tasker
MIL9599	Funstons	N301XRP	United Counties	N710EUR	Arriva The Shires	OBD67V	Smith-Ivins
MIW3853	Richard Taylor's	N302XRP	United Counties	N711EUR	Arriva The Shires	OBX453Y	Buckby's-Coopers
MJI6251	Alec Head	N303XRP	United Counties	N712EUR	Arriva The Shires	OCK367K	Classic Coaches
MJI7854	Seamarks	N304XRP	United Counties	N713EUR	Arriva The Shires	OCU801R	Cedar Coaches
MJI7855	Seamarks	N305DHE	Country Lion	N714EUR	Arriva The Shires	OCU804R	Cedar Coaches
MJI7856	Seamarks	N305XRP	United Counties	N715EUR	Arriva The Shires	OCU808R	Cedar Coaches
MJI7857	Seamarks	N306XRP	United Counties	N715FLN	Expresslines	OCY916R	Arriva The Shires
MJI8660	Seamarks	N307XRP	United Counties	N716EUR	Arriva The Shires	ODO837Y	Beeslty Enterprises
MJI8662	Seamarks	N308XRP	United Counties	N770EOD	Hallmark	ODO918Y	Robinsons
MJU797W	Country Lion	N309VAV	Sovereign	N783SJU	Martin	OGS1V	Greenway Travel
MNC495W	Bryans of Enfield	N309XRP	United Counties	N784JBM	Red Rose Travel	OHP10W	Smith-Ivins
MNH572V	Central Cars	N310VAV	Sovereign	N789SJU	Jeffs	OHR185R	Classic Coaches
MNH577V	Arriva The Shires	N310XRP	United Counties	N790SJU	Jeffs	OHR186R	Classic Coaches
MPE772P	Jeffs	N311VAV	Sovereign	N802GRV	Red Rose Travel	OHV706Y	Sovereign
MPP747	Cedar Coaches	N311XRP	United Counties	N803GRV	Red Rose Travel	OJD141R	Buffalo Travel
MSK287	Hallmark	N312VAV	Sovereign	N895VEG	Richmond's	OJD143R	Starline
MUE314V	P P H	N312XRP	United Counties	N906ETM	Arriva The Shires	OJD216R	Keystone
MUH284X	Arriva The Shires	N313XRP	United Counties	N907ETM	Arriva The Shires	OJD351R	Shoreys
MUH287X	Arriva The Shires	N314XRP	United Counties	N908ETM	Arriva The Shires	OJD357R	Shoreys
MUH290X	Arriva The Shires	N315XRP	United Counties	N909ETM	Arriva The Shires	OJD414R	Buffalo Travel
MXX223	Timebus	N316XRP	United Counties	N910ETM	Arriva The Shires	OJD414R	Buffalo Travel
MXX468	Timebus	N317XRP	United Counties	N911ETM	Arriva The Shires	OJD463R	Motts
MXX481	Bryans of Enfield	N318XRP	United Counties	N912ETM	Arriva The Shires	OJI2830	Buffalo Travel
N1HMC	Hallmark	N319XRP	United Counties	N913ETM	Arriva The Shires	OJR338	Rover Luxury Travel
N3HMC	Hallmark	N320XRP	United Counties	N914ETM	Arriva The Shires	ONH925V	Arriva The Shires
N4CRC	Chambers	N321XRP	United Counties	N915ETM	Arriva The Shires	ONH928V	Arriva The Shires
N4HMC	Hallmark	N322XRP	United Counties	N916ETM	Arriva The Shires	ONH929V	Arriva The Shires
N4LWB	Len Wright	N323XRP	United Counties	N917ETM	Arriva The Shires	OOW233	Yorks
N5HMC	Hallmark	N324XRP	United Counties	N918ETM	Arriva The Shires	OPT829	Rover Luxury Travel
N5LWB	Len Wright	N325XRP	United Counties	N919ETM	Arriva The Shires	OSR204R	Cedar Coaches
N5RDC	Reynolds Diplomat	N326XRP	United Counties	N934HPX	Shire Coaches	OUC49R	Buffalo Travel
N6HMC	Hallmark	N359EAR	Hallmark	N937FLE	Country Lion	OUF65W	Cedar Coaches
N6RDC	Reynolds Diplomat	N366JGS	Arriva The Shires	N986FWT	Luton Airport	OVV851R	Arriva The Shires
N7HMC	Hallmark	N367JGS	Arriva The Shires	N990FNK	Reg's	OVV852R	Arriva The Shires
N8HMC	Hallmark	N368JGS	Arriva The Shires	N991FNK	Reg's	OVV853R	Arriva The Shires
N9HMC	Hallmark	N369JGS	Arriva The Shires	N996BWJ	Simmonds	OWG368X	Motts
N10HMC	Hallmark	N370JGS	Arriva The Shires	NBD304V	Jeffs	P3ERN	Anita's
N15CAN	Hallmark	N371JGS	Arriva The Shires	NBD305V	Jeffs	P4CLN	Country Lion
N20CCH	Cantabrica	N372JGS	Arriva The Shires	NBD306V	Jeffs	P4CRC	Chambers
N28KGS	Arriva The Shires	N373JGS	Arriva The Shires	NBD307V	Jeffs	P5CLN	Country Lion
N29KGS	Arriva The Shires	N374JGS	Arriva The Shires	NBD309V	Jeffs	P17HMC	Hallmark
N31KGS	Arriva The Shires	N375JGS	Arriva The Shires	NBD310V	Jeffs	P18HMC	Hallmark
N32KGS	Arriva The Shires	N376JGS	Arriva The Shires	NBD311V	Jeffs	P19HMC	Hallmark
N35JPP	Arriva The Shires	N377JGS	Arriva The Shires	NCY626	Layston Coaches	P20HMC	Hallmark
N36JPP	Arriva The Shires	N378JGS	Arriva The Shires	NDL637M	Classic Coaches	P22HMC	Hallmark
N37JPP	Arriva The Shires	N379JGS	Arriva The Shires	NDL869	Classic Coaches	P26KOP	Arriva The Shires
N38JPP	Arriva The Shires	N380JGS	Arriva The Shires	NFW37V	Cedar Coaches	P44HMC	Hallmark
N39JPP	Arriva The Shires	N381JGS	Arriva The Shires	NHU2	Classic Coaches	P52KCA	West London Travel
N41JPP	Arriva The Shires	N382JGS	Arriva The Shires	NIB8459	Arriva The Shires	P55HMC	Hallmark
N41RRP	First Northampton	N383JGS	Arriva The Shires	NIL774	J&L Travel	P56BTF	Cliffs Coaches
N42JPP	Arriva The Shires	N384JGS	Arriva The Shires	NIL1787	Alec Head	P100LOW	Arriva The Shires
N42RRP	First Northampton	N385JGS	Arriva The Shires	NIL2883	Buffalo Travel	P112RGS	Sovereign
N43JPP	Arriva The Shires	N386JGS	Arriva The Shires	NIW4405	Reynolds Diplomat	P117ORP	Yorks
N43RRP	First Northampton	N387JGS	Arriva The Shires	NJF204W	Arriva The Shires	P127RWR	Luton Airport
N45JPP	Arriva The Shires	N421ENM	Universitybus	NJI8869	T & M Travel	P128RWR	Luton Airport
N46JPP	Arriva The Shires	N422ENM	Universitybus	NLP172V	Smith-Ivins	P129RWR	Luton Airport
N57MDW	Seamarks	N423ENM	Universitybus	NMJ268V	Welham Travel	P130RWR	Luton Airport
N58MDW	Seamarks	N424ENM	Universitybus	NML627E	Sovereign	P131RWR	Luton Airport
N61MDW	Seamarks	N499ADC	Beeslty Enterprises	NPJ480R	Kellys Coaches	P171KBD	United Counties
N63FWU	Berkeleys	N506FVS	Hallmark	NRO265V	Greenway Travel	P172KBD	United Counties
		N507FVS	Hallmark			P173KBD	United Counties

Reg	Operator	Reg	Operator	Reg	Operator	Reg	Operator
P173NAK	Martin	P772BJF	Martin	R173VBM	Arriva The Shires	R565DRP	United Counties
P174DNH	United Counties	P859ADO	Berkeleys	R174VBM	Arriva The Shires	R566DRP	United Counties
P175DNH	United Counties	P860PBH	Arriva The Shires	R175VBM	Arriva The Shires	R567DRP	United Counties
P175SRO	Arriva The Shires	P861PBH	Arriva The Shires	R176VBM	Arriva The Shires	R568DRP	United Counties
P176DNH	United Counties	P88HMC	Hallmark	R177DNH	United Counties	R602WMJ	Sovereign
P176SRO	Arriva The Shires	P890PWW	Berkeleys	R177VBM	Arriva The Shires	R603WMJ	Sovereign
P177SRO	Arriva The Shires	P955DNR	Tates	R178DNH	United Counties	R604WMJ	Sovereign
P178SRO	Arriva The Shires	P960DNR	Hallmark	R178VBM	Arriva The Shires	R606WMJ	Sovereign
P179SRO	Arriva The Shires	P961DNR	Hallmark	R179DNH	United Counties	R607WMJ	Sovereign
P180ANR	Jeffs	P970DNR	Hallmark	R179VBM	Arriva The Shires	R608CNM	Sovereign
P180DNH	Arriva The Shires	P975HWF	Hallmark	R180DNH	United Counties	R636VNN	Yorks
P181ANR	Jeffs	P980PTM	Universitybus	R180VBM	Arriva The Shires	R648VMJ	Universitybus
P181SRO	Arriva The Shires	P981PKX	Arriva The Shires	R181DNH	United Counties	R649VBM	Universitybus
P182SRO	Arriva The Shires	P982HWF	Hallmark	R181VBM	Arriva The Shires	R650RKX	Cliffs Coaches
P183SRO	Arriva The Shires	P983HWF	Hallmark	R182DNH	United Counties	R650VBM	Universitybus
P184SRO	Arriva The Shires	P984HWF	Hallmark	R182VBM	Arriva The Shires	R651VBM	Universitybus
P185SRO	Arriva The Shires	PAZ3276	Travel Line	R183DNH	United Counties	R652VBM	Universitybus
P186SRO	Arriva The Shires	PBC98G	Classic Coaches	R183VBM	Arriva The Shires	R653VBM	Universitybus
P187SRO	Arriva The Shires	PBC113G	Classic Coaches	R184DNH	United Counties	R654VBM	Universitybus
P188SRO	Arriva The Shires	PBD42R	Country Lion	R184VBM	Arriva The Shires	R693DNH	United Counties
P189SRO	Arriva The Shires	PBD345R	Souls	R185DNH	United Counties	R694DNH	United Counties
P190SRO	Arriva The Shires	PBH539R	Red Kite	R185DNM	United Counties	R695DNH	United Counties
P198OLC	Simmonds	PBZ1450	South Mimms Travel	R186DNH	United Counties	R696DNH	United Counties
P201RUM	Hallmark	PBZ1451	Paul Dale	R186DNM	United Counties	R697DNH	United Counties
P202RUM	Hallmark	PBZ9152	Reg's	R187DNM	Arriva The Shires	R698DNH	United Counties
P203RUM	Hallmark	PBZ9153	Reg's	R188DNM	Arriva The Shires	R699DNH	United Counties
P204RUM	Hallmark	PBZ9154	Reg's	R189DNM	Arriva The Shires	R701DNH	United Counties
P205RUM	Hallmark	PBZ9155	Reg's	R190DNM	Arriva The Shires	R702DNH	United Counties
P215RWR	Berkeleys	PHN178L	Classic Coaches	R191DNM	Arriva The Shires	R703DNH	United Counties
P216RWR	Berkeleys	PIA892	Shoreys	R191RBM	Arriva The Shires	R796GSF	Red Rose Travel
P235MBM	Funstons	PIW4127	Souls	R192DNM	Arriva The Shires	R831COT	Hallmark
P313CVE	Sovereign	PJF227R	Jeffs	R192RBM	Arriva The Shires	R832COT	Hallmark
P314CVE	Sovereign	PJF909R	Langston & Tasker	R193DNM	Arriva The Shires	R902EDO	Motts
P315DVE	Sovereign	PJI3531	Richard Taylor's	R193RBM	Arriva The Shires	R951RCH	Martin
P316RGS	Sovereign	PJJ345S	Classic Coaches	R194DNM	Arriva The Shires	R968RCH	Motts
P317RGS	Sovereign	PKG651R	Langston & Tasker	R194RBM	Arriva The Shires	R981SKX	Hallmark
P318RGS	Sovereign	PMB47Y	Harris	R195DNM	Arriva The Shires	R985KKN	Hallmark
P365RGV	Martin	PMR361M	Beeslty Enterprises	R195RBM	Arriva The Shires	R986KKN	Hallmark
P432JDT	Layston Coaches	PNB782W	Thompson Travel	R196DNM	Arriva The Shires	R989SKX	Hallmark
P450KRP	United Counties	PPJ162W	Prestwood Travel	R196RBM	Arriva The Shires	RAZ3785	Souls
P451KRP	United Counties	PRP3V	Country Lion	R197DNM	Arriva The Shires	RAZ5954	Richard Taylor's
P452KRP	United Counties	PRP802M	Arriva The Shires	R197RBM	Arriva The Shires	RAZ6948	South Mimms Travel
P479FAN	Shire Coaches	PSU353	Funstons	R198DNM	Arriva The Shires	RBD215	Alec Head
P501MVV	First Northampton	PSU630	First Northampton	R198RBM	Arriva The Shires	RBD287Y	Yorks
P501MVV	First Northampton	PSV499	South Mimms Travel	R199RBM	Arriva The Shires	RBM2W	Greenway Travel
P501VRO	Sovereign	PTT106R	Jeffs	R201RBM	Arriva The Shires	RBP847S	Balmoral Autos
P502MVV	First Northampton	PUK641R	Classic Coaches	R202RBM	Arriva The Shires	RBW396	Souls
P502MVV	First Northampton	PVV888J	Country Lion	R203RBM	Arriva The Shires	RBY46L	Hats & Herts Coaches
P503MVV	First Northampton	PXI8935	First Northampton	R204RBM	Arriva The Shires	RBZ4224	Barfordian
P503MVV	First Northampton	PYJ458L	Cedar Coaches	R205RBM	Arriva The Shires	RCH511R	Alec Head
P504MVV	First Northampton	Q956UOE	Red Rose Travel	R205VJF	Shire Coaches	RDS83W	Arriva The Shires
P504MVV	First Northampton	R2CRC	Chambers	R206GMJ	Arriva The Shires	RDS84W	Arriva The Shires
P505MVV	First Northampton	R4FWM	Marshall's	R207GMJ	Arriva The Shires	RDV424H	Classic Coaches
P505MVV	First Northampton	R5FWM	Marshall's	R208GMJ	Arriva The Shires	RHE992X	Jeffs
P506MVV	First Northampton	R5HMC	Hallmark	R209GMJ	Arriva The Shires	RIB1739	Kellys Coaches
P506MVV	First Northampton	R6FWM	Marshall's	R210GMJ	Arriva The Shires	RIB6838	Exodus
P507NWU	Red Rose Travel	R6HMC	Hallmark	R211GMJ	Arriva The Shires	RIB8815	T & M Travel
P512MBD	Buckby's-Coopers	R7FWM	Marshall's	R212GMJ	Arriva The Shires	RIJ3987	Jeffs
P526NOT	Shire Coaches	R7LWB	Len Wright	R213GMJ	Arriva The Shires	RIW9473	Buckby's-Coopers
P569EFL	United Counties	R8FWM	Marshall's	R214GMJ	Arriva The Shires	RJI1649	Alec Head
P570EFL	United Counties	R9CCC	Cedar Coaches	R215GMJ	Arriva The Shires	RJI1662	South Mimms Travel
P570TBH	Arriva The Shires	R9FWM	Marshall's	R291NYG	Tates	RJI4669	Prestwood Travel
P571EFL	United Counties	R10FWM	Marshall's	R341SUT	First Northampton	RJI4670	Prestwood Travel
P571TBH	Arriva The Shires	R11FWM	Marshall's	R342SUT	First Northampton	RJI6616	Buffalo Travel
P601RGS	Sovereign	R12FWM	Marshall's	R343SUT	First Northampton	RJI6861	Arriva The Shires
P647SBH	Universitybus	R46GNW	Hallmark	R418YWJ	Martin	RJI6862	Arriva The Shires
P664PNM	Universitybus	R47GNW	Hallmark	R447SKX	Arriva The Shires	RKE154W	T & M Travel
P665PNM	Universitybus	R68KFL	Hallmark	R448SKX	Arriva The Shires	RKY878R	Abbey Coaches
P667PNM	Universitybus	R71KFL	Hallmark	R449SKX	Arriva The Shires	RND617X	Buffalo Travel
P668PNM	Universitybus	R72JTM	Universitybus	R450SKX	Arriva The Shires	RNK749M	Buffalo Travel
P669PNM	Arriva The Shires	R74GNW	Luton Airport	R451SKX	Arriva The Shires	RNV303V	Souls
P670PNM	Arriva The Shires	R75GNW	Berkeleys	R452SKX	Arriva The Shires	RRP862R	United Counties
P671OPP	Arriva The Shires	R91GTM	Sovereign	R453SKX	Arriva The Shires	RRP863R	United Counties
P671PNM	Arriva The Shires	R92GTM	Sovereign	R454SKX	Arriva The Shires	RTA693M	Classic Coaches
P672OPP	Arriva The Shires	R120HNK	Sovereign	R455SKX	Arriva The Shires	RTH927S	Rodgers
P673OPP	Arriva The Shires	R121HNK	Sovereign	R456SKX	Arriva The Shires	RXI9280	Welham Travel
P674OPP	Arriva The Shires	R122HNK	Sovereign	R490UFP	Jeffs	S1CRC	Chambers
P686JBD	United Counties	R123HNK	Sovereign	R503SCH	Shire Coaches	S106KJF	Shire Coaches
P687JBD	United Counties	R124HNK	Sovereign	R532YRP	Universitybus	S146KNK	Arriva The Shires
P688JBD	United Counties	R125HNK	Sovereign	R560DRP	United Counties	S147KNK	Arriva The Shires
P689JBD	United Counties	R126HNK	Sovereign	R561DRP	United Counties	S148KNK	Arriva The Shires
P690JBD	United Counties	R127HNK	Sovereign	R562DRP	United Counties	S149KNK	Arriva The Shires
P691JBD	United Counties	R171VBM	Arriva The Shires	R563DRP	United Counties	S150KNK	Arriva The Shires
P692JBD	United Counties	R172VBM	Arriva The Shires	R564DRP	United Counties	S151KNK	Arriva The Shires

Reg	Operator	Reg	Operator	Reg	Operator	Reg	Operator
S152KNK	Arriva The Shires	TCL142R	United Counties	VIB6181	Paul Dale	WYV57T	Sovereign
S153KNK	Arriva The Shires	TDL419S	ABC Travel	VIJ4021	Souls	XAK909T	Classic Coaches
S154KNK	Arriva The Shires	TEX405R	Red Kite	VJD44S	Enfieldian	XAK911T	Classic Coaches
S156KNK	Arriva The Shires	TEX872R	Red Kite	VJI2779	Barfordian	XAM109A	Geoff Amos
S157KNK	Arriva The Shires	TFN980T	Classic Coaches	VJI3982	Barfordian	XAM116A	Geoff Amos
S158KNK	Arriva The Shires	TFU62T	Buffalo Travel	VJT612X	Langston & Tasker	XAM124A	Geoff Amos
S159KNK	Arriva The Shires	TFX663	Barfordian	VJT618X	Langston & Tasker	XAM730A	Geoff Amos
S160KNK	Arriva The Shires	TGY698	Jeffs	VJT622X	Thompson Travel	XAM731A	Geoff Amos
S161KNK	Arriva The Shires	THX261S	Universitybus	VKX510	Jeffs	XAY272S	South Mimms Travel
S582VOB	Seamarks	THX283S	Shoreys	VLT255	United Counties	XBC445X	J&L Travel
S583VOB	Seamarks	THX304S	Shoreys	VLV815	Tates	XBR657R	T & M Travel
S584VOB	Seamarks	THX493S	Buffalo Travel	VNP893	Jeffs	XCP144X	Buffalo Travel
SBD524R	Arriva The Shires	THX509S	Bryans of Enfield	VRP45S	Jeffs	XEA745	Yorks
SCN255S	Cedar Coaches	THX533S	Buffalo Travel	VRP51S	Jeffs	XEL587	Drury
SDA710S	Office Travel	THX580S	Shoreys	VRS152L	Cedar Coaches	XEU858T	Classic Coaches
SDA714S	Office Travel	THX605S	Buffalo Travel	VUD483	Souls	XGV226	P P H
SFU718	Rover Luxury Travel	TIB4873	Arriva The Shires	VVV61S	Country Lion	XHE753T	New Greens
SGS505W	Kellys Coaches	TIB4886	Arriva The Shires	VVV66S	Jeffs	XHO856	Yorks
SHO695M	Office Travel	TIB5906	Arriva The Shires	VVV70S	First Northampton	XIB1906	Smith's of Tring
SHP689R	Beeslty Enterprises	TIB7835	Arriva The Shires	VVV949W	United Counties	XIB1907	Smith's of Tring
SIB3708	Paul Dale	TIB8567	Alec Head	VVV950W	United Counties	XIB1908	Smith's of Tring
SIB4846	Arriva The Shires	TIB8570	Z & S Coaches	VVV951W	Arriva The Shires	XIB1909	Smith's of Tring
SIB7480	Arriva The Shires	TIW3902	Buffalo Travel	VVV952W	United Counties	XLC516	Yorks
SIB7481	Arriva The Shires	TJH882Y	ABC Travel	VVV956W	Arriva The Shires	XMW285	P P H
SIB8349	L B Travel	TJI4501	Smith's of Tring	VVV957W	Arriva The Shires	XNV890S	Red Kite
SIB8529	Arriva The Shires	TJI6574	Hats & Herts Coaches	VVV960W	Arriva The Shires	XPC14S	Classic Coaches
SIW1931	Barfordian	TJI6575	Travel Line	VVV961W	United Counties	XPO987	Yorks
SIW1932	Barfordian	TJI6756	Travel Line	VVV962W	United Counties	XPT569V	Classic Coaches
SIW1936	Barfordian	TJI7508	Office Travel	VVV963W	United Counties	XRN716R	ABC Travel
SIW1937	Barfordian	TJI8299	Rover Luxury Travel	VVV965W	United Counties	XRN716R	Red Kite
SJI3928	Geoff Amos	TJT788	P P H	VVV966W	United Counties	XTM482S	P P H
SJI3929	Geoff Amos	TMJ637R	Classic Coaches	VVV967W	United Counties	XTW856S	Sworder's
SJI5617	Welham Travel	TMJ643R	Layston Coaches	VXT571	Jeffs	XUY159R	Langston & Tasker
SJI8100	Marshall's	TNH865R	Arriva The Shires	VYU758S	Jeffs	XVY392	Yorks
SJI8102	Marshall's	TRR892R	Smith-Ivins	WDA689T	ABC Travel	XWG254	Jeffs
SJI8103	Marshall's	TSU477	Taylor's Reliance	WDA968T	ABC Travel	XWG639T	Drury
SJI8106	Marshall's	TVP891S	Office Travel	WDA999T	Central Cars	XYN591	Yorks
SKN491R	Sworder's	TVV170W	Geoff Amos	WEX929S	United Counties	YAA130V	Thompson Travel
SLU261	Arriva The Shires	TVY659	Yorks	WIB1113	Arriva The Shires	YAY81	Barfordian
SMJ521	Taylor's Reliance	TWN803S	Classic Coaches	WIB1114	Arriva The Shires	YDK225L	Harris
SMK663F	Sovereign	TXI2427	Alec Head	WIB4784	Richard Taylor's	YDN504	Starline
SMK668F	Sovereign	TXI2898	Cedar Coaches	WIB7180	Smith's of Tring	YDX100Y	First Northampton
SMK674F	Sovereign	UBH394W	Luton Airport	WIJ297	Tates	YEB105T	Exodus
SMK686F	Sovereign	UBH395W	Luton Airport	WJI5277	Marshall's	YER469	Richmond's
SMK694F	Sovereign	UBH396W	Luton Airport	WLT512	United Counties	YFC16V	Jeffs
SMK719F	Sovereign	UDM448V	Arriva The Shires	WLT528	United Counties	YFC17V	Jeffs
SMK756F	Sovereign	UFC221	Yorks	WLT682	United Counties	YIB2396	Arriva The Shires
SNV930W	United Counties	UFW38W	Cedar Coaches	WLT908	United Counties	YIB2397	Arriva The Shires
SNV931W	United Counties	UFW40W	First Northampton	WPH132Y	Red Rose Travel	YIJ387	Harris
SNV932W	Arriva The Shires	UFW41W	First Northampton	WPW201S	Red Kite	YMB938T	Arriva The Shires
SNV933W	Arriva The Shires	UIA8946	Village Bus	WRO438S	Prestwood Travel	YNF333Y	Chambers
SNV934W	Arriva The Shires	UJI1758	Buffalo Travel	WRR396Y	Cedar Coaches	YNG208S	Red Kite
SNV935W	United Counties	UJI2463	Geoff Amos	WRY216X	Enfieldian	YNH1W	Country Lion
SNV936W	United Counties	UMO180N	Classic Coaches	WSU368	Cedar Coaches	YOD567L	Acclaim Travel
SNV937W	United Counties	UND126	Souls	WSU448	P P H	YOX69K	Classic Coaches
SNV938W	Arriva The Shires	UPB307S	Classic Coaches	WSU450	P P H	YPD128Y	Keystone
SOA663S	Classic Coaches	UPB340S	Classic Coaches	WSU451	New Greens	YPL72T	Office Travel
SUK431Y	P P H	URP939W	United Counties	WSU452	P P H	YRP161W	Souls
SUR283R	Motts	URP940W	United Counties	WSU453	P P H	YSV306	Exodus
SVL834R	United Counties	URP941W	United Counties	WSU481	First Northampton	YSV375	Exodus
SVO89	Taylor's Reliance	URP942W	Red Kite	WSV509	Alec Head	YSV727	Exodus
SVV588W	Arriva The Shires	URP944W	United Counties	WSY601	Reg's	YSV815	Jeffs
SWC24K	Classic Coaches	URP945W	United Counties	WSY602	Reg's	YSV994	Exodus
SXI6397	J&L Travel	URP946W	Arriva The Shires	WSY691	Reg's	YTA612S	Alec Head
SYK901	Yorks	URP947W	Arriva The Shires	WTH960T	Rodgers	YVN522T	Shoreys
TAZ4995	Souls	URY598	Buffalo Travel	WUM106S	Cedar Coaches	YVN522T	Shoreys
TBU30G	Classic Coaches	UTN3Y	Harris	WUT866	L B Travel	YVV893S	Arriva The Shires
TBZ5791	Geoff Amos	UWG820Y	Luton Airport	WVV827S	Jeffs	YVV894S	Arriva The Shires
TBZ5793	Geoff Amos	VBT201V	Welham Travel	WVV829S	Jeffs	YVV895S	Arriva The Shires
TBZ5873	Geoff Amos	VBW846	Jeffs	WVV830S	Jeffs	YVV896S	Red Kite
TCD375J	Classic Coaches	VDV104S	Cedar Coaches	WWN191	Classic Coaches		
TCD376J	Classic Coaches	VDY379	J&L Travel	WXI4357	Buffalo Travel		
TCG333M	Z & S Coaches	VHM847	Yorks	WXI4359	Westways		

ISBN 1 897990 39 1   First Edition, September 1998
Published by *British Bus Publishing Ltd*
The Vyne, 16 St Margaret's Drive
Wellington, Telford, TF1 3PH
Fax and evening order-line 01952 255669